BAHÁ'U'LLÁH AND THE NEW ERA

Bahá'u'lláh and the New Era

By J. E. Esslemont

An Introduction to the Bahá'í Faith

1970

BAHÁ'Í PUBLISHING TRUST • WILMETTE, ILLINOIS

Standard Book No.: 0-87743-001-2
Library of Congress Catalog Card No.: 73-112791

First edition, George Allen & Unwin Ltd., London, 1923
First revised edition, Bahá'í Publishing Committee, New York, 1937
Second revised edition, Bahá'í Publishing Committee, Wilmette, 1950
Third revised edition, Bahá'í Publishing Trust, Wilmette, 1970

Preface to 1937 Edition

With the publication of *Bahá'u'lláh and the New Era* more than ten years ago, the Bahá'í Faith was given its first well-conceived, thorough exposition by a student of the teachings. Recognizing its value as the most satisfactory introduction to the Cause, Bahá'ís in both East and West have found Dr. Esslemont's book so helpful that it has been translated into some thirty different languages.

As Dr. Esslemont himself recognized, the Faith entered a new phase of its history after the ascension of 'Abdu'l-Bahá. The result is that the author's views, some of them written prior to 1921, no longer on certain aspects of the subject correspond to the evolutionary character of the Faith. His treatment of events and social conditions then existing, moreover, no longer appears fully relevant. Unavoidably, a few errors of fact had entered his text, while his explanation of the stations of the Báb and of 'Abdu'l-Bahá have been replaced in the minds of Bahá'ís by the authoritative interpretations since made by the first Guardian of the Faith, Shoghi Effendi.

The present edition therefore represents a revision made by the American National Spiritual Assembly, acting under the advice and approval of Shoghi Effendi.

These revisions in no respect alter the original plan of Dr. Esslemont's book, nor affect the major portion of his text. Their purpose has been to amplify the author's discussion in a few passages by the addition of material representing the fuller knowledge available since his lamented death, and newer translations of his quotations from Bahá'í Sacred Writings.

January, 1937

Bahá'í Publishing Committee

v

Preface to 1950 Edition

With this edition the American Bahá'í Publishing Committee takes over copyright and other interests in *Bahá'u'lláh and the New Era* from Messrs. George Allen & Unwin Ltd., of London, England, through whom the late Dr. J. E. Esslemont published his famous book more than twenty years ago. Under arrangement with the British publishers, the Committee has since 1928 brought out eleven printings, in addition to the first American edition imported by Brentano's of New York.

This edition does not displace the text as it has appeared since major revision was made in the book under the direction of the Guardian of the Faith in 1937, as the time has not come for anything like a thorough recasting of the book to make its references to world conditions completely contemporaneous. Dr. Esslemont's work endures as a trustworthy introduction to the history and teachings of the Bahá'í Faith. Its translation into some thirty different languages attests its appeal to students in the East as well as the West.

It should be added that any further revision of the text in the future is subject to approval by Shoghi Effendi. The Committee has no authority to pass upon revisions which may be desired by Bahá'ís of other countries for their particular need.

December, 1950

Bahá'í Publishing Committee

Preface to 1970 Edition

Since 1937 no revision has been made to the text of Dr. Esslemont's book, although in 1950 some minor corrections were introduced. On the other hand, the diffusion and development of the Bahá'í Faith since that time have been tremendous, and there has been added to Bahá'í bibliography a rich legacy of incomparable expositions, translations, and historical accounts from the pen of Shoghi Effendi, Guardian of the Faith and the appointed interpreter of its Sacred Writings.

It has therefore been deemed necessary to bring the book up to date in order to maintain its usefulness for modern readers. This has been done with a minimum of alteration to the text, and chiefly by the use of footnotes and of an epilogue giving the current statistics and new developments in the organic unfoldment of the Bahá'í Faith.

Dr. Esslemont's book continues to be one of the most widely used introductory books on the Bahá'í Faith, as evidenced by the fact that since 1937 the number of its translations has increased from thirty to fifty-eight.

Bahá'í Publishing Trust

Introduction

In December 1914, through a conversation with friends who had met 'Abdu'l-Bahá, and the loan of a few pamphlets, I first became acquainted with the Bahá'í teachings. I was at once struck by their comprehensiveness, power, and beauty. They impressed me as meeting the great needs of the modern world more fully and satisfactorily than any other presentation of religion which I had come across—an impression which subsequent study has only served to deepen and confirm.

In seeking for fuller knowledge about the Movement I found considerable difficulty in obtaining the literature I wanted, and soon conceived the idea of putting together the gist of what I learned in the form of a book, so that it might be more easily available for others. When communication with Palestine was reopened after the war, I wrote to 'Abdu'l-Bahá and enclosed a copy of the first nine chapters of the book, which was then almost complete in rough draft. I received a very kind and encouraging reply, and a cordial invitation to visit Him in Haifa and bring the whole of my manuscript with me. The invitation was gladly accepted, and I had the great privilege of spending two and a half months as the guest of 'Abdu'l-Bahá during the winter of 1919-1920. During this visit 'Abdu'l-Bahá discussed the book with me on various occasions. He gave several valuable suggestions for its improvement and proposed that, when I had revised the manuscript, He would have the whole of it translated into Persian so that He could read it through and amend or correct it where necessary. The revisal and translation were carried out as suggested, and 'Abdu'l-Bahá found time, amid His busy life, to correct some three and a half chapters (Chapters I, II, V, and part of III) before He passed away. It is a matter of profound regret to me that 'Abdu'l-Bahá was not able to complete the correction of the manuscript, as the value of the book would thereby have been greatly enhanced. The whole of the manuscript has been carefully revised, however, by a committee of the National Bahá'í Assembly of England, and its publication approved by that Assembly.

I am greatly indebted to Miss E. J. Rosenberg, Mrs. Claudia S. Coles, Mírzá Luṭfu'lláh S. Ḥakím, Messrs. Roy Wilhelm and Mountfort Mills, and many other kind friends for valuable help in the preparation of the work.

As regards the transliteration of Arabic and Persian names and words, the system adopted in this book is that recently recommended by Shoghi Effendi for use throughout the Bahá'í world.

J. E. ESSLEMONT

Fairford, Cults,
  By Aberdeen.

Contents

		PAGE
Preface to 1937 Edition		v
Preface to 1950 Edition		vii
Preface to 1970 Edition		ix
Introduction		xi

CHAPTER

1.	The Glad Tidings	1
2.	The Báb: Forerunner	11
3.	Bahá'u'lláh: The Glory of God	23
4.	'Abdu'l-Bahá: The Servant of Bahá	51
5.	What Is a Bahá'í?	71
6.	Prayer	88
7.	Health and Healing	101
8.	Religious Unity	116
9.	True Civilization	133
10.	The Way to Peace	156
11.	Various Ordinances and Teachings	175
12.	Religion and Science	197
13.	Prophecies Fulfilled by the Bahá'í Movement	211
14.	Prophecies of Bahá'u'lláh and 'Abdu'l-Bahá	234
15.	Retrospect and Prospect	252
Epilogue		283
Basic References on the Bahá'í Faith		287
Index		289

The Glad Tidings/1

The Promised One of all the peoples of the world hath appeared. All peoples and communities have been expecting a Revelation, and He, Bahá'u'lláh, is the foremost Teacher and Educator of all mankind.—'ABDU'L-BAHÁ.

The Greatest Event in History

If we study the story of the "ascent of man" as recorded in the pages of history, it becomes evident that the leading factor in human progress is the advent, from time to time, of men who pass beyond the accepted ideas of their day and become the discoverers and revealers of truths hitherto unknown among mankind. The inventor, the pioneer, the genius, the prophet—these are the men on whom the transformation of the world primarily depends. As Carlyle says:—

> The plain truth, very plain, we think, is, that. . . . One that has a higher Wisdom, a hitherto unknown spiritual Truth in him, is stronger, not than ten men that have it not, nor than ten thousand, but than all men that have it not; and stands among them with a quite ethereal, angelic power, as if with a sword out of Heaven's own armory, which no buckler, and no tower of brass will finally withstand.—*Signs of the Times*

In the history of science, of art, of music, we see abundant illustrations of this truth, but in no domain is the supreme importance of the great man and his message more clearly evident than in that of religion. All down the ages, whenever the spiritual life of men has become degenerate and their morals corrupt, that most wonderful and mysterious of men, the prophet, makes his appearance. Alone against the world, without a single human being capable of teaching, of guiding, of fully understanding him, or of sharing his responsibility, he

1

arises, like a seer among blind men, to proclaim his gospel of righteousness and truth.

Amongst the prophets some stand out with special pre-eminence. Every few centuries a great divine Revealer—a Krishna, a Zoroaster, a Moses, a Jesus, a Muḥammad—appears in the East, like a spiritual sun, to illumine the darkened minds of men and awaken their dormant souls. Whatever our views as to the relative greatness of these religion Founders, we must admit that They have been the most potent factors in the education of mankind. With one accord these Prophets declare that the words They utter are not from Themselves, but are a Revelation through Them, a divine Message of which They are the Bearers. Their recorded utterances abound, too, in hints and promises of a great world Teacher Who will appear "in the fullness of time" to carry on Their work and bring it to fruition, One Who will establish a reign of peace and justice upon earth, and bring into one family all races, religions, nations, and tribes, "that there may be one fold and one Shepherd" and that all may know and love God "from the least even unto the greatest."

Surely the advent of this "Educator of mankind," in the latter days, when He appears, must be the greatest event in human history. *And the Bahá'í Movement is proclaiming to the world the glad tidings that this Educator has in fact appeared, that His Revelation has been delivered and recorded and may be studied by every earnest seeker, that the "Day of the Lord" has already dawned and the "Sun of Righteousness" arisen.* As yet only a few on the mountaintops have caught sight of the glorious Orb, but already its rays are illumining heaven and earth, and erelong it will rise above the mountains and shine with full strength on the plains and valleys too, giving life and guidance to all.

The Changing World

That the world, during the nineteenth and the early part of the twentieth centuries,[1] has been passing through the death

---

[1] Written shortly after the First World War.

pangs of an old era and the birth pangs of a new, is evident to all. The old principles of materialism and self-interest, the old sectarian and patriotic prejudices and animosities, are perishing, discredited, amidst the ruins they have wrought, and in all lands we see signs of a new spirit of faith, of brotherhood, of internationalism, that is bursting the old bonds and overrunning the old boundaries. Revolutionary changes of unprecedented magnitude have been occurring in every department of human life. The old era is not yet dead. It is engaged in a life and death struggle with the new. Evils there are in plenty, gigantic and formidable, but they are being exposed, investigated, challenged, and attacked with new vigor and hope. Clouds there are in plenty, vast and threatening, but the light is breaking through, and is illumining the path of progress and revealing the obstacles and pitfalls that obstruct the onward way.

In the eighteenth century it was different. Then the spiritual and moral gloom that enshrouded the world was relieved by hardly a ray of light. It was like the darkest hour before the dawn, when the few lamps and candles that remain alight do little more than make the darkness visible. Carlyle in his *Frederick the Great* writes of the eighteenth century thus:—

A century which has no history and can have little or none. A century so opulent in accumulated falsities . . . as never century before was! Which had no longer the consciousness of being false, so false had it grown; and was so steeped in falsity, and impregnated with it to the very bone, that—in fact the measure of the thing was full, and a French Revolution had to end it. . . . A very fit termination, as I thankfully feel, for such a century. . . . For there was need once more of a Divine Revelation to the torpid, frivolous children of men, if they were not to sink altogether into the ape condition.—*Frederick the Great,* Book I, Chap. 1.

Compared with the eighteenth century the present time is as the dawn after darkness, or as the spring after winter. The world is stirring with new life, thrilling with new ideals and hopes. Things that but a few years ago seemed impossible dreams are now accomplished facts. Others that seemed centuries ahead of us have already become matters of "practical politics." We fly in the air and make voyages under the sea. We send messages around the world with the speed of lightning. Within a few decades we have seen miracles too numerous to mention.

The Sun of Righteousness

What is the cause of this sudden awakening throughout the world? Bahá'ís believe that it is due to a great outpouring of the Holy Spirit through the Prophet Bahá'u'lláh, Who was born in Persia in 1817 and passed away in the Holy Land in 1892.

Bahá'u'lláh taught that the Prophet, or "Manifestation of God," is the light-bringer of the spiritual world, as the sun is the light-bringer of the natural world. Just as the material sun shines over the earth and causes the growth and development of material organisms, so also, through the Divine Manifestation, the Sun of Truth shines upon the world of heart and soul, and educates the thoughts, morals, and characters of men. And just as the rays of the natural sun have an influence which penetrates into the darkest and shadiest corners of the world, giving warmth and life even to creatures that have never seen the sun itself, so also, the outpouring of the Holy Spirit through the Manifestation of God influences the lives of all, and inspires receptive minds even in places and among peoples where the names of the Prophet is quite unknown. The advent of the Manifestation is like the coming of the spring. It is a day of resurrection in which the spiritually dead are raised to new life, in which the reality of the divine religions is renewed and reestablished, in which appear "new heavens and a new earth."

But, in the world of nature, the spring brings about not only the growth and awakening of new life, but also the destruction and removal of the old and effete; for the same sun, that makes the flowers to spring and the trees to bud, causes also the decay and disintegration of what is dead and useless; it loosens the ice and melts the snow of winter, and sets free the flood and the storm that cleanse and purify the earth. So is it also in the spiritual world. The spiritual sunshine causes similar commotion and change. Thus the Day of Resurrection is also the Day of Judgment, in which corruptions and imitations of the truth and outworn ideas and customs are discarded and destroyed, in which the ice and snow of prejudice and superstition, which accumulated during the season of winter, are melted and transformed, and energies long frozen and pent up are released to flood and renovate the world.

The Mission of Bahá'u'lláh

Bahá'u'lláh declared, plainly and repeatedly, that He was the long-expected Educator and Teacher of all peoples, the channel of a wondrous grace that would transcend all previous outpourings, in which all previous forms of religion would become merged, as rivers merge in the ocean. He laid a foundation which affords a firm basis for unity throughout the whole world and the inauguration of that glorious age of peace on earth, goodwill among men, of which prophets have told and poets sung.

Search after truth, the oneness of mankind, unity of religions, of races, of nations, of East and West, the reconciliation of religion and science, the eradication of prejudices and superstitions, the equality of men and women, the establishment of justice and righteousness, the setting up of a supreme international tribunal, the unification of languages, the compulsory diffusion of knowledge—these, and many other teachings like these, were revealed by the pen of Bahá'u'lláh during the latter half of the nineteenth century, in innumerable books and epistles several of which were addressed to the kings and rulers of the world.

His Message, unique in its comprehensiveness and scope, is wonderfully in accord with the signs and needs of the times. Never were the new problems confronting men so gigantic and complex as now. Never were the proposed solutions so numerous and conflicting. Never was the need of a great world Teacher so urgent or so widely felt. Never, perhaps, was the expectancy of such a Teacher so confident or so general.

Fulfillment of Prophecies

'Abdu'l-Bahá writes:—

When Christ appeared, twenty centuries ago, although the Jews were eagerly awaiting His coming, and prayed every day, with tears, saying: "O God, hasten the revelation of the Messiah," yet when the Sun of Truth dawned, they denied Him and rose against Him with the greatest enmity, and eventually crucified that divine Spirit, the Word of God, and named Him Beelzebub, the evil one, as is recorded in the Gospel. The reason for this was that they said: "The revelation of Christ, according to the clear text of the Torah, will be attested by certain signs, and so long as these signs have not appeared, whoso layeth claim to be a Messiah is an impostor. Among these signs is this, that the Messiah should come from an unknown place, yet we all know this man's house in Nazareth, and can any good thing come out of Nazareth? The second sign is that He shall rule with a rod of iron, that is, He must act with the sword, but this Messiah has not even a wooden staff. Another of the conditions and signs is this: He must sit upon the throne of David and establish David's sovereignty. Now, far from being enthroned, this man has not even a mat to sit on. Another of the conditions is this: the promulgation of all the laws of the Torah; yet this man has abrogated these laws, and has even broken the sabbath day, although it is the clear text of the Torah that whosoever layeth claim to prophethood and revealeth miracles and breaketh the sabbath day, must be put to death. Another of the signs is this, that in His reign justice will be so advanced that righteousness and well-doing will extend from the human even to the animal world—the snake and the mouse will share one hole, and the eagle and the partridge one nest, the lion and the gazelle shall dwell in one pasture, and the wolf and the kid shall drink from one fountain. Yet now, injustice and tyranny have waxed so great in his time that they have crucified him! Another of the conditions is this, that in the days of the Messiah the Jews will prosper and triumph over all the peoples of the world, but now they are living in the utmost abasement and servitude in the empire of the Romans. Then how can this be the Messiah promised in the Torah?"

In this wise did they object to that Sun of Truth, although that Spirit of God was indeed the One promised in the Torah. But as they did not understand the meaning of these signs, they crucified the Word of God. Now the Bahá'ís hold that the recorded signs did come to pass in the Manifestation of Christ, although not in the sense which the Jews understood, the description in the Torah being allegorical. For instance, among the signs is that of sovereignty. For Bahá'ís say that the sovereignty of Christ was a heavenly, divine, everlasting sovereignty, not a Napoleonic sovereignty that vanisheth in a short time. For well-nigh two thousand years this sovereignty of Christ hath been established, and until now it endureth, and to all eternity that holy Being will be exalted upon an everlasting throne.

In like manner all the other signs have been made manifest, but the Jews did not understand. Although nearly twenty centuries have elapsed since Christ appeared with divine splendor, yet the Jews are still awaiting the coming of the Messiah and regard themselves as true and Christ as false.—Written by 'Abdu'l-Bahá for this chapter.

Had the Jews applied to Christ He would have explained to them the true meaning of the prophecies concerning Himself. Let us profit by their example, and before deciding that the prophecies concerning the manifestation of the latter-day Teacher have not been fulfilled, let us turn to what Bahá'u'lláh Himself has written regarding their interpretation, for many of the prophecies are admittedly "sealed" sayings, and the true Educator Himself is the only one who can break the seals and show the real meanings contained in the casket of words.

Bahá'u'lláh has written much in explanation of the prophecies of old, but it is not on these that He depends for proof of His Prophethood. The sun is its own proof, to all that have the power of perception. When it rises we need no ancient predictions to assure us of its shining. So with the Manifestation of God when He appears. Were all the former prophecies swept into oblivion, He would still be His own abundant and sufficient proof to all whose spiritual senses are open.

Proofs of Prophethood

Bahá'u'lláh asked no one to accept His statements and His tokens blindly. On the contrary, He put in the very forefront of His teachings emphatic warnings against blind acceptance of authority, and urged all to open their eyes and ears, and use their own judgment, independently and fearlessly, in order to ascertain the truth. He enjoined the fullest investigation and never concealed Himself, offering, as the supreme proofs of His Prophethood, His words and works and their effects in transforming the lives and characters of men. The tests He proposed are the same as those laid down by His great predecessors. Moses said:—

> When a prophet speaketh in the name of the Lord, if the thing follow not, nor come to pass, that is the thing which the Lord hath not spoken, but the prophet hath spoken it presumptuously: thou shalt not be afraid of him.—Deut. xviii, 22.

Christ put His test just as plainly, and appealed to it in proof of His own claim. He said:—

> Beware of false prophets, which come to you in sheep's clothing, but inwardly they are ravening wolves. Ye shall know them by their fruits. Do men gather grapes of thorns, or figs of thistles? Even so every good tree bringeth forth good fruit; but a corrupt tree bringeth forth evil fruit. . . . Wherefore by their fruits ye shall know them. —Matt. vii, 15-20.

In the chapters that follow, we shall endeavor to show whether Bahá'u'lláh's claim to Prophethood stands or falls by application of these tests: whether the things that He had spoken have followed and come to pass, and whether His fruits have been good or evil; in other words, whether His prophecies are being fulfilled and His ordinances established, and whether His lifework has contributed to the education and upliftment of humanity and the betterment of morals, or the contrary.

Difficulties of Investigation

There are, of course, difficulties in the way of the student who seeks to get at the truth about this Cause. Like all great moral and spiritual reformations, the Bahá'í Faith has been grossly misrepresented. About the terrible persecutions and sufferings of Bahá'u'lláh and His followers, both friends and enemies are in entire agreement. About the value of the Movement, however, and the character of its Founders, the statements of the believers and the accounts of the deniers are utterly at variance. It is just as in the time of Christ. Concerning the crucifixion of Jesus and the persecution and martyrdom of His followers both Christian and Jewish historians are in agreement, but whereas the believers say that Christ fulfilled and developed the teachings of Moses and the prophets, the deniers declare that He broke the laws and ordinances and was worthy of death.

In religion, as in science, truth reveals her mysteries only to the humble and reverent seeker, who is ready to lay aside every prejudice and superstition—to sell all that he has, in order that he may buy the "one pearl of great price." To understand the Bahá'í Faith in its full significance, we must undertake its study in the spirit of sincere and selfless devotion to truth, persevering in the path of search and relying on divine guidance. In the Writings of its Founders we shall find the master key to the mysteries of this great spiritual awakening, and the ultimate criterion of its value. Unfortunately, here again there are difficulties in the way of the student who is unacquainted with the Persian and Arabic languages in which the teachings are written. Only a small proportion of the Writings has been translated into English, and many of the translations which have appeared leave much to be desired, both in accuracy and style. But despite the imperfection and inadequacy of historical narratives and translations, the greatest essential truths which form the massive and firm foundations of this Cause stand out like mountains from the mists of uncertainty.[1]

Aim of Book

The endeavor in the following chapters will be to set forth, as far as possible, fairly and without prejudice, the salient features of the history and more especially of the teachings of the Bahá'í Cause, so that readers may be enabled to form an intelligent judgment as to their importance, and perhaps be induced to search into the subject more deeply for themselves.

Search after truth, however, important though it be, is not the whole aim and end of life. The truth is no dead thing, to be placed in a museum when found—to be labeled, classified, cataloged, exhibited, and left there, dry and sterile. It is something vital which must take root in men's hearts and bear fruit in their lives ere they reap the full reward of their search.

The real object, therefore, in spreading the knowledge of a prophetic revelation is that those who become convinced of its truth may proceed to practice its principles, to "lead the life" and diffuse the glad tidings, thus hastening the advent of that blessed day when God's will shall be done on earth as it is in heaven.

---

[1] There are now the incomparable translations by Shoghi Effendi from the Persian and Arabic, of the Writings of Bahá'u'lláh and 'Abdu'l-Bahá. These, together with his own considerable writings covering the history of the Faith, the statements and implications of its fundamental verities, and the unfoldment of its Administrative Order, make the modern inquirer's task infinitely easier than in Dr. Esslemont's time.

The Báb:[1] Forerunner/2

Verily the oppressor hath slain the Beloved of the worlds that he might thereby quench the light of God amidst His creatures and withhold mankind from the stream of celestial life in the days of his Lord, the Gracious, the Bountiful.— BAHÁ'U'LLÁH, *Tablet to Ra'ís.*

Birthplace of the New Revelation

Persia, the birthplace of the Bahá'í Revelation, has occupied a unique place in the history of the world. In the days of her early greatness she was a veritable queen among nations, unrivaled in civilization, in power, and in splendor. She gave to the world great kings and statesmen, prophets and poets, philosophers and artists. Zoroaster, Cyrus and Darius, Ḥáfiz and Firdawsí, Sa'dí and 'Umar Khayyám are but a few of her many famous sons. Her craftsmen were unsurpassed in skill; her carpets were matchless, her steel blades unequaled, her pottery world famous. In all parts of the Near and Middle East she has left traces of her former greatness.

Yet, in the eighteenth and nineteenth centuries she had sunk to a condition of deplorable degradation. Her ancient glory seemed irretrievably lost. Her government was corrupt and in desperate financial straits; some of her rulers were feeble, and others monsters of cruelty. Her priests were bigoted and intolerant, her people ignorant and superstitious. Most of them belonged to the Shí'ih sect,[2] of Muḥammadans, but there were also considerable numbers of Zoroastrians, Jews, and Chris-

---

[1] The "a" pronounced as in Sháh.

[2] One of the two great factions—Shí'ih and Sunní—into which Islám fell soon after the death of Muḥammad. The Shí'ihs claim that 'Alí, the son-in-law of Muḥammad, was the first legitimate successor of the Prophet, and that only his descendants are the rightful caliphs.

11

tians, of diverse and antagonistic sects. All professed to follow sublime teachers who exhorted them to worship the one God and to live in love and unity, yet they shunned, detested, and despised each other, each sect regarding the others as unclean, as dogs or heathens. Cursing and execration were indulged in to a fearful extent. It was dangerous for a Jew or a Zoroastrian to walk in the street on a rainy day, for if his wet garment should touch a Muḥammadan, the Muslim was defiled, and the other might have to atone for the offense with his life. If a Muḥammadan took money from a Jew, Zoroastrian, or Christian he had to wash it before he could put it in his pocket. If a Jew found his child giving a glass of water to a poor Muḥammadan beggar he would dash the glass from the child's hand, for curses rather than kindness should be the portion of infidels! The Muslims themselves were divided into numerous sects, among whom strife was often bitter and fierce. The Zoroastrians did not join much in these mutual recriminations, but lived in communities apart, refusing to associate with their fellow countrymen of other faiths.

Social as well as religious affairs were in a state of hopeless decadence. Education was neglected. Western science and art were looked upon as unclean and contrary to religion. Justice was travestied. Pillage and robbery were of common occurrence. Roads were bad and unsafe for travel. Sanitary arrangements were shockingly defective.

Yet, notwithstanding all this, the light of spiritual life was not extinct in Persia. Here and there, amid the prevailing worldliness and superstition, could still be found some saintly souls, and in many a heart the longing for God was cherished, as in the hearts of Anna and Simeon before the appearance of Jesus. Many were eagerly awaiting the coming of a promised Messenger of God, and confident that the time of His advent was at hand. Such was the state of affairs in Persia when the Báb, the Herald of a new era, set all the country in commotion with His Message.

Early Life

Mírzá 'Alí Muḥammad, Who afterwards assumed the title of Báb (i.e. Gate), was born at Shíráz, in the south of Persia, on the 20th of October, A.D.[1] 1819. He was a Siyyid, that is, a descendant of the Prophet Muḥammad. His father, a well-known merchant, died soon after His birth, and He was then placed under the care of a maternal uncle, a merchant of Shíráz, who brought Him up. In childhood He learned to read, and received the elementary education customary for children.[2] At the age of fifteen He went into business, at first with His guardian, and afterwards with another uncle who lived at Búshihr, on the shore of the Gulf of Persia.

As a youth He was noted for great personal beauty and charm of manner, and also for exceptional piety, and nobility of character. He was unfailing in His observance of the prayers, fasts, and other ordinances of the Muḥammadan religion, and not only obeyed the letter, but lived in the spirit of the Prophet's teachings. He married when about twenty-two years of age. Of this marriage one son was born, who died while still an infant, in the first year of the Báb's public ministry.

---

[1] First day of Muharram, A.H. 1235.

[2] On this point a historian remarks: "The belief of many people in the East, especially the believers in the Báb (now Bahá'ís) was this: that the Báb received no education, but that the Mullás, in order to lower Him in the eyes of the people, declared that such knowledge and wisdom as He possessed were accounted for by the education He had received. After deep search into the truth of this matter we have found evidence to show that in childhood for a short time He used to go to the house of Shaykh Muḥammad (also known as 'Ábid) where He was taught to read and write in Persian. It was this to which the Báb referred when He wrote in the book of Bayán: 'O Muḥammad, O My teacher! . . .'

"The remarkable thing is this, however, that this Shaykh, who was His teacher, became a devoted disciple of his own pupil, and the uncle of the Báb who was like a father to Him, whose name was Ḥájí Siyyid 'Alí, also became a devout believer and was martyred as a Bábí.

"The understanding of these mysteries is given to seekers after truth, but we know this, that such education as the Báb received was but elementary, and that whatever signs of unusual greatness and knowledge appeared in Him were innate and from God."

Declaration

On reaching His twenty-fifth year, in response to divine command, He declared that "God the Exalted had elected Him to the station of Bábhood." In "A Traveller's Narrative"[1] we read that:—"What He intended by the term 'Báb' was this: that He was the channel of grace from some great Person still behind the veil of glory, Who was the possessor of countless and boundless perfections, by Whose will He moved, and to the bond of Whose love He clung."—*A Traveller's Narrative* (Episode of the Báb), p. 3.

In those days belief in the imminent appearance of a Divine Messenger was especially prevalent among a sect known as the Shaykhís, and it was to a distinguished divine belonging to this sect, called Mullá Husayn Bushrú'í, that the Báb first announced His mission. The exact date of this announcement is given in the *Bayán,* one of the Báb's Writings, as two hours and eleven minutes after sunset on the eve preceding the fifth day of the month of Jamádíyu'l-Avval A.H. 1260[2] 'Abdu'l-Bahá was born in the course of the same night, but the exact hour of His birth has not been ascertained. After some days of anxious investigation and study, Mullá Husayn became firmly convinced that the Messenger long expected by the Shí'ihs had indeed appeared. His eager enthusiasm over this discovery was soon shared by several of his friends. Before long the majority of the Shaykhís accepted the Báb, becoming known as Bábís; and soon the fame of the young prophet began to spread like wildfire throughout the land.

Spread of the Bábí Movement

The first eighteen disciples of the Báb (with Himself as nineteenth) became known as "Letters of the Living." These

[1] *A Traveller's Narrative Written to Illustrate the Episode of the Báb* with an introduction by E. G. Browne, referred to subsequently as *Episode of the Báb.*
[2] May 23, A.D. 1844.

disciples He sent to different parts of Persia and Turkistán to spread the news of His advent. Meantime He Himself set out on a pilgrimage to Mecca, where He arrived in December 1844, and there openly declared His mission. On His return to Búshihr great excitement was caused by the announcement of His Bábhood. The fire of His eloquence, the wonder of His rapid and inspired writings, His extraordinary wisdom and knowledge, His courage and zeal as a reformer, aroused the greatest enthusiasm among His followers, but excited a corresponding degree of alarm and enmity among the orthodox Muslims. The Shí'ih doctors vehemently denounced Him, and persuaded the Governor of Fárs, namely Husayn Khán, a fanatical and tyrannical ruler, to undertake the suppression of the new heresy. Then commenced for the Báb a long series of imprisonments, deportations, examinations before tribunals, scourgings, and indignities, which ended only with His martyrdom in 1850.

Claims of Báb

The hostility aroused by the claim of Bábhood was redoubled when the young Reformer proceeded to declare that He was Himself the Mihdí (Mahdi) Whose coming Muhammad had foretold. The Shí'ihs identified this Mihdí with the 12th Imám [1] who, according to their beliefs, had mysteriously disappeared from the sight of men about a thousand years previously. They believed that he was still alive and would reappear in the same body as before, and they interpreted in a material sense the prophecies regarding his dominion, his glory, his conquests, and the "signs" of his advent, just as the Jews in the time of Christ interpreted similar prophecies re-

---

[1] The Imám of the Shí'ihs is the divinely ordained successor of the Prophet whom all the faithful must obey. Eleven persons successively held the office of Imám, the first being 'Alí, the cousin and son-in-law of the Prophet. The majority of the Shí'ihs hold that the twelfth Imám, called by them the Imám Mihdí, disappeared as a child into an underground passage in A.H. 329, and that in the fullness of time he will come forth, overthrow the infidels, and inaugurate an era of blessedness.

garding the Messiah. They expected that he would appear with earthly sovereignty and an innumerable army and declare his revelation, that he would raise dead bodies and restore them to life, and so on. As these signs did not appear, the Shí'ihs rejected the Báb with the same fierce scorn which the Jews displayed towards Jesus. The Bábís, on the other hand, interpreted many of the prophecies figuratively. They regarded the sovereignty of the Promised One, like that of the Galilean "Man of Sorrows," as a mystical sovereignty; His glory as spiritual, not earthly glory; His conquests as conquests over the cities of men's hearts; and they found abundant proof of the Báb's claim in His wonderful life and teachings, His unshakable faith, His invincible steadfastness, and His power of raising to newness of spiritual life those who were in the graves of error and ignorance.

But the Báb did not stop even with the claim of Mihdíhood. He adopted the sacred title of "Nuqtiyiúlá" or "Primal Point." This was a title applied to Muhammad Himself by His followers. Even the Imáms were secondary in importance to the "Point," from Whom they derived their inspiration and authority. In assuming this title, the Báb claimed to rank, like Muhammad, in the series of great Founders of religion, and for this reason, in the eyes of the Shí'ihs, He was regarded as an impostor, just as Moses and Jesus before Him had been regarded as impostors. He even inaugurated a new calendar, restoring the solar year, and dating the commencement of the new era from the year of His own Declaration.

Persecution Increases

In consequence of these declarations of the Báb and the alarming rapidity with which people of all classes, rich and poor, learned and ignorant, were eagerly responding to His teaching, attempts at suppression became more and more ruthless and determined. Houses were pillaged and destroyed. Women were seized and carried off. In Tihrán, Fárs, Mázindarán, and other places great numbers of the believers were put to death. Many were beheaded, hanged, blown from the mouths of cannon, burnt, or chopped to pieces. Despite all attempts at repression, however, the Movement progressed. Nay, through this very oppression the assurance of the believers increased, for thereby many of the prophecies concerning the coming of the Mihdí were literally fulfilled. Thus in a tradition recorded by Jábir, which the Shí'ihs regard as authentic, we read:—

> In him shall be the perfection of Moses, the preciousness of Jesus, and the patience of Job; his saints shall be abased in his time, and their heads shall be exchanged as presents, even as the heads of the Turk and the Deylamite are exchanged as presents; they shall be slain and burned, and shall be afraid, fearful and dismayed; the earth shall be dyed with their blood, and lamentation shall prevail amongst their women; these are my saints indeed.—*New History of the Báb,* translated by Prof. E. G. Browne, p. 132.

Martyrdom of the Báb

On the 9th of July, 1850,[1] the Báb Himself, Who was then in His thirty-first year, fell a victim to the fanatical fury of His persecutors. With a devoted young follower named Áqá Muḥammad 'Alí, who had passionately begged to be allowed to share His martyrdom, He was led to the scaffold in the old barrack square of Tabríz. About two hours before noon the two were suspended by ropes under their armpits in such a way that the head of Muḥammad 'Alí rested against the breast of his beloved Master. A regiment of Armenian soldiers was drawn up and received the order to fire. Promptly the volleys rang out, but when the smoke cleared, it was found that the Báb and His companion were still alive. The bullets had but severed the ropes by which they were suspended, so that they dropped to the ground unhurt. The Báb proceeded to a room

---

[1] Friday, 28th Sha'bán, A.H. 1266.

nearby, where He was found talking to one of His friends. About noon they were again suspended. The Armenians, who considered the result of their volleys a miracle, were unwilling to fire again, so another regiment of soldiers had been brought on the scene, who fired when ordered. This time the volleys took effect. The bodies of both victims were riddled by bullets and horribly mutilated, although their faces were almost untouched.

By this foul deed the barrack square of Tabríz became a second Calvary. The enemies of the Báb enjoyed a guilty thrill of triumph, thinking that this hated tree of the Bábí Faith was now severed at the root, and its complete eradication would be easy! But their triumph was short-lived! They did not realize that the Tree of truth cannot be felled by any material ax. Had they but known, this very crime of theirs was the means of giving greater vigor to the Cause. The martyrdom of the Báb fulfilled His own cherished wish and inspired His followers with increased zeal. Such was the fire of their spiritual enthusiasm that the bitter winds of persecution but fanned it to a fiercer blaze: The greater the efforts at extinction, the higher mounted the flames.

Tomb on Mount Carmel

After the Báb's martyrdom, His remains, with those of His devoted companion, were thrown on the edge of the moat outside the city wall. On the second night they were rescued at midnight by some of the Bábís, and after being concealed for years in secret depositories in Persia, were ultimately brought, with great danger and difficulty, to the Holy Land. There they are now interred in a tomb beautifully situated on the slope of Mount Carmel, not far from the Cave of Elijah, and only a few miles from the spot where Bahá'u'lláh spent His last years and where His remains now lie. Among the thousands of pilgrims from all parts of the world who come to pay homage at the Holy Tomb of Bahá'u'lláh, none omit to offer a prayer also at the Shrine of His devoted lover and Forerunner, the Báb.

Writings of Báb

The Writings of the Báb were voluminous, and the rapidity with which, without study or premeditation, He composed elaborate commentaries, profound expositions, or eloquent prayers was regarded as one of the proofs of His divine inspiration.

The purport of His various Writings has been summarized as follows:—

Some of these (the Báb's Writings) were commentaries on, and interpretations of, the verses of the Qur'án; some were prayers, homilies, and hints of (the true significance of certain) passages; others were exhortations, admonitions, dissertations on the different branches of the doctrine of the Divine Unity . . . encouragements to amendment of character, severance from worldly states, and dependence on the inspirations of God. But the essence and purport of His compositions were the praises and descriptions of that Reality soon to appear which was His only object and aim, His darling, and His desire. For He regarded His own appearance as that of a harbinger of good tidings, and considered His own real nature merely as a means for the manifestation of the greater perfections of that One. And indeed He ceased not from celebrating Him by night or day for a single instant, but used to signify to all His followers that they should expect His arising, in such wise that He declares in His Writings: "I am a letter out of that most mighty Book and a dewdrop from that limitless Ocean, and when He shall appear, My true nature, My mysteries, riddles, and intimations will become evident, and the embryo of this religion shall develop through the grades of its being and ascent, attain to the station of 'the most comely of forms' and become adorned with the robe of 'blessed be God, the best of Creators!' " . . . and so inflamed was He with His flame that commemoration of Him was the bright candle of

His dark nights in the fortress of Máh-Kú, and remembrance of Him was the best of companions in the straits of the prison of C̲h̲ihríq. Thereby He obtained spiritual enlargements; with His wine was He inebriated; and at remembrance of Him did He rejoice.—*A Traveller's Narrative* (Episode of the Báb), p. 54.

He Whom God Shall Make Manifest

The Báb has been compared to John the Baptist, but the station of the Báb is not merely that of the Herald or Forerunner. In Himself the Báb was a Manifestation of God, the Founder of an independent religion, even though that religion was limited in time to a brief period of years. The Bahá'ís believe that the Báb and Bahá'u'lláh were Co-Founders of their Faith, the following words of Bahá'u'lláh testifying to this truth: "That so brief a span should have separated this most mighty and wondrous Revelation from Mine own previous Manifestation, is a secret that no man can unravel and a mystery such as no mind can fathom. Its duration had been foreordained, and no man shall ever discover its reason unless and until he be informed of the contents of My Hidden Book." In His references to Bahá'u'lláh, however, the Báb revealed an utter selflessness, declaring that, in the day of "Him Whom God shall manifest":—"If one should hear a single verse from Him and recite it, it is better than that he should recite the *Bayán* (i.e. the Revelation of the Báb) a thousand times."— *A Traveller's Narrative* (Episode of the Báb), p. 349.

He counted Himself happy in enduring any affliction, if by so doing He could smooth the path, by ever so little, for "Him Whom God shall make manifest," Who was, He declared, the sole source of His inspiration as well as the sole object of His love.

Resurrection, Paradise, and Hell

An important part of the Báb's teaching is His explanation of the terms Resurrection, Day of Judgment, Paradise, and

Hell. By the Resurrection is meant, He said, the appearance of a new Manifestation of the Sun of Truth. The raising of the dead means the spiritual awakening of those who are asleep in the graves of ignorance, heedlessness, and lust. The Day of Judgment is the Day of the new Manifestation, by acceptance or rejection of Whose Revelation the sheep are separated from the goats, for the sheep know the voice of the Good Shepherd and follow Him. Paradise is the joy of knowing and loving God, as revealed through His Manifestation, thereby attaining to the utmost perfection of which one is capable, and, after death, obtaining entrance to the Kingdom of God and the life everlasting. Hell is simply deprivation of that knowledge of God with consequent failure to attain divine perfection, and loss of the eternal favor. He definitely declared that these terms have no real meaning apart from this; and that the prevalent ideas regarding the resurrection of the material body, a material heaven and hell, and the like, are mere figments of the imagination. He taught that man has a life after death, and that in the afterlife progress towards perfection is limitless.

Social and Ethical Teachings

In His Writings the Báb tells His followers that they must be distinguished by brotherly love and courtesy. Useful arts and crafts must be cultivated. Elementary education should be general. In the new and wondrous Dispensation now commencing, women are to have fuller freedom. The poor are to be provided for out of the common treasury, but begging is strictly forbidden, as is the use of intoxicating liquors for beverage purposes.

The guiding motive of the true Bábí must be pure love, without hope of reward or fear of punishment. Thus He says in the *Bayán:*—

> So worship God that if the recompense of your worship were to be the Fire, no alteration of your worship of Him would be produced. If you worship God from fear, that is unworthy of the threshold of the holiness of God. . . .

So also, if your gaze is on Paradise, and if you worship in hope of that; for then you have made God's creation a partner with Him.—*Bábís of Persia,* II, by Prof. E. G. Browne, J.R.A.S., vol. xxi, p. 931.

Passion and Triumph

This last quotation reveals the spirit which animated the Báb's whole life. To know and love God, to mirror forth His attributes, and to prepare the way for His coming Manifestation—these were the sole aim and object of His being. For Him life had no terrors and death no sting, for love had cast out fear, and martyrdom itself was but the rapture of casting His all at the feet of His Beloved.

Strange! that this pure and beautiful Soul, this inspired Teacher of divine Truth, this devoted lover of God and of His fellowmen should be so hated, and done to death by the professedly religious of His day! Surely nothing but unthinking or willful prejudice could blind men to the fact that here was indeed a Prophet, a Holy Messenger of God. Worldly greatness and glory He had none, but how can spiritual power and dominion be proved except by the ability to dispense with all earthly assistance, and to triumph over all earthly opposition, even the most potent and virulent? How can divine love be demonstrated to an unbelieving world save by its capacity to endure to the uttermost the blows of calamity and the darts of affliction, the hatred of enemies and the treachery of seeming friends, to rise serene above all these and, undismayed and unembittered, still to forgive and bless?

The Báb has endured and the Báb has triumphed. Thousands have testified to the sincerity of their love for Him by sacrificing their lives and their all in His service. Kings might well envy His power over men's hearts and lives. Moreover, "He Whom the Lord shall make manifest" has appeared, has confirmed the claims and accepted the devotion of His Forerunner, and made Him partaker of His glory.

Bahá'u'lláh:[1] The Glory of God/3

O thou who art waiting, tarry no longer, for He is come. Behold His Tabernacle and His Glory dwelling therein. It is the Ancient Glory, with a new Manifestation.—BAHÁ'U'-LLÁH.

Birth and Early Life

Mírzá Husayn 'Alí, Who afterwards assumed the title of Bahá'u'lláh (i.e. Glory of God), was the eldest son of Mírzá 'Abbás of Núr, a Vazír or Minister of State. His family was wealthy and distinguished, many of its members having occupied important positions in the Government and in the civil and military services of Persia. He was born in Ṭihrán (Teheran), the capital city of Persia, between dawn and sunrise on the 12th of November, 1817.[2] He never attended school or college, and what little teaching He received was given at home. Nevertheless, even as a child He showed wonderful wisdom and knowledge. While He was still a youth His father died, leaving Him responsible for the care of His younger brothers and sisters, and for the management of the extensive family estates.

On one occasion 'Abdu'l-Bahá, the eldest son of Bahá'u'-lláh, related to the writer the following particulars about His Father's early days:—

> From childhood He was extremely kind and generous. He was a great lover of outdoor life, most of His time being spent in the garden or the fields. He had an extraordinary power of attraction, which was felt by all. People

---

[1] Pronounced with the accent on the second and fourth syllables, the first syllable being almost mute and both l's distinctly sounded.

[2] 2nd of Muḥarram, A.H. 1233.

23

always crowded around Him. Ministers and people of the Court would surround Him, and the children also were devoted to Him. When He was only thirteen or fourteen years old He became renowned for His learning. He would converse on any subject and solve any problem presented to Him. In large gatherings He would discuss matters with the 'ulamá (leading mullás) and would explain intricate religious questions. All of them used to listen to Him with the greatest interest.

When Bahá'u'lláh was twenty-two years old, His father died, and the Government wished Him to succeed to His father's position in the Ministry, as was customary in Persia, but Bahá'u'lláh did not accept the offer. Then the Prime Minister said: "Leave Him to Himself. Such a position is unworthy of Him. He has some higher aim in view. I cannot understand Him, but I am convinced that He is destined for some lofty career. His thoughts are not like ours. Let Him alone."

Imprisoned as Bábí

When the Báb declared His mission in 1844, Bahá'u'lláh, Who was then in His twenty-seventh year, boldly espoused the Cause of the new Faith, of which He soon became recognized as one of the most powerful and fearless exponents.

He had already twice suffered imprisonment for the Cause, and on one occasion had undergone the torture of the bastinado, when in August 1852, an event occurred fraught with terrible consequences for the Bábís. One of the Báb's followers, a youth named Ṣádiq, had been so affected by the martyrdom of his beloved Master, of which he was an eyewitness, that his mind became deranged, and, in revenge, he waylaid the Sháh and fired a pistol at him. Instead of using a bullet, however, he charged his weapon with small shot, and although a few pellets struck the Sháh, no serious harm was done. The youth dragged the Sháh from his horse, but was promptly seized by the attendants of His Majesty and put to death on the spot. The whole body of Bábís was unjustly held responsible for the deed, and frightful massacres ensued. Eighty of them were forthwith put to death in Ṭihrán with the most revolting tortures. Many others were seized and put into prisons, among them being Bahá'u'lláh. He afterwards wrote:—

By the righteousness of God! We were in no wise connected with that evil deed, and Our innocence was indisputably established by the tribunals. Nevertheless, they apprehended Us, and from Níyávarán, which was then the residence of His Majesty, conducted Us, on foot and in chains, with bared head and bare feet, to the dungeon of Ṭihrán. A brutal man, accompanying Us on horseback, snatched off Our hat, whilst We were being hurried along by a troop of executioners and officials. We were consigned for four months to a place foul beyond comparison. As to the dungeon in which this wronged One and others similarly wronged were confined, a dark and narrow pit were preferable. Upon Our arrival We were first conducted along a pitch-black corridor, from whence We descended three steep flights of stairs to the place of confinement assigned to Us. The dungeon was wrapped in thick darkness, and Our fellow prisoners numbered nearly a hundred and fifty souls: thieves, assassins and highwaymen. Though crowded, it had no other outlet than the passage by which We entered. No pen can depict that place, nor any tongue describe its loathsome smell. Most of these men had neither clothes nor bedding to lie on. God alone knoweth what befell Us in that most foul-smelling and gloomy place!

Day and night, while confined in that dungeon, We meditated upon the deeds, the condition, and the conduct of the Bábís, wondering what could have led a people so high-minded, so noble, and of such intelligence, to perpetrate such an audacious and outrageous act against the person of His Majesty. This wronged One, thereupon, decided to arise, after His release from prison, and undertake, with the utmost vigor, the task of regenerating this people.

One night, in a dream, these exalted words were heard on every side: "Verily, We shall render Thee victorious by Thyself and by Thy pen. Grieve Thou not for that which hath befallen Thee, neither be Thou afraid, for Thou art in safety. Erelong will God raise up the treasures of the earth—men who will aid Thee through Thyself and through Thy Name, wherewith God hath revived the hearts of such as have recognized Him."—*Epistle to the Son of the Wolf*, pp. 20-21.

Exile to Baghdád

This terrible imprisonment lasted four months, but Bahá'u'lláh and His companions remained zealous and enthusiastic, in the greatest of happiness. Almost every day one or more of them was tortured or put to death and the others reminded that their turn might come next. When the executioners came to fetch one of the friends, the one whose name was called would literally dance with joy, kiss the hands of Bahá'u'lláh, embrace the rest of his fellow believers, and then hasten with glad eagerness to the place of martyrdom.

It was conclusively proved that Bahá'u'lláh had no share in the plot against the Sháh, and the Russian Minister testified to the purity of His character. He was, moreover, so ill that it was thought He would die. Instead, therefore, of sentencing Him to death, the Sháh ordered that He should be exiled to 'Iráq-i-'Arab, in Mesopotamia; and thither, a fortnight later, Bahá'u'lláh set out, accompanied by His family and a number of other believers. They suffered terribly from cold and other hardships on the long winter journey, and arrived in Baghdád in a state of almost utter destitution.

As soon as His health permitted, Bahá'u'lláh began to teach inquirers and to encourage and exhort the believers, and soon peace and happiness reigned among the Bábís.[1] This, however, was short-lived. Bahá'u'lláh's half brother, Mírzá Yaḥyá, also

---

[1] This was early in the year 1853, or nine years after the Báb's Declaration, thus fulfilling certain prophecies of the Báb concerning "the year nine."

known as Ṣubḥ-i-Azal, arrived in Baghdád, and soon afterwards differences, secretly instigated by him, began to grow,
just as similar divisions had arisen among the disciples of
Christ. These differences (which later, in Adrianople, became
open and violent) were very painful to Bahá'u'lláh, Whose
whole aim in life was the promotion of unity among the
people of the world.

Two Years in the Wilderness

About a year after coming to Baghdád, He departed alone
into the wilderness of Sulaymáníyyih, taking with Him nothing
but a change of clothes. Regarding this period He writes in the
Book of Íqán [1] as follows:—

In the early days of Our arrival in this land, when
We discerned the signs of impending events, We decided,
ere they happened, to retire. We betook Ourselves to the
wilderness, and there, separated and alone, led for two
years a life of complete solitude. From Our eyes there
rained tears of anguish, and in Our bleeding heart there
surged an ocean of agonizing pain. Many a night We had
no food for sustenance, and many a day Our body found
no rest. By Him Who hath My being between His hands!
notwithstanding these showers of afflictions and unceas-
ing calamities, Our soul was wrapt in blissful joy, and Our
whole being evinced an ineffable gladness. For in Our
solitude We were unaware of the harm or benefit, the
health or ailment, of any soul. Alone, We communed with
Our spirit, oblivious of the world and all that is therein.
We knew not, however, that the mesh of divine destiny
exceedeth the vastest of mortal conceptions, and the dart
of His decree transcendeth the boldest of human designs.
None can escape the snares He setteth, and no soul can
find release except through submission to His will. By the
righteousness of God! Our withdrawal contemplated no

---

[1] *Book of Íqán, Íqán, Kitáb-i-Íqán,* and *Book of Certitude* all refer to the
same book.

return, and Our separation hoped for no reunion. The one
object of Our retirement was to avoid becoming a subject
of discord among the faithful, a source of disturbance
unto Our companions, the means of injury to any soul,
or the cause of sorrow to any heart. Beyond these, We
cherished no other intention, and apart from them, We
had no end in view. And yet, each person schemed after
his own desire, and pursued his own idle fancy, until the
hour when, from the mystic Source, there came the summons bidding Us return whence We came. Surrendering
Our will to His, We submitted to His injunction.
What pen can recount the things We beheld upon Our
return! Two years have elapsed during which Our
enemies have ceaselessly and assiduously contrived to
exterminate Us, whereunto all witness.—*Kitáb-i-Íqán,*
pp. 250-252.

Opposition of Mullás

After His return from this retirement, His fame became
greater than ever and people flocked to Baghdád from far and
near to see Him and hear His teachings. Jews, Christians, and
Zoroastrians, as well as Muḥammadans, became interested in
the new Message. The mullás (Muḥammadan doctors), however, took up a hostile attitude and persistently plotted to effect
His overthrow. On a certain occasion they sent one of their
number to interview Him and submit to Him certain questions.
The envoy found the answers of Bahá'u'lláh so convincing and
His wisdom so amazing, although evidently not acquired by
study, that he was obliged to confess that in knowledge and
understanding Bahá'u'lláh was peerless. In order, however,
that the mullás who had sent him should be satisfied as to the
reality of Bahá'u'lláh's Prophethood, he asked that some miracle should be produced as a proof. Bahá'u'lláh expressed His
willingness to accept the suggestion on certain conditions,
declaring that if the mullás would agree regarding some
miracle to be performed, and would sign and seal a document
to the effect that on performance of this miracle they would
confess the validity of His mission and cease to oppose Him,

He would furnish the desired proof or else stand convicted of imposture. Had the aim of the mullás been to get at the truth, surely here was their opportunity; but their intention was far otherwise. Rightly or wrongly, they meant to secure a decision in their own favor. They feared the truth and fled from the daring challenge. This discomfiture, however, only spurred them on to devise fresh plots for the eradication of the oppressed sect. The consul general of Persia in Baghdád came to their assistance and sent repeated messages to the Sháh to the effect that Bahá'u'lláh was injuring the Muhammadan religion more than ever, still exerting a malign influence in Persia, and that He ought therefore to be banished to some more distant place.

It was characteristic of Bahá'u'lláh that, at this crisis, when at the instigation of the Muhammadan mullás the Persian and Turkish Governments were combining their efforts to eradicate the Movement, He remained calm and serene, encouraging and inspiring His followers and writing imperishable words of consolation and guidance. 'Abdu'l-Bahá relates how the *Hidden Words* were written at this time. Bahá'u'lláh would often go for a walk along the bank of the Tigris. He would come back looking very happy and write down those lyric gems of wise counsel which have brought help and healing to thousands of aching and troubled hearts. For years, only a few manuscript copies of the *Hidden Words* were in existence, and these had to be carefully concealed lest they should fall into the hands of the enemies that abounded, but now this little volume is probably the best known of all Bahá'u'lláh's works, and is read in every quarter of the globe. *The Book of Íqán is* another well-known work of Bahá'u'lláh's written about the same period, towards the end of His sojourn at Baghdád (A.D. 1862-1863).

Declaration at Ridván ¹ near Baghdád

After much negotiation, at the request of the Persian Government, an order was issued by the Turkish Government

---

¹ Pronounced Rizwán.

summoning Bahá'u'lláh to Constantinople. On receipt of this news His followers were in consternation. They besieged the house of their beloved Leader to such an extent that the family encamped in the garden of Najíb Páshá outside the town for twelve days, while the caravan was being prepared for the long journey. It was during these twelve days (April 22 to May 3, 1863, i.e. nineteen years after the Báb's Declaration) that Bahá'u'lláh announced to several of His followers the glad tidings that He was the One Whose coming had been foretold by the Báb—the Chosen of God, the Promised One of all the Prophets. The garden where this memorable Declaration took place has become known to Bahá'ís as the "Garden of Ridván," and the days Bahá'u'lláh spent there are commemorated in the "Feast of Ridván," which is held annually on the anniversary of those twelve days. During those days Bahá'u'lláh, instead of being sad or depressed, showed the greatest joy, dignity, and power. His followers became happy and enthusiastic, and great crowds came to pay their respects to Him. All the notables of Baghdád, even the Governor himself, came to honor the departing Prisoner.

Constantinople and Adrianople

The journey to Constantinople lasted between three and four months, the party consisting of Bahá'u'lláh with members of His family and twenty-six disciples. Arrived in Constantinople they found themselves prisoners in a small house in which they were very much overcrowded. Later they got somewhat better quarters, but after four months they were again moved on, this time to Adrianople. The journey to Adrianople, although it lasted but a few days, was the most terrible they had yet undertaken. Snow fell heavily most of the time, and as they were destitute of proper clothing and food, their sufferings were extreme. For the first winter in Adrianople, Bahá'u'lláh and His family, numbering twelve persons, were accommodated in a small house of three rooms, comfortless and vermin infested. In the spring they were given a more comfortable abode. They remained in Adrianople over four and a half years. Here Bahá'u'lláh resumed His teaching and gathered about Him a large following. He publicly announced His mission and was enthusiastically *accepted by the majority of the Bábís, who were known thereafter as Bahá'ís.* A minority, however, under the leadership of Bahá'u'lláh's half brother, Mírzá Yahyá, became violently opposed to Him and joined with their former enemies, the Shí'ihs, in plotting for His overthrow. Great troubles ensued, and at last the Turkish Government banished both Bábís and Bahá'ís from Adrianople, exiling Bahá'u'lláh and His followers to 'Akká, in Palestine, where they arrived (according to Nabíl) [1] on August 31, 1868, while Mírzá Yahyá and his party were sent to Cyprus.

Letters to Kings

About this time Bahá'u'lláh wrote His famous letters to the Sultán of Turkey, many of the crowned heads of Europe, the Pope, and the Sháh of Persia. Later, in His *Kitáb-i-Aqdas* [2] He addressed other sovereigns, the rulers and presidents of America, the leaders of religion in general, and the generality of mankind. To all, He announced His mission and called upon them to bend their energies to the establishment of true religion, just government, and international peace. In His letter to the Sháh He powerfully pleaded the cause of the oppressed Bábís and asked to be brought face to face with those who had instigated their persecution. Needless to say, this request was not complied with; Badí, the young and devoted Bahá'í who delivered the letter of Bahá'u'lláh, was seized and martyred with fearful tortures, hot bricks being pressed on his flesh!

In the same letter Bahá'u'lláh gives a most moving account of His own sufferings and longings:—

O king, I have seen in the way of God what no eye hath seen and no ear hath heard. Friends have disclaimed Me;

---

[1] Author of an early history of the Faith, *The Dawn-Breakers,* Nabíl was a participant in some of the scenes he describes and was personally acquainted with many of the early believers.

[2] *The Aqdas, Kitáb-i-Aqdas, The Book of Aqdas,* and *The Most Holy Book* all refer to the same book.

ways are straitened unto Me; the pool of safety is dried
up; the plain of ease is scorched yellow. How many
calamities have descended, and how many will descend!
I walk advancing toward the Mighty, the Bounteous,
while behind Me glides the serpent. My eyes rain down
tears until My bed is drenched; but My sorrow is not for
Myself. By God, My head longeth for the spears for the
love of its Lord, and I never pass by a tree but My heart
addresseth it saying, "O would that thou wert cut down
in My name and My body were crucified upon thee in
the way of My Lord!" Yea, because I see mankind going
astray in their intoxication and they know it not: they
have exalted their lusts and put aside their God, as though
they took the command of God for a mockery, a sport,
and a plaything; and they think that they do well, and
that they are harbored in the citadel of security. The
matter is not as they suppose: tomorrow they shall see
what they now deny.

We are about to shift from this most remote place of
banishment (Adrianople) unto the prison of 'Akká. And
according to what they say, it is assuredly the most
desolate of the cities of the world, the most unsightly of
them in appearance, the most detestable in climate, and
the foulest in water; it is as though it were the metropolis
of the owl; there is naught heard therein save the sound
of its hooting. And in it they intend to imprison this
Servant, and to shut in our faces the doors of leniency
and take away from us the good things of the life of the
world during what remaineth of our days. By God,
though weariness should weaken Me, and hunger should
destroy Me, though My couch should be made of the
hard rock and My associates of the beasts of the desert, I
will not blench, but will be patient, as the resolute and
determined are patient, in the strength of God, the King
of Preexistence, the Creator of the nations; and under
all circumstances I give thanks unto God. And We hope
of His graciousness (exalted is He) . . . that He will
render all men's faces sincere towards Him, the Mighty,

the Bounteous. Verily He answereth him who prayeth unto Him, and is near unto him who calleth on Him. And We ask Him to make this dark calamity a buckler for the body of His saints, and to protect them thereby from the sharp swords and piercing blades. Through affliction hath His light shone and His praise been bright unceasingly: this hath been His method through past ages and bygone times. *A Traveller's Narrative* (Episode of the Báb), pp. 145-147.

Imprisonment in 'Akká

At that time 'Akká (Acre) was a prison city to which the worst criminals were sent from all parts of the Turkish Empire. On arriving there, after a miserable sea journey, Bahá'u'lláh and His followers, about eighty to eighty-four in number, including men, women, and children, were imprisoned in the army barracks. The place was dirty and cheerless in the extreme. There were no beds or comforts of any sort. The food supplied was wretched and inadequate, so much so that after a time the prisoners begged to be allowed to buy their food for themselves. During the first few days the children were crying continually, and sleep was almost impossible. Malaria, dysentery, and other diseases soon broke out, and everyone in the company fell sick, with the exception of two. Three succumbed to their sickness, and the sufferings of the survivors were indescribable.[1]

This rigorous imprisonment lasted for over two years, during which time none of the Bahá'ís were allowed outside the prison door, except four men, carefully guarded, who went out daily to buy food.

During the imprisonment in the barracks, visitors were rigidly excluded. Several of the Bahá'ís of Persia came all the way on foot for the purpose of seeing their beloved Leader, but

---

[1] In order to bury two of those who died, Bahá'u'lláh gave His own carpet to be sold for the expenses of their burial, but instead of using this money for that purpose the soldiers appropriated it, and thrust the bodies into a hole in the ground.

were refused admittance within the city walls. They used to go to a place on the plain outside the third moat, from which they could see the windows of Bahá'u'lláh's quarters. He would show Himself to them at one of the windows and after gazing on Him from afar, they would weep and return to their homes, fired with new zeal for sacrifice and service.

Restrictions Relaxed

At last the imprisonment was mitigated. A mobilization of Turkish troops occurred and the barracks were required for soldiers. Bahá'u'lláh and His family were transferred to a house by themselves and the rest of the party were accommodated in a caravanserai in the town. Bahá'u'lláh was confined for seven more years in this house. In a small room near that in which He was imprisoned, thirteen of His household, including both sexes, had to accommodate themselves as best they could! In the earlier part of their stay in this house they suffered greatly from insufficiency of accommodation, inadequate food supply, and lack of the ordinary conveniences of life. After a time, however, a few additional rooms were placed at their disposal and they were able to live in comparative comfort. From the time Bahá'u'lláh and His companions left the barracks, visitors were allowed to see them, and gradually the severe restrictions imposed by the imperial firmans were more and more left in abeyance, although now and then reimposed for a time.

Prison Gates Opened

Even when the imprisonment was at its worst, the Bahá'ís were not dismayed, and their serene confidence was never shaken. While in the barracks at 'Akká, Bahá'u'lláh wrote to some friends, "Fear not. These doors shall be opened. My tent shall be pitched on Mount Carmel, and the utmost joy shall be realized." This declaration was a great source of consolation to His followers, and in due course it was literally fulfilled. The story of how the prison doors were opened had best be told in the words of 'Abdu'l-Bahá, as translated by His grandson, Shoghi Effendi:—

Bahá'u'lláh loved the beauty and verdure of the country. One day He passed the remark: "I have not gazed on verdure for nine years. The country is the world of the soul, the city is the world of bodies." When I heard indirectly of this saying I realized that He was longing for the country, and I was sure that whatever I could do towards the carrying out of His wish would be successful. There was in 'Akká at that time a man called Muḥammad Páshá Ṣafwat, who was very much opposed to us. He had a palace called Mazra'ih, about four miles north of the city, a lovely place, surrounded by gardens and with a stream of running water. I went and called on this Páshá at his home. I said: "Páshá, you have left the palace empty, and are living in 'Akká." He replied: "I am an invalid and cannot leave the city. If I go there it is lonely and I am cut off from my friends." I said: "While you are not living there and the place is empty, let it to us." He was amazed at the proposal, but soon consented. I got the house at a very low rent, about five pounds per annum, paid him for five years and made a contract. I sent laborers to repair the place and put the garden in order and had a bath built. I also had a carriage prepared for the use of the Blessed Beauty.[1] One day I determined to go and see the place for myself. Notwithstanding the repeated injunctions given in successive firmans that we were on no account to pass the limits of the city walls, I walked out through the city gate. Gendarmes were on guard, but they made no objection, so I proceeded straight to the palace. The next day I again went out, with some friends and officials, unmolested and unopposed, although the guards and sentinels stood on both sides of the city gates. Another day I arranged a banquet, spread a table under the pine trees of Bahjí, and gathered round

---

[1] Jamál-i-Mubárak (lit. Blessed Beauty) was a title frequently applied to Bahá'u'lláh by his followers and friends.

it the notables and officials of the town. In the evening
we all returned to the town together.

One day I went to the holy presence of the Blessed
Beauty and said: "The palace at Mazra'ih is ready for
You, and a carriage to drive You there." (At that time
there were no carriages in 'Akká or Haifa.) He refused to
go, saying: "I am a prisoner." Later I requested Him
again, but got the same answer. I went so far as to ask
Him a third time, but He still said "No!" and I did not
dare to insist further. There was, however, in 'Akká a
certain Muḥammadan Shaykh, a well-known man with
considerable influence, who loved Bahá'u'lláh and was
greatly favored by Him. I called this Shaykh and explained the position to him. I said, "You are daring. Go
tonight to His holy presence, fall on your knees before
Him, take hold of His hands and do not let go until He
promises to leave the city!" He was an Arab. . . . He
went directly to Bahá'u'lláh and sat down close to His
knees. He took hold of the hands of the Blessed Beauty
and kissed them and asked: "Why do you not leave the
city?" He said: "I am a prisoner." The Shaykh replied:
"God forbid! Who has the power to make You a prisoner?
You have kept Yourself in prison. It was Your own will to
be imprisoned, and now I beg You to come out and go to
the palace. It is beautiful and verdant. The trees are lovely,
and the oranges like balls of fire!" As often as the Blessed
Beauty said: "I am a prisoner, it cannot be," the Shaykh
took His hands and kissed them. For a whole hour he kept
on pleading. At last Bahá'u'lláh said, "Khaylí khub (very
good)" and the Shaykh's patience and persistence were
rewarded. He came to me with great joy to give the glad
news of His Holiness's consent. In spite of the strict fir-
man of 'Abdu'l-'Azíz which prohibited my meeting or
having any intercourse with the Blessed Perfection, I took
the carriage the next day and drove with Him to the palace. No one made any objection. I left Him there and returned myself to the city.

For two years He remained in that charming and

lovely spot. Then it was decided to remove to another place, at Bahjí. It so happened that an epidemic disease had broken out at Bahjí, and the proprietor of the house fled away in distress, with all his family, ready to offer the house free of charge to any applicant. We took the house at a very low rent, and there the doors of majesty and true sovereignty were flung wide open. Bahá'u'lláh was nominally a prisoner (for the drastic firmans of Sultán 'Abdu'l-'Azíz were never repealed), yet in reality He showed forth such nobility and dignity in His life and bearing that He was reverenced by all, and the rulers of Palestine envied His influence and power. Governors and mutaṣarrifs, generals and local officials, would humbly request the honor of attaining His presence—a request to which He seldom acceded.

On one occasion a Governor of the city implored this favor on the ground of his being ordered by higher authorities to visit, with a certain general, the Blessed Perfection. The request being granted, the general, who was a very corpulent individual, a European, was so impressed by the majestic presence of Bahá'u'lláh that he remained kneeling on the ground near the door. Such was the diffidence of both visitors that it was only after repeated invitations from Bahá'u'lláh that they were induced to smoke the narguileh (hubble-bubble pipe) offered to them. Even then they only touched it with their lips, and then, putting it aside, folded their arms and sat in an attitude of such humility and respect as to astonish all those who were present.

The loving reverence of friends, the consideration and respect that were shown by all officials and notables, the inflow of pilgrims and seekers after truth, the spirit of devotion and service that was manifest all around, the majestic and kingly countenance of the Blessed Perfection, the effectiveness of His command, the number of His zealous devotees—all bore witness to the fact that Bahá'u'lláh was in reality no prisoner, but a King of Kings. Two despotic sovereigns were against Him, two

powerful autocratic rulers, yet, even when confined in
their own prisons, He addressed them in very austere
terms, like a king addressing his subjects. Afterwards, in
spite of the severe firmans, He lived at Bahjí like a prince.
Often He would say: "Verily, verily, the most wretched
prison has been converted into a Paradise of Eden."
Surely, such a thing has not been witnessed since the
creation of the world.

Life at Bahjí

Having in His earlier years of hardship shown how to glorify God in a state of poverty and ignominy, Bahá'u'lláh in His
later years at Bahjí showed how to glorify God in a state of
honor and affluence. The offerings of hundreds of thousands
of devoted followers placed at His disposal large funds which
He was called upon to administer. Although His life at Bahjí
has been described as truly regal, in the highest sense of the
word, yet it must not be imagined that it was characterized by
material splendor or extravagance. The Blessed Perfection and
His family lived in very simple and modest fashion, and expenditure on selfish luxury was a thing unknown in that household. Near His home the believers prepared a beautiful garden
called Riḍván, in which He often spent many consecutive days
or even weeks, sleeping at night in a little cottage in the garden. Occasionally He went further afield. He made several visits to 'Akká and Haifa, and on more than one occasion pitched
His tent on Mount Carmel, as He had predicted when imprisoned in the barracks at 'Akká. The time of Bahá'u'lláh was
spent for the most part in prayer and meditation, in writing
the sacred Books, revealing Tablets, and in the spiritual education of the friends. In order to give Him entire freedom for
this great work, 'Abdu'l-Bahá undertook the arrangement of
all other affairs, even meeting the mullás, poets, and members
of the Government. All of these were delighted and happy
through meeting 'Abdu'l-Bahá, and entirely satisfied with His
explanation and talks, and although they had not met Bahá'u'-
lláh Himself, they became full of friendly feeling towards Him,

through their acquaintanceship with His Son, for 'Abdu'l-
Bahá's attitude caused them to understand the station of His
Father.

The distinguished Orientalist, the late Professor Edward G.
Browne, of the University of Cambridge, visited Bahá'u'lláh at
Bahjí in the year 1890, and recorded his impressions as fol-
lows:—

My conductor paused for a moment while I removed
my shoes. Then, with a quick movement of the hand, he
withdrew, and, as I passed, replaced the curtain; and I
found myself in a large apartment, along the upper end of
which ran a low divan, while on the side opposite to the
door were placed two or three chairs. Though I dimly
suspected whither I was going and Whom I was to behold (for no distinct intimation had been given to me),
a second or two elapsed ere, with a throb of wonder and
awe, I became definitely conscious that the room was not
untenanted. In the corner where the divan met the wall
sat a wondrous and venerable Figure, crowned with a felt
headdress of the kind called táj by dervishes (but of unusual height and make), round the base of which was
wound a small white turban. The face of Him on Whom I
gazed I can never forget, though I cannot describe it.
Those piercing eyes seemed to read one's very soul;
power and authority sat on that ample brow; while the
deep lines on the forehead and face implied an age which
the jet black hair and beard flowing down in indistin-
guishable luxuriance almost to the waist seemed to belie.
No need to ask in Whose presence I stood, as I bowed
myself before One Who is the object of a devotion and
love which kings might envy and emperors sigh for in
vain!

A mild dignified voice bade me be seated, and then
continued: "Praise be to God that thou hast attained!
. . . Thou hast come to see a prisoner and an exile. . . .
We desire but the good of the world and the happiness of
the nations; yet they deem Us a stirrer-up of strife and se-

dition worthy of bondage and banishment. . . . That all nations should become one in faith, and all men as brothers; that the bonds of affection and unity between the sons of men should be strengthened; that diversity of religion should cease, and differences of race be annulled—what harm is there in this? . . . Yet so it shall be; these fruitless strifes, these ruinous wars shall pass away, and the Most Great Peace shall come. . . . Do not you in Europe need this also? Is not this that which Christ foretold? . . . Yet do We see your kings and rulers lavishing their treasures more freely on means for the destruction of the human race than on that which would conduce to the happiness of mankind. . . . These strifes and this bloodshed and discord must cease, and all men be as one kindred and one family. . . . Let not a man glory in this, that he loves his country; let him rather glory in this, that he loves his kind. . . ."

Such, so far as I can recall them, were the words which, besides many others, I heard from Bahá. Let those who read them consider well with themselves whether such doctrines merit death and bonds, and whether the world is more likely to gain or lose by their diffusion.—Introduction to *A Traveller's Narrative* (Episode of the Báb), p. xxxix.

Ascension

Thus simply and serenely did Bahá'u'lláh pass the evening of His life on earth until, after an attack of fever, He passed away on the 29th of May, 1892, at the age of seventy-five. Among the last Tablets He revealed was His Will and Testament, which He wrote with His own hand and duly signed and sealed. Nine days after His death the seals were broken by His eldest son, in the presence of members of the family and a few friends, and the contents of the short but remarkable document were made known. By this Will 'Abdu'l-Bahá was constituted His Father's representative and the expounder of His teachings, and the family and relatives of Bahá'u'lláh and all believers were instructed to turn to Him and obey Him. By this arrangement sectarianism and division were provided against and the unity of the Cause assured.

Prophethood of Bahá'u'lláh

It is important to have clear ideas of Bahá'u'lláh's Prophethood. His utterances, like those of other divine "Manifestations," may be divided into two classes, in one of which He writes or speaks simply as a man who has been charged by God with a message to His fellows, while in the other class the words purport to be the direct utterance of God Himself.

He writes in the *Book of Íqán:*—

We have already in the foregoing pages assigned two stations unto each of the Luminaries arising from the Daysprings of eternal holiness. One of these stations, the station of essential unity, We have already explained. "No distinction do We make between any of them." (Qur'án 2:136.) The other is the station of distinction, and pertaineth to the world of creation and to the limitations thereof. In this respect, each Manifestation of God hath a distinct individuality, a definitely prescribed mission, a predestined Revelation, and specially designated limitations. Each one of Them is known by a different name, is characterized by a special attribute, fulfills a definite mission, and is entrusted with a particular Revelation. Even as He saith: "Some of the Apostles We have caused to excel the others. To some God hath spoken, some He hath raised and exalted. And to Jesus, Son of Mary, We gave manifest signs, and We strengthened Him with the Holy Spirit." (Qur'án 2:253.) . . .

Thus, viewed from the standpoint of Their oneness and sublime detachment, the attributes of Godhead, Divinity, Supreme Singleness, and Inmost Essence, have been and are applicable to those Essences of being, inasmuch as They all abide on the throne of divine Revelation, and are established upon the seat of divine Concealment.

Through Their appearance the Revelation of God is made manifest, and by Their countenance the beauty of God is revealed. Thus it is that the accents of God Himself have been heard uttered by these Manifestations of the divine Being.

Viewed in the light of Their second station—the station of distinction, differentiation, temporal limitations, characteristics and standards—They manifest absolute servitude, utter destitution and complete self-effacement. Even as He saith: "I am the servant of God. I am but a man like you.". . .

Were any of the all-embracing Manifestations of God to declare: "I am God!" He verily speaketh the truth, and no doubt attacheth thereto. For it hath been repeatedly demonstrated that through Their Revelation, Their attributes and names, the Revelation of God, His Name and His attributes, are made manifest in the world. Thus, He hath revealed: "Those shafts were God's, not Thine!" (Qur'án 8:17.) And also He saith: "In truth, they who plighted fealty unto Thee, really plighted that fealty unto God." (Qur'án 48:10.) And were any of Them to voice the utterance: "I am the Messenger of God," He also speaketh the truth, the indubitable truth. Even as He saith: "Muḥammad is not the father of any man among you, but He is the Messenger of God." Viewed in this light, They are all but Messengers of that ideal King, that unchangeable Essence. And were They all to proclaim: "I am the Seal of the Prophets," They verily utter but the truth, beyond the faintest shadow of doubt. For They are all but one person, one soul, one spirit, one being, one revelation. They are all the manifestation of the "Beginning" and the "End," the "First" and the "Last," the "Seen" and "Hidden"—all of which pertain to Him Who is the innermost Spirit of Spirits and eternal Essence of Essences. And were They to say: "We are the servants of God," (Qur'án 33:40) this also is a manifest and indisputable fact. For They have been made manifest in the uttermost state of servitude, a servitude the like of which no man can possibly attain. Thus in moments in which these Essences of being were deeply immersed beneath the oceans of ancient and everlasting holiness, or when They soared to the loftiest summits of divine mysteries, They claimed Their utterance to be the Voice of Divinity, the call of God Himself. Were the eye of discernment to be opened, it would recognize that in this very state, They have considered Themselves utterly effaced and non-existent in the face of Him Who is the All-Pervading, the Incorruptible. Methinks, They have regarded Themselves as utter nothingness, and deemed Their mention in that Court an act of blasphemy. For the slightest whisperings of self, within such a Court, is an evidence of self-asser-tion and independent existence. In the eyes of Them that have attained unto that Court, such a suggestion is itself a grievous transgression. How much more grievous would it be, were aught else to be mentioned in that Presence, were man's heart, his tongue, his mind, or his soul, to be busied with anyone but the Well-Beloved, were his eyes to behold any countenance other than His beauty, were his ear to be inclined to any melody but His voice, and were his feet to tread any way but His way.

In this day the breeze of God is wafted, and His spirit hath pervaded all things. Such is the outpouring of His grace that the pen is stilled and the tongue is speechless.

By virtue of this station, They have claimed for Them-selves the Voice of Divinity and the like, whilst by virtue of Their station of Messengership, They have declared Themselves the Messengers of God. In every instance They have voiced an utterance that would conform to the requirements of the occasion, and have ascribed all these declarations to Themselves, declarations ranging from the realm of divine Revelation to the realm of creation, and from the domain of Divinity even unto the domain of earthly existence. Thus it is that whatsoever be Their ut-terance, whether it pertain to the realm of Divinity, Lord-ship, Prophethood, Messengership, Guardianship, Apos-tleship or Servitude, all is true, beyond the shadow of a doubt. Therefore, these sayings which We have quoted in support of Our argument must be attentively considered, that the divergent utterances of the Manifestations of the Unseen and Daysprings of holiness may cease to agitate the soul and perplex the mind.—*Kitáb-i-Íqán,* 176-181.

When Bahá'u'lláh speaks as a man, the station He claims for Himself is that of utter humility, of "annihilation in God." What distinguishes the Manifestation, in His human personality, from other men is the completeness of His self-abnegation as well as the perfection of His powers. Under all circumstances He is able to say, as did Jesus in the Garden of Gethsemane, "Nevertheless not my will, but thine, be done." Thus in His epistle to the Sháh, Bahá'u'lláh says:—

O king! I was but a man like others, asleep upon My couch, when lo, the breezes of the All-Glorious were wafted over Me, and taught Me the knowledge of all that hath been. This thing is not from Me, but from One Who is Almighty and All-Knowing. And He bade Me lift up My voice between earth and heaven, and for this there befell Me what hath caused the tears of every man of understanding to flow. The learning current amongst men I studied not; their schools I entered not. . . . This is but a leaf which the winds of the will of thy Lord, the Almighty, the All-Praised, have stirred. Can it be still when the tempestuous winds are blowing? Nay, by Him Who is the Lord of all names and attributes! They move it as they list. The evanescent is as nothing before Him Who is the Ever-Abiding. His all-compelling summons hath reached Me, and caused Me to speak His praise amidst all people. I was indeed as one dead when His behest was uttered. The hand of the will of thy Lord, the Compassionate, the Merciful, transformed Me. Can any one speak forth of his own accord that for which all men, both high and low, will protest against him? Nay, by Him Who taught the Pen the eternal mysteries, save him whom the grace of the Almighty, the All-Powerful, hath strengthened. —*The Tablet to the <u>Sh</u>áh* as quoted in *The Promised Day Is Come,* pp. 40-41.

As Jesus washed His disciples' feet, so Bahá'u'lláh used sometimes to cook food and perform other lowly offices for His followers. He was a servant of the servants, and gloried only in servitude, content to sleep on a bare floor if need be, to live on bread and water, or even, at times, on what He called "the divine nourishment, that is to say, hunger!" His perfect humility was seen in His profound reverence for nature, for human nature, and especially for the saints, prophets, and martyrs. To Him, all things spoke of God, from the meanest to the greatest.

His human personality had been chosen by God to become the Divine Mouthpiece and Pen. It was not of His own will that He had assumed this position of unparalleled difficulty and hardship. As Jesus said: "Father, if it be possible, let this cup pass from me," so Bahá'u'lláh said: "Had another exponent or speaker been found, We would not have made Ourself an object of censure, derision and calumnies on the part of the people" (*Tablet of I<u>sh</u>ráqát*). But the divine call was clear and imperative and He obeyed. God's will became His will, and God's pleasure, His pleasure; and with "radiant acquiescence" He declared:—"Verily I say: Whatever befalleth in the path of God is the beloved of the soul and the desire of the heart. Deadly poison in His path is pure honey, and every tribulation a draught of crystal water."—*Epistle to the Son of the Wolf,* p. 17.

At other times, as we have mentioned, Bahá'u'lláh speaks "from the station of Deity." In these utterances His human personality is so completely subservient that it is left out of account altogether. Through Him God addresses His creatures, proclaiming His love for them, teaching them His attributes, making known His will, announcing His laws for their guidance, and pleading for their love, their allegiance, and service.

In the Writings of Bahá'u'lláh, the utterance frequently changes from one of these forms to another. Sometimes it is evidently the man who is discoursing, then without a break the writing continues as if God were speaking in the first person. Even when speaking as a man, however, Bahá'u'lláh speaks as God's Messenger, as a living example of entire devotion to God's will. His whole life is actuated by the Holy Spirit. Hence no hard and fast line can be drawn between the human and divine elements in His life or teachings. God tells Him:—

> Say: "Naught is seen in My temple but the Temple of God, and in My beauty but His beauty, and in My being but His being, and in Myself but Himself, and in My movement but His movement, and in My acquiescence but His acquiescence, and in My pen but His pen, the precious, the extolled."
> Say: "There hath not been in My soul but the truth, and in Myself naught could be seen but God."—*Súratu'l-Haykal,* p. 30.

His Mission

Bahá'u'lláh's mission in the world is to bring about unity—unity of all mankind in and through God. He says:—"Of the Tree of Knowledge the all-glorious fruit is this exalted Word: Of one tree are all ye the fruits and of one bough the leaves. Let not man glory in this that he loves his country, but let him rather glory in this that he loves his kind."

Previous Prophets have heralded an age of peace on earth, goodwill among men, and have given Their lives to hasten its advent, but each and all of Them have plainly declared that this blessed consummation would be reached only after the "coming of the Lord" in the latter days, when the wicked would be judged and the righteous rewarded.

Zoroaster foretold three thousand years of conflict before the advent of Sháh Bahrám, the world Savior, Who would overcome Ahríman the spirit of evil, and establish a reign of righteousness and peace.

Moses foretold a long period of exile, persecution, and oppression for the children of Israel, before the Lord of Hosts would appear to gather them from all the nations, to destroy the oppressors and establish His Kingdom upon earth.

Christ said: "Think not that I am come to send peace upon earth: I came not to send peace but a sword" (Matt. x, 34), and He predicted a period of wars and rumors of wars, of tribulations and afflictions that would continue till the coming of the Son of Man "in the glory of the Father."

Muḥammad declared that, because of their wrongdoings, Alláh had put enmity and hatred among both Jews and Christians that would last until the Day of Resurrection, when He would appear to judge them all.

Bahá'u'lláh, on the other hand, announces that He is the Promised One of all these Prophets—the Divine Manifestation in Whose era the reign of peace will actually be established. This statement is unprecedented and unique, yet it fits in wonderfully with the signs of the times, and with the prophecies of all the great Prophets. Bahá'u'lláh revealed with incomparable clearness and comprehensiveness the means for bringing about peace and unity amongst mankind.

It is true that, since the advent of Bahá'u'lláh, there have been, until now, war and destruction on an unprecedented scale, but this is just what all the Prophets have said would happen at the dawn of the "great and terrible Day of the Lord," and is, therefore, but a confirmation of the view that the "coming of the Lord" is not only at hand, but is already an accomplished fact. According to the parable of Christ, the Lord of the Vineyard must miserably destroy the wicked husbandmen before He gives the Vineyard to others who will render Him the fruits in their seasons. Does not this mean that at the coming of the Lord dire destruction awaits those despotic governments, avaricious and intolerant priests, mullás, or tyrannical leaders who through the centuries have, like wicked husbandmen, misruled the earth and misappropriated its fruits?

There may be terrible events, and unparalleled calamities yet awhile on the earth, but Bahá'u'lláh assures us "that erelong, these fruitless strifes, these ruinous wars shall pass away and the Most Great Peace shall come." War and strife have become so intolerable in their destructiveness that mankind *must* find deliverance from them or perish. "The fullness of time" has come and with it the promised Deliverer!

His Writings

The Writings of Bahá'u'lláh are most comprehensive in their range, dealing with every phase of human life, individual and social, with things material and things spiritual, with the interpretation of ancient and modern scriptures, and with prophetic anticipations of both the near and distant future.

The range and accuracy of His knowledge was amazing. He could quote and expound the scriptures of the various religions with which His correspondents or questioners were familiar, in convincing and authoritative manner, although apparently He had never had the ordinary means of access to many of the books referred to. He declares, in *The Epistle to the Son of the Wolf,* that He had never read the *Bayán,* although in His own Writings He shows the most perfect knowledge and understanding of the Báb's Revelation. (The Báb, as we have seen, declared that His Revelation, the *Bayán,* was inspired by and emanated from "Him Whom God shall make manifest"!) With the single exception of a visit from Professor Edward Granville Browne, to whom in the year 1890 He accorded four interviews, each lasting twenty to thirty minutes, He had no opportunities of intercourse with enlightened Western thinkers, yet His Writings show a complete grasp of the social, political, and religious problems of the Western world, and even His enemies had to admit that His wisdom and knowledge were incomparable. The well-known circumstances of His long imprisonment render it impossible to doubt that the wealth of knowledge shown in His Writings must have been acquired from some spiritual source, quite independent of the usual means of study or instruction and the help of books or teachers.[1]

---

[1] When asked whether Bahá'ulláh had made a special study of Western writings and founded His teachings in accordance with them 'Abdu'l-Bahá said that the books of Bahá'u'lláh, *written* and *printed as long ago as the 1870's,* contained the ideals now so familiar to the West, although at that time these ideas had not been printed or thought of in the West.

Sometimes He wrote in modern Persian, the ordinary language of His fellow countrymen, which is largely admixed with Arabic. At other times, as when addressing learned Zoroastrians, He wrote in the purest classical Persian. He also wrote with equal fluency in Arabic, sometimes in very simple language, sometimes in classical style somewhat similar to that of the Qur'án. His perfect mastery of these different languages and styles was remarkable because of His entire lack of literary education.

In some of His Writings the way of holiness is pointed out in such simple terms that "the wayfaring men, though fools, shall not err therein" (Isaiah xxxv, 8). In others there is a wealth of poetic imagery, profound philosophy, and allusions to Muhammadan, Zoroastrian, and other Scriptures, or to Persian and Arabic literature and legends, such as only the poet, the philosopher, or the scholar can adequately appreciate. Still others deal with advanced stages of the spiritual life and are to be understood only by those who have already passed through the earlier stages. His works are like a bountiful table provided with foods and delicacies suited to the needs and tastes of all who are genuine truth seekers.

It is because of this that His Cause had effect among the learned and cultured, spiritual poets, and well-known writers. Even some of the leaders of the Ṣúfís and of other sects, and some of the political ministers who were writers, were attracted by His words, for they exceeded those of all other writers in sweetness and depth of spiritual meaning.

The Bahá'í Spirit

From His place of confinement in distant 'Akká, Bahá'u'lláh stirred His native land of Persia to its depths; and not only Persia; He stirred and is stirring the world. The spirit that animated Him and His followers was unfailingly gentle, courteous, and patient, yet it was a force of astonishing vitality and transcendent power. It achieved the seemingly impossible. It changed human nature. Men who yielded to its influence became new creatures. They were filled with a love, a faith, and enthusiasm, compared with which earthly joys and sorrows were but as dust in the balance. They were ready to face lifelong suffering or violent death with perfect equanimity, nay, with radiant joy, in the strength of fearless dependence on God. Most wonderful of all, their hearts were so brimming over with the joy of a new life as to leave no room for thoughts of bitterness or vindictiveness against their oppressors. They entirely abandoned the use of violence in self-defense, and instead of bemoaning their fate, they considered themselves the most fortunate of men in being privileged to receive this new and glorious Revelation and to spend their lives or shed their blood in testifying to its truth. Well might their hearts sing with joy, for they believed that God, the Supreme, the Eternal, the Beloved, had spoken to them through human lips, had called them to be His servants and friends, had come to establish His Kingdom upon earth, and to bring the priceless boon of peace to a warworn, strife-stricken world.

Such was the faith inspired by Bahá'u'lláh. He announced His own mission, as the Báb had foretold that He would, and, thanks to the devoted labors of His great Forerunner, there were thousands ready to acclaim His advent—thousands who had shaken off superstitions and prejudices, and were waiting with pure hearts and open minds for the Manifestation of God's promised glory. Poverty and chains, sordid circumstances, and outward ignominy could not hide from them the spiritual glory of their Lord—nay, these dark earthly surroundings only served to enhance the brilliance of His real splendor.

'Abdu'l-Bahá: The Servant of Bahá/4

When the ocean of My presence hath ebbed and the Book of My Revelation is ended, turn your faces toward Him Whom God hath purposed, Who hath branched from this Ancient Root.—BAHÁ'U'LLÁH, *Kitáb-i-Aqdas.*

Birth and Childhood

'Abbás Effendi, Who afterwards assumed the title of 'Abdu'l-Bahá (i.e. Servant of Bahá), was the eldest son of Bahá'u'lláh. He was born in Ṭihrán before midnight on the eve of the 23rd of May, 1844,[1] the very same night in which the Báb declared His mission.

He was nine years of age when His Father, to Whom even then He was devotedly attached, was thrown into the dungeon in Ṭihrán. A mob sacked their house, and the family were stripped of their possessions and left in destitution. 'Abdu'l-Bahá tells how one day He was allowed to enter the prison yard to see His beloved Father when He came out for His daily exercise. Bahá'u'lláh was terribly altered, so ill He could hardly walk, His hair and beard unkempt, His neck galled and swollen from the pressure of a heavy steel collar, His body bent by the weight of His chains, and the sight made a never-to-be-forgotten impression on the mind of the sensitive boy.

During the first year of their residence in Baghdád, ten years before the open Declaration by Bahá'u'lláh of His mission, the keen insight of 'Abdu'l-Bahá, Who was then but nine years of age, already led Him to the momentous discovery that His Father was indeed the Promised One Whose manifestation all the Bábís were awaiting. Some sixty years afterwards He thus described the moment in which this conviction suddenly overwhelmed His whole nature:—

---

[1] Thursday, 5th Jamádí I, A.H. 1260.

51

I am the Servant of the Blessed Perfection. In Ba<u>gh</u>dád I was a child. Then and there He announced to me the Word, and I believed in Him. As soon as He proclaimed to me the Word, I threw myself at His holy feet and implored and supplicated Him to accept my blood as a sacrifice in His pathway. Sacrifice! How sweet I find that word! There is no greater bounty for me than this! What greater glory can I conceive than to see this neck chained for His sake, these feet fettered for His love, this body mutilated or thrown into the depths of the sea for His Cause! If in reality we are His sincere lovers—if in reality I am His sincere servant, then I must sacrifice my life, my all at His blessed threshold.—*Diary of Mírzá Aḥmad Sohrab,* January 1914.

About this time He began to be called by His friends "the Mystery of God," a title given to Him by Bahá'u'lláh, by which He was commonly known during the period of residence in Ba<u>gh</u>dád.

When His Father went away for two years in the wilderness, 'Abbás was heartbroken. His chief consolation consisted in copying and committing to memory the Tablets of the Báb, and much of His time was spent in solitary meditation. When at last His Father returned, the boy was overwhelmed with joy.

Youth

From that time onwards, He became his Father's closest companion and, as it were, protector. Although a mere youth, He already showed astonishing sagacity and discrimination, and undertook the task of interviewing all the numerous visitors who came to see His Father. If He found they were genuine truth seekers, He admitted them to His Father's presence, but otherwise He did not permit them to trouble Bahá'u'lláh. On many occasions He helped His Father in answering the questions and solving the difficulties of these visitors. For example, when one of the Ṣúfí leaders, named 'Alí <u>Sh</u>awkat Pá<u>sh</u>á, asked for an explanation of the phrase: "I was a hidden mystery," which occurs in a well-known Muḥammadan tradition,[1] Bahá'u'lláh turned to the "Mystery of God," 'Abbás, and asked Him to write the explanation. The boy, who was then about fifteen or sixteen years of age, at once wrote an important epistle giving an exposition so illuminating as to astonish the Páshá. This epistle is now widely spread among the Bahá'ís, and is well known to many outside the Bahá'í Faith. About this time 'Abbás was a frequent visitor to the mosques, where He would discuss theological matters with the doctors and learned men. He never attended any school or college, His only teacher being His Father. His favorite recreation was horseback riding, which He keenly enjoyed.

After Bahá'u'lláh's Declaration in the garden outside Baghdád, 'Abdu'l-Bahá's devotion to His Father became greater than ever. On the long journey to Constantinople He guarded Bahá'u'lláh night and day, riding by His wagon and watching near His tent. As far as possible He relieved His Father of all domestic cares and responsibilities, becoming the mainstay and comfort of the entire family.

During the years spent in Adrianople, 'Abdu'l-Bahá endeared Himself to everyone. He taught much, and became generally known as the "Master." At 'Akká, when nearly all the party were ill with typhoid, malaria, and dysentery, He washed the patients, nursed them, fed them, watched with them, taking no rest, until, utterly exhausted, He Himself took dysentery, and for about a month remained in a dangerous condition. In 'Akká, as in Adrianople, all classes, from the Governor to the most wretched beggar, learned to love and respect Him.

Marriage

The following particulars regarding the marriage of 'Abdu'l-Bahá were kindly supplied to the writer by a Persian historian of the Bahá'í Faith:—

"During the youth of 'Abdu'l-Bahá the question of a suitable marriage for Him was naturally one of great interest to the believers, and many people came forward,

---

[1] The tradition is quoted in a Tablet of Bahá'u'lláh; see Chapter 5 of this book.

wishing to have this crown of honor for their own family. For a long time, however, 'Abdu'l-Bahá showed no inclination for marriage, and no one understood the wisdom of this. Afterwards it became known that there was a girl who was destined to become the wife of 'Abdu'l-Bahá, one whose birth came about through the blessing which the Báb gave to her parents in Iṣfáhán. Her father was Mírzá Muḥammad 'Alí, who was the uncle of the "King of Martyrs" and the "Beloved of Martyrs," and she belonged to one of the great and noble families of Iṣfáhán. When the Báb was in Iṣfáhán, Mírzá Muḥammad 'Alí had no children, but his wife was longing for a child. On hearing of this, the Báb gave him a portion of His food and told him to share it with his wife. After they had eaten of that food, it soon became apparent that their long-cherished hopes of parenthood were about to be fulfilled, and in due course a daughter was born to them, who was given the name of Munírih Khánum.[1] Later on a son was born, to whom they gave the name of Siyyid Yaḥyá, and afterwards they had some other children. After a time Munírih's father died, her cousins were martyred by Ẓillu's-Sulṭán and the mullás, and the family fell into great troubles and bitter persecutions because of their being Bahá'ís. Bahá'u'lláh then permitted Munírih and her brother Siyyid Yaḥyá to come to 'Akká for protection. Bahá'u'lláh and His wife, Navváb, the mother of 'Abdu'l-Bahá, showed such kindness and favor to Munírih that others understood that they wished her to become the wife of 'Abdu'l-Bahá. The wish of His Father and mother became the wish of 'Abdu'l-Bahá, too. He had a warm feeling of love and affection for Munírih which was fully reciprocated, and erelong they became united in marriage.

The marriage proved exceedingly happy and harmonious. Of the children born to them four daughters have survived the rigors of their long imprisonment, and, through their beautiful

---

[1] It is interesting to compare this story with that of the birth of John the Baptist; see St. Luke's Gospel, Chapter I.

lives of service, have endeared themselves to all who have been privileged to know them.

Center of the Covenant

Bahá'u'lláh indicated in many ways that 'Abdu'l-Bahá was to direct the Cause after His own ascension. Many years before His death He declared this in a veiled manner in His *Kitáb-i-Aqdas*. He referred to 'Abdu'l-Bahá on many occasions as "the Center of My Covenant," "the Most Great Branch," "the Branch from the Ancient Root." He habitually spoke of Him as "the master" and required all His family to treat Him with marked deference; and in His Will and Testament He left explicit instructions that all should turn to Him and obey Him.

After the death of the "Blessed Beauty" (as Bahá'u'lláh was generally called by His family and believers), 'Abdu'l-Bahá assumed the position which His Father had clearly indicated for Him as head of the Cause and authoritative Interpreter of the teachings, but this was resented by certain of His relatives and others, who became as bitterly opposed to 'Abdu'l-Bahá as Ṣubḥ-i-Azal had been to Bahá'u'lláh. They tried to stir up dissensions among the believers, and, failing in that, proceeded to make various false charges against 'Abdu'l-Bahá to the Turkish Government.

In accordance with instructions received from His Father, 'Abdu'l-Bahá was erecting a building on the side of Mount Carmel, above Haifa, which was intended to be the permanent resting-place of the remains of the Báb, and also to contain a number of rooms for meetings and services. They represented to the authorities that this building was intended as a fort, and that 'Abdu'l-Bahá and His followers meant to entrench themselves there, defy the Government, and endeavor to gain possession of the neighboring region of Syria.

Strict Imprisonment Renewed

In consequence of this and other equally unfounded charges, in 1901, 'Abdu'l-Bahá and His family, who for more than twenty years had been allowed the freedom of the country for some miles around 'Akká, were again, for over seven years, strictly confined within the walls of the prison city. This did not prevent Him, however, from effectively spreading the Bahá'í Message through Asia, Europe, and America. Mr. Horace Holley writes of this period as follows:—

> To 'Abdu'l-Bahá, as a teacher and friend, came men and women from every race, religion and nation, to sit at His table like favored guests, questioning Him about the social, spiritual or moral program each had most at heart; and after a stay lasting from a few hours to many months, returning home, inspired, renewed and enlightened. The world surely never possessed such a guesthouse as this.
>
> Within its doors the rigid castes of India melted away, the racial prejudice of Jew, Christian and Muḥammadan became less than a memory; and every convention save the essential law of warm hearts and aspiring minds broke down, banned and forbidden by the unifying sympathy of the master of the house. It was like a King Arthur and the Round Table . . . but an Arthur who knighted women as well as men, and sent them away not with the sword but with the Word.—*The Modern Social Religion*, Horace Holley, p. 171.

During these years 'Abdu'l-Bahá carried on an enormous correspondence with believers and inquirers in all parts of the world. In this work He was greatly assisted by His daughters and also by several interpreters and secretaries.

Much of His time was spent in visiting the sick and the afflicted in their own homes; and in the poorest quarters of 'Akká no visitor was more welcome than the "Master." A pilgrim who visited 'Akká at this time writes:—

> It is the custom of 'Abdu'l-Bahá each week, on Friday morning, to distribute alms to the poor. From His own scanty store He gives a little to each one of the needy who come to ask assistance. This morning about one hundred

were ranged in line, seated and crouching upon the
ground in the open street of the court where 'Abdu'l-
Bahá's house stands. And such a nondescript collection of
humanity they were. All kinds of men, women and children—poor, wretched, hopeless in aspect, half-clothed,
many of them crippled and blind, beggars indeed, poor
beyond expression—waiting expectant—until from the
doorway came 'Abdu'l-Bahá. . . . Quickly moving from
one to another, stopping sometimes to leave a word of
sympathy and encouragement, dropping small coins into
each eager outstretched palm, touching the face of a
child, taking the hand of an old woman who held fast to
the hem of His garment as He passed along, speaking
words of light to old men with sightless eyes, inquiring
after those too feeble and wretched to come for their pit-
tance of help, and sending them their portion with a message of love and uplift.—*Glimpses of 'Abdu'l-Bahá,*
M. J. M., p. 13.

'Abdu'l-Bahá's personal wants were few. He worked late
and early. Two simple meals a day sufficed Him. His wardrobe
consisted of a very few garments of inexpensive material. He
could not bear to live in luxury while others were in want.

He had a great love for children, for flowers, and for the
beauties of nature. Every morning about six or seven, the family party used to gather to partake of the morning tea together,
and while the Master sipped His tea, the little children of the
household chanted prayers. Mr. Thornton Chase writes of
these children:—"Such children I have never seen, so courteous, unselfish, thoughtful for others, unobtrusive, intelligent,
and swiftly self-denying in the little things that children love."
—*In Galilee,* p. 51.

The "ministry of flowers" was a feature of the life at 'Akká,
of which every pilgrim brought away fragrant memories. Mrs.
Lucas writes:—"When the Master inhales the odor of flowers,
it is wonderful to see Him. It seems as though the perfume of
the hyacinths were telling Him something, as He buries His
face in the flowers. It is like the effort of the ear to hear a beau-

tiful harmony—a concentrated attention."—*A Brief Account of My Visit to 'Akká,* p. 26.

He loved to present beautiful and sweet-smelling flowers to His numerous visitors.

Mr. Thornton Chase sums up his impression of the prison life at 'Akká as follows:—

> Five days we remained within those walls, prisoners with Him Who dwells in that "Greatest Prison." It is a prison of peace, of love and service. No wish, no desire is there save the good of mankind, the peace of the world, the acknowledgment of the Fatherhood of God and the mutual rights of men as His creatures, His children. Indeed, the real prison, the suffocating atmosphere, the separation from all true heart desires, the bond of world conditions, is outside of those stone walls, while within them is the freedom and pure aura of the spirit of God. All troubles, tumults, worries or anxieties for worldly things are barred out there.—*In Galilee,* p. 24.

To most people the hardships of prison life would appear as grievous calamities, but for 'Abdu'l-Bahá they had no terrors. When in prison He wrote:—

> Grieve not because of my imprisonment and calamity; for this prison is my beautiful garden, my mansioned paradise and my throne of dominion among mankind. My calamity in my prison is a crown to me in which I glory among the righteous.
>
> Anyone can be happy in the state of comfort, ease, success, health, pleasure and joy; but if one be happy and contented in the time of trouble, hardship and prevailing disease, that is the proof of nobility.—*Tablets of 'Abdu'l-Bahá,* vol. ii, pp. 258, 263.

Turkish Commissions of Investigation

In 1904 and 1907 commissions were appointed by the Turkish Government to inquire into the charges against 'Abdu'l-Bahá, and lying witnesses gave evidence against Him.

'Abdu'l-Bahá, while refuting the charges, expressed His entire readiness to submit to any sentence the tribunal chose to impose. He declared that if they should throw Him into jail, drag Him through the streets, curse Him, spit upon Him, stone Him, heap upon Him all sorts of ignominy, hang Him, or shoot Him, He would still be happy.

Between the sittings of the Commissions of Investigation He pursued His ordinary life with the utmost serenity, planting fruit trees in a garden and presiding at a marriage feast with the dignity and radiance of spiritual freedom. The Italian Consul offered to provide Him a safe passage to any foreign port He cared to select, but this offer He gratefully but firmly refused, saying that whatever the consequences, He must follow in the footsteps of the Báb and the Blessed Perfection, Who never tried to save Themselves or run away from Their enemies. He encouraged most of the Bahá'ís, however, to leave the neighborhood of 'Akká, which had become very dangerous for them, and remained alone, with a few of the faithful, to await His destiny.

The four corrupt officials who constituted the last investigating commission arrived in 'Akká in the early part of the winter of 1907, stayed one month, and departed for Constantinople, after finishing their so-called "investigation," prepared to report that the charges against 'Abdu'l-Bahá had been substantiated and to recommend His exile or execution. No sooner had they got back to Turkey, however, than the revolution broke out there, and the four commissioners, who belonged to the old regime, had to flee for their lives. The Young Turks established their supremacy, and all political and religious prisoners in the Ottoman Empire were set free. In September 1908 'Abdu'l-Bahá was released from prison, and in the following year 'Abdu'l-Ḥamíd, the Sulṭán, became himself a prisoner.

Western Tours

After His release, 'Abdu'l-Bahá continued the same holy life of ceaseless activity in teaching, correspondence, ministering to the poor and the sick, with merely the change from 'Akká to Haifa and from Haifa to Alexandria, until August 1911, when

He started on His first visit to the Western world. During His tours in the West, 'Abdu'l-Bahá met men of every shade of opinion and amply fulfilled the command of Bahá'u'lláh to "consort with all the people with joy and fragrance." He reached London early in September 1911, and spent a month there, during which, besides daily talks with inquirers and many other activities, He addressed the congregations of the Rev. R. J. Campbell at the City Temple, and of Archdeacon Wilberforce at St. John's, Westminster, and breakfasted with the Lord Mayor. He then proceeded to Paris, where His time was occupied in giving daily addresses and talks to eager listeners of many nationalities and types. In December He returned to Egypt, and next spring, in response to the earnest entreaty of the American friends, He proceeded to the United States, arriving in New York in April 1912. During the next nine months He traveled through America, from coast to coast, addressing all sorts and conditions of men—university students, socialists, Mormons, Jews, Christians, agnostics, Esperantists, peace societies, New Thought clubs, women's suffrage societies, and speaking in churches of almost every denomination, in each case giving addresses suited to the audience and the occasion. On December 5 He sailed for Great Britain, where He passed six weeks, visiting Liverpool, London, Bristol, and Edinburgh. In Edinburgh He gave a notable address to the Esperanto Society, in which He announced that He had encouraged the Bahá'ís of the East to study Esperanto in order to further better understanding between the East and the West. After two months in Paris, spent as before in daily interviews and conferences, He proceeded to Stuttgart, where He held a series of very successful meetings with the German Bahá'ís; thence to Budapest and Vienna, founding new groups in these places, returning, in May 1913, to Egypt, and on December 5, 1913, to Haifa.

Return to Holy Land

He was then in His seventieth year, and His long and arduous labors, culminating in these strenuous Western tours, had

worn out His physical frame. After His return He wrote the
following pathetic Tablet to the believers in East and West:—

Friends, the time is coming when I shall be no longer
with you. I have done all that could be done. I have
served the Cause of Bahá'u'lláh to the utmost of my ability. I have labored night and day all the years of my life.
Oh, how I long to see the believers shouldering the responsibilities of the Cause! Now is the time to proclaim
the Kingdom of Abhá (i.e. the Most Glorious!). Now is
the hour of union and concord! Now is the day of the
spiritual harmony of the friends of God! . . .

I am straining my ears toward the East and toward the
West, toward the North and toward the South, that haply
I may hear the songs of love and fellowship raised in the
meetings of the believers. My days are numbered, and
save this there remains none other joy for me.

Oh, how I yearn to see the friends united, even as a
shining strand of pearls, as the brilliant Pleiades, as the
rays of the sun, the gazelles of one meadow!

The mystic nightingale is singing for them; will they
not listen? The bird of Paradise is warbling; will they not
hear? The Angel of the Kingdom of Abhá is calling to
them; will they not hearken? The Messenger of the Covenant is pleading; will they not heed?

Ah! I am waiting, waiting to hear the glad news that
the believers are the embodiment of sincerity and loyalty,
the incarnation of love and amity and the manifestation of
unity and concord!

Will they not rejoice my heart? Will they not satisfy
my yearnings? Will they not heed my pleadings? Will they
not fulfill my hopes? Will they not answer my call?

I am waiting, I am patiently waiting!

The enemies of the Bahá'í Cause, whose hopes had risen
high when the Báb fell a victim to their fury, when Bahá'u'lláh
was driven from His native land and made a prisoner for life,
and again at the passing of Bahá'u'lláh—these enemies once
more took heart when they saw the physical weakness and

weariness of 'Abdu'l-Bahá after His return from His Western travels. But again their hopes were doomed to disappointment. In a short time 'Abdu'l-Bahá was able to write:—

Unquestionably this physical body and human energy would have been unable to stand the constant wear and tear . . . but the aid and help of the Desired One were the guardian and protector of the weak and humble 'Abdu'l-Bahá. . . . Some have asserted that 'Abdu'l-Bahá is on the eve of bidding his last farewell to the world, that his physical energies are depleted and drained and that erelong these complications will put an end to his life. This is far from the truth. Although in the outward estimation of the Covenant-breakers and defective-minded the body is weak on account of ordeals in the blessed path, yet, praise be to God! through the providence of the Blessed Perfection the spiritual forces are in the utmost rejuvenation and strength. Thanks be to God that now, through the blessing and benediction of Bahá'u'lláh, even the physical energies are fully restored, divine joy is obtained, the supreme glad tidings are resplendent and ideal happiness overflowing.—*Star of the West,* vol. v, No. 14, p. 213.

Both during the European War and after its close 'Abdu'l-Bahá, amidst countless other activities, was able to pour forth a series of great and inspiring letters which, when communications were reopened, roused believers throughout the world to new enthusiasm and zeal for service. Under the inspiration of these letters the Cause progressed by leaps and bounds and everywhere the Faith showed signs of new vitality and vigor.

War Time at Haifa

A remarkable instance of the foresight of 'Abdu'l-Bahá was supplied during the months immediately preceding the war. During peacetimes there was usually a large number of pilgrims at Haifa, from Persia and other regions of the globe. About six months before the outbreak of war one of the old

Bahá'ís living at Haifa presented a request from several believers of Persia for permission to visit the Master. 'Abdu'l-Bahá did not grant the permission, and from that time onwards gradually dismissed the pilgrims who were at Haifa, so that by the end of July 1914 none remained. When, in the first days of August, the sudden outbreak of the Great War startled the world, the wisdom of His precaution became apparent.

When the war broke out, 'Abdu'l-Bahá, Who had already spent fifty-five years of His life in exile and prison, became again virtually a prisoner of the Turkish Government. Communication with friends and believers outside Syria was almost completely cut off, and He and His little band of followers were again subjected to straitened circumstances, scarcity of food, and great personal danger and inconvenience.

During the war 'Abdu'l-Bahá had a busy time in ministering to the material and spiritual wants of the people about Him. He personally organized extensive agricultural operations near Tiberias, thus securing a great supply of wheat, by means of which famine was averted, not only for the Bahá'ís but for hundreds of the poor of all religions in Haifa and 'Akká, whose wants He liberally supplied. He took care of all, and mitigated their sufferings as far as possible. To hundreds of poor people He would give a small sum of money daily. In addition to money He gave bread. If there was no bread He would give dates or something else. He made frequent visits to 'Akká to comfort and help the believers and poor people there. During the time of war He had daily meetings of the believers, and through His help the friends remained happy and tranquil throughout those troublous years.

Sir 'Abdu'l-Bahá 'Abbás, K.B.E.

Great was the rejoicing in Haifa when, on the 23rd day of September, 1918, at 3 P.M., after some twenty-four hours' fighting, the city was taken by British and Indian cavalry, and the horrors of war conditions under the Turkish rule came to an end.

From the beginning of the British occupation, large numbers

of soldiers and government officials of all ranks, even the highest, sought interviews with 'Abdu'l-Bahá, delighting in His illuminating talks, His breadth of view and depth of insight, His dignified courtesy and genial hospitality. So profoundly impressed were the government representatives by His noble character and His great work in the interests of peace conciliation, and the true prosperity of the people, that a knighthood of the British Empire was conferred on 'Abdu'l-Bahá, the ceremony taking place in the garden of the Military Governor of Haifa on the 27th day of April, 1920.

Last Years

During the winter of 1919-1920 the writer had the great privilege of spending two and a half months as the guest of 'Abdu'l-Bahá at Haifa and intimately observing His daily life. At that time, although nearly seventy-six years of age, He was still remarkably vigorous, and accomplished daily an almost incredible amount of work. Although often very weary He showed wonderful powers of recuperation, and His services were always at the disposal of those who needed them most. His unfailing patience, gentleness, kindliness, and tact made His presence like a benediction. It was His custom to spend a large part of each night in prayer and meditation. From early morning until evening, except for a short siesta after lunch, He was busily engaged in reading and answering letters from many lands and in attending to the multitudinous affairs of the household and of the Cause. In the afternoon He usually had a little relaxation in the form of a walk or a drive, but even then He was usually accompanied by one or two, or a party, of pilgrims with whom He would converse on spiritual matters, or He would find opportunity by the way of seeing and ministering to some of the poor. After His return He would call the friends to the usual evening meeting in His salon. Both at lunch and supper He used to entertain a number of pilgrims and friends, and charm His guests with happy and humorous stories as well as precious talks on a great variety of subjects. "My home is the home of laughter and mirth," He declared, and indeed it was so. He delighted in gathering together people of various races, colors, nations, and religions in unity and cordial friendship around His hospitable board. He was indeed a loving father not only to the little community at Haifa, but to the Bahá'í community throughout the world.

The Passing of 'Abdu'l-Bahá

'Abdu'l-Bahá's manifold activities continued with little abatement despite increasing bodily weakness and weariness up till the last day or two of His life. On Friday, November 25, 1921, He attended the noonday prayer at the mosque in Haifa, and afterwards distributed alms to the poor with His own hands, as was His wont. After lunch He dictated some letters. When He had rested He walked in the garden and had a talk with the gardener. In the evening He gave His blessing and counsel to a loved and faithful servant of the household who had been married that day, and afterwards He attended the usual meeting of the friends in His own salon. Less than three days later, about 1:30 A.M. on Monday, November 28, He passed away so peacefully that, to the two daughters watching by His bedside, it seemed as if He had gone quietly to sleep.

The sad news soon spread throughout the town and was flashed over the wires to all parts of the world. The next morning (Tuesday, November 29) the funeral took place:

A funeral the like of which Haifa, nay, Palestine itself, had surely never seen . . . so deep was the feeling that brought so many thousands of mourners together, representative of so many religions, races and tongues.

The High Commissioner, Sir Herbert Samuel, the Governor of Jerusalem, the Governor of Phœnicia, the chief officials of the Government, the consuls of the various countries, resident in Haifa, the heads of the various religious communities, the notables of Palestine, Jews, Christians, Moslems, Druses, Egyptians, Greeks, Turks, Kurds, and a host of His American, European and native friends, men, women and children, both of high and low

degree . . . all, about ten thousand in number, mourning
the loss of their beloved One. . . . "O God, our God!"
the people wailed with one accord, "Our father has left
us, our father has left us!" . . .
They slowly wended their way up Mount Carmel, the
vineyard of God. . . . After two hours' walking, they
reached the garden of the Tomb of the Báb. . . . As the
vast concourse pressed around, representatives of the
various denominations, Moslems, Christians and Jews, all
hearts being ablaze with fervent love of 'Abdu'l-Bahá,
some on the impulse of the moment, others prepared,
raised their voices in eulogy and regret, paying their last
homage of farewell to their loved One. So united were
they in their acclamation of Him, as the wise educator and
reconciler of the human race in this perplexed and sor-
rowful age, that there seemed to be nothing left for the
Bahá'ís to say.—*The Passing of 'Abdu'l-Bahá,* by Lady
Blomfield and Shoghi Effendi.

Nine speakers, all of them prominent representatives of the
Muslim, Christian, and Jewish communities, bore eloquent
and moving witness to their love and admiration of the pure
and noble life which had just drawn to its close. Then the
casket was slowly passed to its simple and hallowed resting-
place.

Surely here was a fitting tribute to the memory of One Who
had labored all His life for unity of religions, of races, of
tongues—a tribute, and also a proof, that His lifework had not
been in vain, that the ideals of Bahá'u'lláh, which were His
inspiration, nay, His very life, were already beginning to
permeate the world and to break down the barriers of sect and
caste that for centuries had alienated Muslim, Christian, Jew,
and the other diverse factions into which the human family has
been riven.

Writings and Addresses

The Writings of 'Abdu'l-Bahá are very numerous and are
mostly in the form of letters to believers and inquirers. A great

many of His talks and addresses have also been recorded and many have been published. Of the thousands of pilgrims who have visited Him at 'Akká and Haifa a large number have written descriptions of their impressions, and many of these records are now available in printed form.

His teachings are thus very completely preserved, and they cover a very wide range of subjects. With many of the problems of both East and West He dealt more fully than His Father had done, giving more detailed applications of the general principles laid down by Bahá'u'lláh. A number of His Writings have not yet been translated into any Western language, but enough is already available to give deep and full knowledge of the more important principles of His teaching.

He spoke Persian, Arabic, and Turkish. In His Western tours His talks and addresses were always interpreted, obviously losing much of their beauty, eloquence, and force in the process, yet such was the power of the spirit which accompanied His words that all who heard Him were impressed.

Station of 'Abdu'l-Bahá

The unique station assigned to 'Abdu'l-Bahá by the Blessed Perfection is indicated in the following passage written by the latter:—"When the ocean of My presence hath ebbed and the Book of My Revelation is ended, turn your faces toward Him Whom God hath purposed, Who hath branched from this Ancient Root." And again:—". . . refer ye whatsoever ye understand not in the Book to Him Who hath branched from this mighty Stock." 'Abdu'l-Bahá Himself wrote the following:—"In accordance with the explicit text of the *Kitáb-i-Aqdas* Bahá'u'lláh hath made the Center of the Covenant the Interpreter of His Word—a Covenant so firm and mighty that from the beginning of time until the present day no religious Dispensation hath produced its like."

The very completeness of the servitude with which 'Abdu'l-Bahá promulgated the Faith of Bahá'u'lláh in East and West resulted at times in a confusion of belief concerning His station on the part of believers. Realizing the purity of the spirit animating His word and deed, surrounded by religious influences marking the breakdown of their traditional doctrines, a number of Bahá'ís felt that they honored 'Abdu'l-Bahá by likening Him to a Manifestation, or hailing Him as the "return of Christ." Nothing caused Him such intense grief as this failure to perceive that His capacity to serve Bahá'u'lláh proceeded from the purity of the mirror turned to the Sun of Truth, and not from the Sun itself.

Moreover, unlike previous Dispensations, the Faith of Bahá'u'lláh had within it the potency of a universal human society. During 'Abdu'l-Bahá's mission covering the period 1892 to 1921, the Faith evolved through successive stages of development in the direction of a true world order. Its development required continuous direction and specific instruction from 'Abdu'l-Bahá, Who alone knew the fullness of that new potent inspiration brought to earth in this age. Until His own *Will and Testament* was revealed after 'Abdu'l-Bahá's departure from the flesh, and its significance was expounded by Shoghi Effendi, the Guardian of the Faith, the Bahá'ís almost inevitably attributed to their beloved Master's guidance a degree of spiritual authority equaling that of the Manifestation.

The effects of such naive enthusiasm are no longer felt within the Bahá'í community, but with a sounder realization of the mystery of that incomparable devotion and servitude, the Bahá'ís can today all the more consciously appreciate the unique character of the mission which 'Abdu'l-Bahá fulfilled. The Faith which in 1892 seemed so weak and helpless in the physical exile and imprisonment of its Exemplar and Interpreter, has since, with irresistible power, raised up communities in many countries,[1] and challenges the weakness of a decaying civilization with a body of teachings that alone reveal the future of a despairing humanity.

The *Will and Testament of 'Abdu'l-Bahá* itself set forth with complete clarity the mystery of the stations of the Báb and of Bahá'u'lláh, and His own mission:—

---

[1] In 1969, 139 independent states and 173 significant territories and islands. (See Epilogue)

This is the foundation of the belief of the people of Bahá (may my life be offered up for them): "His Holiness, the Exalted One (the Báb), is the Manifestation of the unity and oneness of God and the Forerunner of the Ancient Beauty. His Holiness, the Abhá Beauty (may my life be a sacrifice for His steadfast friends), is the supreme Manifestation of God and the Dayspring of His most divine Essence. All others are servants unto Him and do His bidding."

By this statement, and by numerous others in which 'Abdu'l-Bahá emphasized the importance of basing one's knowledge of the Faith upon His *general* Tablets, a foundation for unity of belief was established, with the result that the differences of understanding caused by reference to His Tablets to individuals, in which the Master answered personal questions, rapidly disappeared. Above all, the establishment of a definite administrative order, with the Guardian at its head, transferred to institutions all authority previously wielded in the form of prestige and influence by individual Bahá'ís in the various local groups.

Exemplar of Bahá'í Life

Bahá'u'lláh was preeminently the Revealer of the Word. His forty years' imprisonment gave Him but limited opportunities of intercourse with His fellowmen. To 'Abdu'l-Bahá, therefore, fell the important task of becoming the exponent of the Revelation, the doer of the Word, the great exemplar of the Bahá'í life in actual contact with the world of today, in the most diverse phases of its myriad activities. He showed that it is still possible, amid the whirl and rush of modern life, amid the self-love and struggle for material prosperity that everywhere prevail, to live the life of entire devotion to God and to the service of one's fellows, which Christ and Bahá'u'lláh and all the Prophets have demanded of men. Through trial and vicissitudes, calumnies, and treachery on the one hand, and through love and praise, devotion, and veneration on the other, He stood like a lighthouse founded on a rock, around which wintry tempests rage and the summer ocean plays, His poise and serenity remaining ever steadfast and unshaken. He lived the life of faith, and calls on His followers to live it here and now. He raised amid a warring world the banner of unity and peace, the standard of a new era, and He assures those who rally to its support that they shall be inspired by the Spirit of the new day. It is the same Holy Spirit which inspired the Prophets and saints of old, but it is a new outpouring of that Spirit, suited to the needs of the new time.

What Is a Bahá'í?/5

Man must show forth fruits. A fruitless man, in the words of His Holiness the Spirit (i.e. Christ), is like a fruitless tree, and a fruitless tree is fit for fire.—BAHÁ'U'LLÁH, *Words of Paradise.*

Herbert Spencer once remarked that by no political alchemy is it possible to get golden conduct out of leaden instincts, and it is equally true that by no political alchemy is it possible to make a golden society out of leaden individuals. Bahá'u'lláh, like all previous Prophets, proclaimed this truth and taught that in order to establish the Kingdom of God in the world, it must first be established in the hearts of men. In examining the Bahá'í teachings, therefore, we shall commence with the instructions of Bahá'u'lláh for individual conduct, and try to form a clear picture of what it means to be a Bahá'í.

Living the Life

When asked on one occasion: "What is a Bahá'í?" 'Abdu'l-Bahá replied: "To be a Bahá'í simply means to love all the world; to love humanity and try to serve it; to work for universal peace and universal brotherhood." On another occasion He defined a Bahá'í as "one endowed with all the perfections of man in activity." In one of His London talks He said that a man may be a Bahá'í even if He has never heard the name of Bahá'u'lláh. He added:—

The man who lives the life according to the teachings of Bahá'u'lláh is already a Bahá'í. On the other hand, a man may call himself a Bahá'í for fifty years, and if he does not live the life he is not a Bahá'í. An ugly man may call himself handsome, but he deceives no one, and a

71

black man may call himself white, yet he deceives no one, not even himself.—*'Abdu'l-Bahá in London,* p. 109.

One who does not know God's Messengers, however, is like a plant growing in the shade. Although it knows not the sun, it is, nevertheless, absolutely dependent on it. The great prophets are spiritual suns, and Bahá'u'lláh is the sun of this "day" in which we live. The suns of former days have warmed and vivified the world, and had those suns not shone, the earth would now be cold and dead, but it is the sunshine of today that alone can ripen the fruits which the suns of former days have kissed into life.

Devotion to God

In order to attain to the Bahá'í life *in all its fullness,* conscious and direct relations with Bahá'u'lláh are as necessary as is sunshine for the unfolding of the lily or the rose. The Bahá'í worships not the human personality of Bahá'u'lláh, but the glory of God manifest through that personality. He reverences Christ and Muḥammad and all God's former Messengers to mankind, but he recognizes Bahá'u'lláh as the Bearer of God's Message for the new age in which we live, as the great world Teacher Who has come to carry on and consummate the work of His predecessors.

Intellectual assent to a creed does not make a man a Bahá'í, nor does outward rectitude of conduct. Bahá'u'lláh requires of His followers wholehearted and complete devotion. God alone has the right to make such a demand, but Bahá'u'lláh speaks as the Manifestation of God, and the Revealer of His will. Previous Manifestations have been equally clear on this point. Christ said: "If any man come after me, let him deny himself, and take up his cross and follow me. For whosoever will save his life shall lose it, and whosoever will lose his life for my sake shall find it." In different words, all the Divine Manifestations have made this same demand from Their followers, and the history of religion shows clearly that as long as the demand has been frankly recognized and accepted, religion has flourished, despite all earthly opposition, despite affliction, persecution, and martyrdom of the believers. On the other hand, whenever compromise has crept in, and "respectability" has taken the place of complete consecration, then religion has decayed. It has become fashionable, but it has lost its power to save and transform, its power to work miracles. True religion has never yet been fashionable. God grant that one day it may become so; but it is still true, as in the days of Christ, that "strait is the gate and narrow is the way that leadeth unto life, and few there be who find it." The gateway of spiritual birth, like the gateway of natural birth, admits men only one by one, and without encumbrances. If, in the future, more people succeed in entering that way than in the past, it will not be because of any widening of the gate, but because of a greater disposition on the part of men to make the "great surrender" which God demands; because long and bitter experience has at last brought them to see the folly of choosing their own way instead of God's way.

Search After Truth

Bahá'u'lláh enjoins justice on all His followers and defines it as:—"The freedom of man from superstition and imitation, so that he may discern the Manifestations of God with the eye of oneness, and consider all affairs with keen sight."—*Words of Wisdom.*

It is necessary that each individual should see and realize for himself the glory of God manifest in the human temple of Bahá'u'lláh, otherwise the Bahá'í Faith would be for him but a name without meaning. The call of the Prophets to mankind has always been that men should open their eyes, not shut them, use their reason, not suppress it. It is clear seeing and free thinking, not servile credulity, that will enable them to penetrate the clouds of prejudice, to shake off the fetters of blind imitation, and attain to the realization of the truth of a new Revelation.

He who would be a Bahá'í needs to be a fearless seeker after truth, but he should not confine his search to the material plane. His spiritual perceptive powers should be awake as well as his physical. He should use all the faculties God has given him for the acquisition of truth, believing nothing without valid and sufficient reason. If his heart is pure, and his mind free from prejudice, the earnest seeker will not fail to recognize the divine glory in whatsoever temple it may become manifest. Bahá'u'lláh further declares:—

> Man should know his own self, and know those things that lead to loftiness or to baseness, to shame or to honor, to wealth or to poverty.—*Tablet of Ṭarázát.*

> The source of all learning is the knowledge of God, exalted be His glory, and this cannot be attained save through the knowledge of His divine Manifestation.— *Words of Wisdom.*

The Manifestation is the *perfect* man, the great Exemplar for mankind, the first fruit of the tree of humanity. Until we know Him we do not know the latent possibilities within ourselves. Christ tells us to consider the lilies how they grow, and declares that Solomon in all his glory was not arrayed like one of these. The lily grows from a very unattractive-looking bulb. If we had never seen a lily in bloom, never gazed on its matchless grace of foliage and flower, how could we know the reality contained in that bulb? We might dissect it most carefully and examine it most minutely, but we should never discover the dormant beauty which the gardener knows how to awaken. So until we have seen the glory of God revealed in the Manifestation, we can have no idea of the spiritual beauty latent in our own nature and in that of our fellows. By knowing and loving the Manifestation of God and following His teachings we are enabled, little by little, to realize the potential perfections within ourselves; then, and not till then, does the meaning and purpose of life and of the universe become apparent to us.

Love of God

To know the Manifestation of God means also to love Him. One is impossible without the other. According to Bahá'u'lláh, the purpose of man's creation is that he may know God and adore Him. He says in one of His Tablets:—

The cause of the creation of all contingent beings has been love, as it is said in the well-known tradition, "I was a hidden treasure and I loved to be known. Therefore I created the creation in order to be known."

And in the *Hidden Words* He says:—

O Son of Being!
Love Me, that I may love thee. If thou lovest Me not, My love can in no wise reach thee. Know this, O servant.

O Son of the Wondrous Vision!
I have breathed within thee a breath of My own spirit, that thou mayest be My lover. Why hast thou forsaken Me and sought a beloved other than Me?

To be God's lover! That is the sole object of life for the Bahá'í. To have God as his closest companion and most intimate friend, his Peerless Beloved, in Whose presence is fullness of joy! And to love God means to love everything and everybody, for all are of God. The real Bahá'í will be the perfect lover. He will love everyone with a pure heart, fervently. He will hate no one. He will despise no one, for he will have learned to see the face of the Beloved in every face, and to find His traces everywhere. His love will know no limit of sect, nation, class, or race. Bahá'u'lláh says:—Of old it hath been revealed: "Love of one's country is an element of the Faith of God." . . . The Tongue of Grandeur hath . . . in the day of His Manifestation proclaimed: "It is not his to boast who loveth his country, but it is his who loveth the world."—*Tablet of the World*. And again:—"Blessed is he who prefers his brother before himself; such an one is of the people of Bahá."
—*Words of Paradise*.

'Abdu'l-Bahá tells us we must be "as one soul in many bodies, for the more we love each other, the nearer we shall be to God." To an American audience He said:—

Likewise the divine religions of the holy Manifestations of God are in reality one though in name and nomenclature they differ. Man must be a lover of the light no matter from what dayspring it may appear. He must be a lover of the rose no matter in what soil it may be growing. He must be a seeker of the truth no matter from what source it come. Attachment to the lantern is not loving the light. Attachment to the earth is not befitting but enjoyment of the rose which develops from the soil is worthy. Devotion to the tree is profitless but partaking of the fruit is beneficial. Luscious fruits no matter upon what tree they grow or where they may be found must be enjoyed. The word of truth no matter which tongue utters it must be sanctioned. Absolute verities no matter in what book they be recorded must be accepted. If we harbor prejudice it will be the cause of deprivation and ignorance. The strife between religions, nations and races arises from misunderstanding. If we investigate the religions to discover the principles underlying their foundations we will find they agree, for the fundamental reality of them is one and not multiple. By this means the religionists of the world will reach their point of unity and reconciliation.

Again He says:—

Every soul of the beloved ones must love the others and withhold not his possessions and life from them, and by all means he must endeavor to make the others joyous and happy. But these others must also be disinterested and self-sacrificing. Thus may this sunrise flood the horizons, this melody gladden and make happy all the people, this divine remedy become the panacea for every disease, this spirit of truth become the cause of life for every soul.—*Tablets of 'Abdu'l-Bahá*, vol. i, p. 147.

Severance

Devotion to God implies also severance from everything that is not of God, severance, that is, from all selfish and worldly, and even other-worldly, desires. The path of God may lie through riches or poverty, health or sickness, through palace or dungeon, rose garden or torture chamber. Whichever it be, the Bahá'í will learn to accept his lot with "radiant acquiescence." Severance does not mean stolid indifference to one's surroundings or passive resignation to evil conditions; nor does it mean despising the good things which God has created. The true Bahá'í will not be callous, nor apathetic, nor ascetic. He will find abundant interest, abundant work, and abundant joy in the path of God, but he will not deviate one hair's breadth from that path in pursuit of pleasure nor hanker after anything that God has denied him. When a man becomes a Bahá'í, God's will becomes his will, for to be at variance with God is the one thing he cannot endure. In the path of God no errors can appal, no troubles dismay him. The light of love irradiates his darkest days, transmutes suffering into joy, and martyrdom itself into an ecstasy of bliss. Life is lifted to the heroic plane and death becomes a glad adventure. Bahá'u'lláh says:—

He that hath in his heart even less than a mustard seed of love for anything beside Me, verily he cannot enter My Kingdom.—*Súratu'l-Haykal.*

O Son of Man!
If thou lovest Me, turn away from thyself; and if thou seekest My pleasure, regard not thine own; that thou mayest die in Me and I may eternally live in thee."

O My Servant!
Free thyself from the fetters of this world, and loose thy soul from the prison of self. Seize thy chance, for it will come to thee no more.—*Hidden Words.*

Obedience

Devotion to God involves implicit obedience to His revealed commands even when the reason for these commands is not understood. The sailor implicitly obeys his captain's orders, even when he does not know the reason for them, but his acceptance of authority is not blind. He knows full well that the captain has served a thorough probation, and given ample proofs of competence as a navigator. Were it not so, he would be foolish indeed to serve under him. So the Bahá'í must implicitly obey the Captain of his salvation, but he will be foolish indeed if he has not first ascertained that this Captain has given ample proofs of trustworthiness. Having received such proofs, however, to refuse obedience would be even greater folly, for only by intelligent and open-eyed obedience to the wise master can we reap the benefits of his wisdom, and acquire this wisdom for ourselves. Be the captain ever so wise, if none of the crew obey him how shall the ship reach its port or the sailors learn the art of navigation? Christ clearly pointed out that obedience is the path of knowledge. He said:—"My doctrine is not mine, but his that sent me. If any man will do his will, he shall know of the doctrine, whether it be of God, or whether I speak of myself."—St. John vii, 16-17. So Bahá'u'lláh says: "Faith in God, and the knowledge of Him, cannot be fully attained except . . . by practicing all that He hath commanded and all that is revealed in the Book from the Pen of Glory."—*Tablet of Tajallíyát.*

Implicit obedience is not a popular virtue in these democratic days, and indeed entire submission to the will of any mere man would be disastrous. But the unity of humanity can be attained only by complete harmony of each and all with the Divine will. Unless that will be clearly revealed, and men abandon all other leaders and obey the Divine Messenger, then conflict and strife will go on, and men will continue to oppose each other, to devote a large part of their energy to frustrating the efforts of their brother men, instead of working harmoniously together for the glory of God and the common good.

Service

Devotion to God implies a life of service to our fellow-creatures. We can be of service to God in no other way. If we turn our backs on our fellowmen, we are turning our backs upon God. Christ said, "Inasmuch as ye did it not unto the least of these My brethren, ye did it not unto Me." So Bahá'u'-lláh says:—"O son of man! If thine eyes be turned towards mercy, forsake the things that profit thee, and cleave unto that which will profit mankind. And if thine eyes be turned towards justice, choose thou for thy neighbor that which thou choosest for thyself."—*Words of Paradise.*

'Abdu'l-Bahá says:—

In the Bahá'í Cause arts, sciences and all crafts are counted as worship. The man who makes a piece of note-paper to the best of his ability, conscientiously, concentrating all his forces on perfecting it, is giving praise to God. Briefly, all effort and exertion put forth by man from the fullness of his heart is worship, if it is prompted by the highest motives and the will to do service to humanity. This is worship: to serve mankind and to minister to the needs of the people. Service is prayer. A physician ministering to the sick, gently, tenderly, free from prejudice, and believing in the solidarity of the human race, is giving praise.—*Wisdom of 'Abdu'l-Bahá* [1]

Teaching

The real Bahá'í will not only believe in the teachings of Bahá'u'lláh, but find in them the guide and inspiration of his whole life and joyfully impart to others the knowledge that is the wellspring of his own being. Only thus will he receive in full measure "the power and confirmation of the Spirit." All cannot be eloquent speakers or ready writers, but all can teach by "living the life." Bahá'u'lláh says:—

The people of Bahá must serve the Lord with wisdom, teach others by their lives, and manifest the light of God in their deeds. The effect of deeds is in truth more powerful than that of words. . . . The effect of the word spoken by the teacher depends upon his purity of purpose and his severance. Some are content with words, but the

---

[1] *Wisdom of 'Abdu'l-Bahá* is also published under the title *Paris Talks.*

truth of words is tested by deeds and dependent upon life. Deeds reveal the station of the man. The words must be according to what has proceeded from the mouth of the Will of God and is recorded in Tablets.—*Words of Wisdom.*

The Bahá'í will, however, on no account force his ideas on those who do not wish to hear them. He will attract people to the Kingdom of God, not try to drive them into it. He will be like the good shepherd who leads his flock, and charms the sheep by his music, rather than like the one who, from behind, urges them on with dog and stick.

Bahá'u'lláh says in the *Hidden Words:*—

O Son of Dust!

The wise are they that speak not unless they obtain a hearing, even as the cupbearer, who proffereth not his cup till he findeth a seeker, and the lover who crieth not out from the depths of his heart until he gazeth upon the beauty of his beloved. Wherefore sow the seeds of wisdom and knowledge in the pure soil of the heart, and keep them hidden, till the hyacinths of divine wisdom spring from the heart and not from mire and clay.

Again He says, in the *Tablet of Ishráqát:*—

O people of Bahá! Ye are the dawning-places of the love and dayprings of the favor of God. Defile not your tongues with cursing or execrating anyone, and guard your eyes from that which is not worthy. Show forth that which ye possess (i.e. Truth). If it be accepted, the aim is attained. If not, to rebuke or interfere with him who rejects is vain. Leave him to himself, and advance towards God, the Protector, the Self-Subsistent. Be not the cause of sorrow, how much less of sedition and strife! It is hoped that ye may be nurtured in the shade of the tree of divine bounty and act as God has willed for you. Ye are all leaves of one tree and drops of one sea.

Courtesy and Reverence

Bahá'u'lláh says:—

O people of God! I exhort you to courtesy. Courtesy is indeed . . . the lord of all virtues. Blessed is he who is adorned with the mantle of Uprightness and illumined with the light of Courtesy. He who is endowed with Courtesy (or Reverence) is endowed with a great station. It is hoped that this wronged One, and all, will attain to it, hold unto it and observe it. This is the irrefutable command which hath flowed from the pen of the Greatest Name.—*Tablet of the World.*

Again and again He repeats:—"Let all the nations of the world consort with each other with joy and fragrance. Consort ye, O people, with the people of all religions with joy and fragrance."

'Abdu'l-Bahá says in a letter to the Bahá'ís of America:—

Beware! Beware! Lest ye offend any heart!
Beware! Beware! Lest ye hurt any soul!
Beware! Beware! Lest ye deal unkindly toward any person!
Beware! Beware! Lest ye be the cause of hopelessness to any creature!
Should one become the cause of grief to any one heart, or of despondency to any one soul, it were better to hide oneself in the lowest depths of the earth than to walk upon the earth.

He teaches that as the flower is hidden in the bud, so a spirit from God dwells in the heart of every man, no matter how hard and unlovely his exterior. The true Bahá'í will treat every man, therefore, as the gardener tends a rare and beautiful plant. He knows that no impatient interference on his part can open the bud into a blossom; only God's sunshine can do that, therefore his aim is to bring that life-giving sunshine into all darkened hearts and homes.

Again, 'Abdu'l-Bahá says:—

> Among the teachings of Bahá'u'lláh is one requiring man, under all conditions and circumstances, to be forgiving, to love his enemy and to consider an ill-wisher as a well-wisher. Not that one should consider another as an enemy and then put up with him . . . and be forbearing toward him. This is hypocrisy and not real love. Nay, rather, you must see your enemies as friends, your ill-wishers as well-wishers and treat them accordingly. Your love and kindness must be real . . . not merely forbearance, for forbearance, if not of the heart, is hypocrisy— *Star of the West*, vol. iv, p. 191.

Such counsel appears unintelligible and self-contradictory until we realize that while the outer, carnal man may be a hater and ill-wisher, there is in everyone an inner, spiritual nature which is the real man, from whom only love and goodwill can proceed. It is to this real, inner man in each of our neighbors that we must direct our thought and love. When he awakens into activity, the outer man will be transformed and renewed.

The Sin-covering Eye

On no subject are the Bahá'í teachings more imperative and uncompromising than on the requirement to abstain from faultfinding. Christ spoke very strongly on the same subject, but it has now become usual to regard the Sermon on the Mount as embodying "counsels of perfection" which the ordinary Christian cannot be expected to live up to. Both Bahá'u'lláh and 'Abdu'l-Bahá are at great pains to make it clear that on this subject They mean all They say. We read in the *Hidden Words*:—

> O Son of Man!
> Breathe not the sins of others so long as thou art thy-

self a sinner. Shouldst thou transgress this command, accursed wouldst thou be, and to this I bear witness.

O Son of Being!
Ascribe not to any soul that which thou wouldst not have ascribed to thee, and say not that which thou doest not. This is My command unto thee, do thou observe it.

'Abdu'l-Bahá tells us:—

To be silent concerning the faults of others, to pray for them, and to help them, through kindness, to correct their faults.

To look always at the good and not at the bad. If a man has ten good qualities and one bad one, to look at the ten and forget the one; and if a man has ten bad qualities and one good one, to look at the one and forget the ten.

Never to allow ourselves to speak one unkind word about another, even though that other be our enemy.

To an American friend He writes:—

The worst human quality and the most great sin is backbiting, more especially when it emanates from the tongues of the believers of God. If some means were devised so that the doors of backbiting could be shut eternally, and each one of the believers of God unsealed his lips in praise of others, then the teachings of His Holiness Bahá'u'lláh would be spread, the hearts illumined, the spirits glorified, and the human world would attain to everlasting felicity.—*Star of the West,* vol. iv, p. 192.

Humility

While we are commanded to overlook the faults of others, and see their virtues, we are commanded, on the other hand, to find out our own faults and take no account of our virtues. Bahá'u'lláh says in the *Hidden Words:*—

O Son of Being!
How couldst thou forget thine own faults and busy

thyself with the faults of others? Whoso doeth this is accursed of Me.

O Emigrants! The tongue I have designed for the mention of Me, defile it not with detraction. If the fire of self overcome you, remember your own faults and not the faults of My creatures, inasmuch as every one of you knoweth his own self better than he knoweth others.

'Abdu'l-Bahá says:—

Let your life be an emanation of the Kingdom of Christ. He came not to be ministered unto, but to minister. . . . In the religion of Bahá'u'lláh all are servants and maidservants, brothers and sisters. As soon as one feels a little better than, a little superior to, the rest, he is in a dangerous position, and unless he casts away the seed of such an evil thought, he is not a fit instrument for the service of the Kingdom.

Dissatisfaction with oneself is a sign of progress. The soul who is satisfied with himself is the manifestation of Satan, and the one who is not contented with himself is the manifestation of the Merciful. If a person has a thousand good qualities he must not look at them; nay, rather he must strive to find out his own defects and imperfections. . . . However much a man may progress, yet he is imperfect, because there is always a point ahead of him. No sooner does he look up towards that point than he becomes dissatisfied with his own condition, and aspires to attain to that. Praising one's own self is the sign of selfishness.—*Diary of Mírzá Ahmad Sohrab,* 1914.

Although we are commanded to recognize and sincerely repent of our sins, the practice of confession to priests and others is definitely forbidden. Bahá'u'lláh says in the *Glad Tidings:*—

The sinner, when his heart is free from all save God, must seek forgiveness from God alone. Confession before the servants (i.e. before men) is not permissible, for it is not the means or the cause of Divine forgiveness. Such confession before the creatures leads to one's humiliation and abasement, and God—exalted be His glory—does not wish for the humiliation of His servants. Verily He is compassionate and beneficent. The sinner must, between himself and God, beg for mercy from the sea of mercy and implore pardon from the heaven of forgiveness.

Truthfulness and Honesty

Bahá'u'lláh says in the *Tablet of Ṭarázát:*—

Verily, honesty is the door of tranquility to all in the world, and the sign of glory from the presence of the merciful One. Whosoever attains thereto has attained to treasures of wealth and affluence. Honesty is the greatest door to the security and tranquility of mankind. The stability of every affair always depends on it, and the worlds of honor, glory and affluence are illumined by its light. . . .

O people of Bahá! Honesty is the best garment for your temples and the most splendid crown for your heads. Adhere thereto by the command of the omnipotent Commander.

Again He says:— "The principle of faith is to lessen words and to increase deeds. He whose words exceed his acts, know verily, that his nonbeing is better than his being, his death better than his life."—*Words of Wisdom.*

'Abdu'l-Bahá says:—

Truthfulness is the foundation of all the virtues of mankind. Without truthfulness, progress and success in all of the worlds are impossible for a soul. When this holy attribute is established in man, all the other divine qualities will also become realized.—*Tablets of 'Abdu'l-Bahá,* vol. ii, p. 459.

Let the light of truth and honesty shine from your

faces so that all may know that your word, in business or pleasure, is a word to trust and be sure of. Forget self and work for the whole (message to the London Bahá'ís, October 1911).

Self-realization

Bahá'u'lláh constantly urges men to realize and give full expression to the perfections latent within them—the true inner self as distinguished from the limited outer self, which at best is but the temple, and too often is the prison of the real man. In the *Hidden Words* He says:—

O Son of Being!

With the hands of power I made thee and with the fingers of strength I created thee; and within thee have I placed the essence of My light. Be thou content with it and seek naught else, for My work is perfect and My command is binding. Question it not, nor have a doubt thereof.

O Son of Spirit!

I created thee rich, why dost thou bring thyself down to poverty? Noble I made thee, wherewith dost thou abase thyself? Out of the essence of knowledge I gave thee being, why seekest thou enlightenment from anyone beside Me? Out of the clay of love I molded thee, how dost thou busy thyself with another? Turn thy sight unto thyself, that thou mayest find Me standing within thee, mighty, powerful and self-subsisting.

O My Servant!

Thou art even as a finely tempered sword concealed in the darkness of its sheath and its value hidden from the artificer's knowledge. Wherefore come forth from the sheath of self and desire that thy worth may be made resplendent and manifest unto all the world.

O My Friend!

Thou art the daystar of the heavens of My holiness,

let not the defilement of the world eclipse thy splendor. Rend asunder the veil of heedlessness, that from behind the clouds thou mayest emerge resplendent and array all things with the apparel of life.

The life to which Bahá'u'lláh calls His followers is surely one of such nobility that in all the vast range of human possibility there is nothing more lofty or beautiful to which man could aspire. Realization of the spiritual self in ourselves means realization of the sublime truth that we are from God and to Him we shall return. This return to God is the glorious goal of the Bahá'í; but to attain this goal the only path is that of obedience to His chosen Messengers, and especially to His Messenger for the time in which we live, Bahá'u'lláh, the Prophet of the new era.

Prayer/6

Prayer is a ladder by which everyone may ascend to heaven.
—MUḤAMMAD.

Conversation with God

"Prayer," says 'Abdu'l-Bahá, "is conversation with God." In order that God may make known His mind and will to men, He must speak to them in a language which they can understand, and this He does by the mouths of His Holy Prophets. While these Prophets are alive in the body They speak with men face to face and convey to them the Message of God, and after Their death Their message continues to reach men's minds through Their recorded sayings and writings. But this is not the only way in which God can speak with men. There is a "language of the spirit," which is independent of speech or writing, by which God can commune with and inspire those whose hearts are seeking after truth, wherever they are, and whatever their native race or tongue. By this language the Manifestation continues to hold converse with the faithful after His departure from the material world. Christ continued to converse with and inspire His disciples after His crucifixion. In fact He influenced them more powerfully than before; and with other Prophets it has been the same. 'Abdu'l-Bahá speaks much of this spiritual language. He says, for instance:—

We should speak in the language of heaven—in the language of the spirit—for there is a language of the spirit and heart. It is as different from our language as our own language is different from that of the animals, who express themselves only by cries and sounds.
It is the language of the spirit which speaks to God. When, in prayer, we are freed from all outward things and

88

turn to God, then it is as if in our hearts we hear the voice of God. Without words we speak, we communicate, we converse with God and hear the answer. . . . All of us, when we attain to a truly spiritual condition, can hear the voice of God (from a talk reported by Miss Ethel J. Rosenberg).

Bahá'u'lláh declares that the higher spiritual truths can be communicated only by means of this spiritual language. The spoken or written word is quite inadequate. In a little book called *The Seven Valleys,* in which He describes the journey of travelers from the earthly dwelling to the divine home, He says, in speaking of the more advanced stages of the journey:—

> The tongue is unable to give an account of these, and utterance falls exceedingly short. The pen is useless in this court, and the ink gives no result but blackness. . . . Heart alone can communicate to heart the state of the knower; this is not the work of a messenger, nor can it be contained in letters.

The Devotional Attitude

In order that we may attain the spiritual condition in which conversation with God becomes possible, 'Abdu'l-Bahá says:—

> We must strive to attain to that condition by being separated from all things and from the people of the world and by turning to God alone. It will take some effort on the part of man to attain to that condition, but he must work for it, strive for it. We can attain to it by thinking and caring less for material things and more for the spiritual. The further we go from the one, the nearer we are to the other. The choice is ours.
>
> Our spiritual perception, our inward sight must be opened, so that we can see the signs and traces of God's spirit in everything. Everything can reflect to us the light of the Spirit (from a talk reported by Miss Ethel J. Rosenberg).

Bahá'u'lláh has written:— "That seeker . . . at the dawn of every day . . . should commune with God, and, with all his soul, persevere in the quest of his Beloved. He should consume every wayward thought with the flame of His loving mention. . . ."—*Gleanings from the Writings of Bahá'u'lláh*, p. 265.

In the same way, 'Abdu'l-Bahá declares:—

When man allows the spirit, through his soul, to enlighten his understanding, then does he contain all creation. . . . But on the other hand, when man does not open his mind and heart to the blessing of the spirit, but turns his soul towards the material side, towards the bodily part of his nature, then is he fallen from his high place and he becomes inferior to the inhabitants of the lower animal kingdom.—*Wisdom of 'Abdu'l-Bahá.*

Again, Bahá'u'lláh writes:—

Deliver your souls, O people, from the bondage of self, and purify them from all attachment to anything besides Me. Remembrance of Me cleanseth all things from defilement, could ye but perceive it. . . . Intone, O My servant, the verses of God that have been received by thee, . . . that the sweetness of thy melody may kindle thine own soul, and attract the hearts of all men. Whoso reciteth, in the privacy of his chamber, the verses revealed by God, the scattering angels of the Almighty shall scatter abroad the fragrance of the words uttered by his mouth.—*Gleanings from the Writings of Bahá'u'lláh*, pp. 294-295.

Necessity for a Mediator

According to 'Abdu'l-Bahá:—

A mediator is necessary between man and the Creator—one who receives the full light of the Divine Splendor and radiates it over the human world, as the earth's atmosphere receives and diffuses the warmth of the sun's rays.—*Divine Philosophy.*

If we wish to pray, we must have some object on which to concentrate. If we turn to God, we must direct our hearts to a certain center. If man worships God otherwise than through His Manifestation, he must first form a conception of God, and that conception is created by his own mind. As the finite cannot comprehend the Infinite, so God is not to be comprehended in this fashion. That which man conceives with his own mind he comprehends. That which he can comprehend is not God. That conception of God which a man forms for himself is but a phantasm, an image, an imagination, an illusion. There is no connection between such a conception and the Supreme Being.

If a man wishes to know God, he must find Him in the perfect mirror, Christ or Bahá'u'lláh. In either of these mirrors he will see reflected the Sun of Divinity.

As we know the physical sun by its splendor, by its light and heat, so we know God, the spiritual Sun, when He shines forth from the temple of Manifestation, by His attributes of perfection, by the beauty of His qualities and by the splendor of His light (from a talk to Mr. Percy Woodcock, at 'Akká, 1909).

Again He says:

Unless the Holy Spirit become intermediary, one cannot attain directly to the bounties of God. Do not overlook the obvious truth, for it is self-evident that a child cannot be instructed without a teacher, and knowledge is one of the bounties of God. The soil is not covered with grass and vegetation without the rain of the cloud; therefore the cloud is the intermediary between the divine bounties and the soil. . . . The light hath a center and if one desire to seek it otherwise than from the center, one can never attain to it. . . . Turn thine attention to the days of Christ; some people imagined that without the Messianic outpourings it was possible to attain to truth, but this very imagination became the cause of their deprivation.—*Tablets of 'Abdu'l-Bahá*, vol. iii, pp. 591, 592.

A man who tries to worship God without turning to His Manifestation is like a man in a dungeon trying through his imagination to revel in the glories of the sunshine.

Prayer Indispensable and Obligatory

The use of prayer is enjoined upon Bahá'ís in no uncertain terms. Bahá'u'lláh says in the *Kitáb-i-Aqdas:*—

Chant (or recite) the words of God every morning and evening. The one who neglects this has not been faithful to the Covenant of God and His agreement, and he who turns away from it today is of those who have turned away from God. Fear God, O my people! Let not too much reading (of the sacred Word) and actions by day or night make you proud. To chant but one verse with joy and gladness is better for you than reading all the Revelations of the omnipotent God with carelessness. Chant the Tablets of God in such measure that ye be not overtaken with fatigue and depression. Burden not the soul so as to cause exhaustion and languor, but rather refresh it that thus it may soar on the wings of Revelation to the dawning-place of proofs. This brings you nearer to God, were ye of those who understand.

'Abdu'l-Bahá says to a correspondent:—"O thou spiritual friend! Know thou that prayer is indispensable and obligatory, and man under no pretext whatever is excused therefrom unless he be mentally unsound or an insurmountable obstacle prevent him."—*Tablets of 'Abdu'l-Bahá,* vol. iii, p. 683.

Another correspondent asked: "Why pray? What is the wisdom thereof, for God has established everything and executes all affairs after the best order—therefore, what is the wisdom in beseeching and supplicating and in stating one's wants and seeking help?"

'Abdu'l-Bahá replied:—

Know thou, verily, it is becoming in a weak one to supplicate to the strong One, and it behooveth a seeker of bounty to beseech the glorious bountiful One. When one supplicates to his Lord, turns to Him and seeks bounty from His ocean, this supplication brings light to his heart, illumination to his sight, life to his soul and exaltation to his being. During thy supplications to God and thy reciting, "Thy Name is my healing," consider how thine heart is cheered, thy soul delighted by the spirit of the love of God, and thy mind attracted to the Kingdom of God! By these attractions one's ability and capacity increase. When the vessel is enlarged the water increases, and when the thirst grows the bounty of the cloud becomes agreeable to the taste of man. This is the mystery of supplication and the wisdom of stating one's wants (from a Tablet to an American believer, translated by 'Alí Kulí <u>Kh</u>án, October 1908).

Bahá'u'lláh has revealed three daily obligatory prayers. The believer is free to choose any one of these three prayers, but is under the obligation of reciting one of them, and in the manner Bahá'u'lláh has prescribed.

Congregational Prayer

The prayers which Bahá'u'lláh has ordained as a daily obligation for Bahá'ís are to be said privately. Only in the case of the Prayer for the Dead has Bahá'u'lláh commanded congregational prayer, and the only requirement is that the believer who reads it aloud, and all others present, should stand. This differs from the Islamic practice of congregational prayer in which the believers stand in rows behind an imám, who leads the prayer, which is prohibited in the Bahá'í Faith.

These ordinances, which are in accordance with Bahá'u'lláh's abolition of professional clergy do not mean that He attached no value to meetings for worship. Regarding the value of gathering for prayer, 'Abdu'l-Bahá spoke as follows:—

Man may say: "I can pray to God whenever I wish, when the feelings of my heart are drawn to God; when I am in the wilderness, when I am in the city, or wherever I may be. Why should I go where others are gathered upon a special day, at a certain hour, to unite my prayers with theirs, when I may not be in a frame of mind for praying?"

To think in this way is useless imagination, for where many are gathered together their force is greater. Separate soldiers fighting alone and individually have not the force of a united army. If all the soldiers in this spiritual war gather together, then their united spiritual feelings help each other, and their prayers become acceptable (from notes taken by Miss Ethel J. Rosenberg).

Prayer the Language of Love

To someone who asked whether prayer was necessary, since presumably God knows the wishes of all hearts, 'Abdu'l-Bahá replied:—

If one friend feels love for another he will wish to say so. Though he knows that the friend is aware that he loves him, he will still wish to say so. . . . God knows the wishes of all hearts, but the impulse to pray is a natural one, springing from man's love to God. . . .

Prayer need not be in words but in thought and attitude. If this love and desire are lacking, it is useless to try and force them. Words without love mean nothing. If a person talks to you as an unpleasant duty, with no love or pleasure in his meeting with you, do you wish to converse with him? (article in *Fortnightly Review,* June 1911, by Miss E. S. Stevens).

In another talk He said:—

In the highest prayer, men pray only for the love of God, not because they fear Him or hell, or hope for bounty or heaven. . . . When a man falls in love with a human being, it is impossible for him to keep from mentioning the name of his beloved. How much more difficult

is it to keep from mentioning the Name of God when one
has come to love Him. . . . The spiritual man finds no
delight in anything save in commemoration of God (from
notes of Miss Alma Robertson and other pilgrims, November and December 1900).

Deliverance from Calamities

According to the teaching of the Prophets, disease and all
other forms of calamity are due to disobedience to the Divine
commands. Even disasters due to floods, hurricanes, and earth-
quakes are attributed by 'Abdu'l-Bahá indirectly to this cause.

The suffering that follows error is not vindictive, however,
but educative and remedial. It is God's voice proclaiming to
man that he has strayed from the right path. If the suffering is
terrible, it is only because the danger of wrongdoing is more
terrible, for "the wages of sin is death."

Just as calamity is due to disobedience, so deliverance
from calamity can be obtained only by obedience. There is no
chance or uncertainty about the matter. Turning *from* God
inevitably brings disaster, and turning *to* God as inevitably
brings blessing.

As the whole of humanity is one organism, however, the
welfare of each individual depends not only on his own be-
havior, but on that of his neighbors. If one does wrong, all
suffer in greater or less degree; while if one does well, all benefit. Each has to bear his neighbor's burdens, to some extent,
and the best of mankind are those who bear the biggest burdens. The saints have always suffered abundantly; the Prophets
have suffered superlatively. Bahá'u'lláh says in the *Book of
Íqán:*—"You must undoubtedly have been informed of the
tribulations, the poverty, the ills, and the degradation that
have befallen every Prophet of God and His companions. You
must have heard how the heads of Their followers were sent
as presents unto different cities."

This is not because the saints and Prophets have merited
punishment above other men. Nay, they often suffer for the
sins of others, and *choose* to suffer, for the sake of others. Their

concern is for the world's welfare, not for their own. The prayer of the true lover of humanity is not that he, as an individual, may escape poverty, ill-health, or disaster, but that mankind may be saved from ignorance and error and the ills that inevitably flow from them. If he wishes health or wealth for himself, it is in order that he may serve the Kingdom, and if physical health and wealth are denied him, he accepts his lot with "radiant acquiescence," well knowing that there is a right wisdom in whatever befalls him in the path of God. 'Abdu'l-Bahá says:—

Grief and sorrow do not come to us by chance; they are sent by the Divine Mercy for our perfecting. When grief and sorrow come, then will a man remember his Father Who is in heaven, Who is able to deliver him from his humiliations. The more a man is chastened, the greater is the harvest of spiritual virtues shown forth by him.— *Wisdom of 'Abdu'l-Bahá,* p. 45.

At first sight it may seem very unjust that the innocent should suffer for the guilty, but 'Abdu'l-Bahá assures us that the injustice is only apparent and that, in the long run, perfect justice prevails. He writes:—

As to the subject of babes and children and weak ones who are afflicted by the hands of the oppressors . . . for those souls there is a recompense in another world . . . that suffering is the greatest mercy of God. Verily that mercy of the Lord is far better than all the comfort of this world and the growth and development appertaining to this place of mortality.—*Tablets of 'Abdu'l-Bahá,* vol. ii, p. 337.

Prayer and Natural Law

Many find a difficulty in believing in the efficacy of prayer because they think that answers to prayer would involve arbitrary interference with the laws of nature. An analogy may help to remove this difficulty. If a magnet be held over some iron filings the latter will fly upwards and cling to it, but this involves no interference with the law of gravitation. The force of gravity continues to act on the filings just as before. What has happened is that a superior force has been brought into play—another force whose action is just as regular and calculable as that of gravity. The Bahá'í view is that prayer brings into action higher forces, as yet comparatively little known; but there seems no reason to believe that these forces are more arbitrary in their action than the physical forces. The difference is that they have not yet been fully studied and experimentally investigated, and their action appears mysterious and incalculable because of our ignorance.

Another difficulty which some find perplexing is that prayer seems too feeble a force to produce the great results often claimed for it. Analogy may serve to clear up this difficulty also. A small force, when applied to the sluice gate of a reservoir, may release and regulate an enormous flow of water-power, or, when applied to the steering gear of an ocean liner, may control the course of the huge vessel. In the Bahá'í view, the power that brings about answers to prayer is the inexhaustible power of God. The part of the suppliant is only to exert the feeble force necessary to release the flow or determine the course of the divine bounty, which is ever ready to serve those who have learned how to draw upon it.

Bahá'í Prayers

Bahá'u'lláh and 'Abdu'l-Bahá have revealed innumerable prayers for the use of Their followers at various times and for various purposes. The greatness of conception and depth of spirituality revealed in these utterances must impress every thoughtful student, but only by making their use a regular and important part of one's daily life can their significance be fully appreciated and their power for good realized. Unfortunately, considerations of space prevent our giving more than a very few short specimens of these prayers. For further examples the reader must be referred to other works.

O my Lord! Make Thy beauty to be my food, and Thy presence my drink, and Thy pleasure my hope, and praise of Thee my action, and remembrance of Thee my companion, and the power of Thy sovereignty my succorer, and Thy habitation my home, and my dwelling-place the seat Thou hast sanctified from the limitations imposed upon them who are shut out as by a veil from Thee. Thou art, verily, the Almighty, the All-Glorious, the Most Powerful.—BAHÁ'U'LLÁH.

I bear witness, O my God, that Thou hast created me to know Thee and to worship Thee. I testify, at this moment, to my powerlessness and to Thy might, to my poverty and to Thy wealth. There is none other God but Thee, the Help in Peril, the Self-Subsisting!— BAHÁ'U'LLÁH.

O my God! O my God! Unite the hearts of Thy servants and reveal to them Thy great purpose. May they follow Thy commandments and abide in Thy law. Help them, O God, in their endeavor, and grant them strength to serve Thee. O God! leave them not to themselves, but guide their steps by the light of knowledge, and cheer their hearts by Thy love. Verily, Thou art their Helper and their Lord.—BAHÁ'U'LLÁH.

O Thou kind Lord! Thou hast created all humanity from the same stock. Thou hast decreed that all shall belong to the same household. In Thy holy presence they are all Thy servants, and all mankind are sheltered beneath Thy Tabernacle; all have gathered together at Thy table of bounty; all are illumined through the light of Thy providence.

O God! Thou art kind to all, Thou hast provided for all, dost shelter all, conferrest life upon all, Thou hast endowed each and all with talents and faculties, and all are submerged in the ocean of Thy mercy.

O Thou kind Lord! Unite all. Let the religions agree and make the nations one, so that they may see each other as one family and the whole earth as one home. May they all live together in perfect harmony.

O God! Raise aloft the banner of the oneness of mankind.

Cement Thou, O God, the hearts together.

O Thou kind Father, O God! Gladden our hearts through the fragrance of Thy love. Brighten our eyes through the light of Thy guidance. Delight our ears with the melody of Thy Word, and shelter us all in the stronghold of Thy providence.

Thou art the Mighty and Powerful, Thou art the Forgiving and Thou art the One Who overlookest the shortcomings of all mankind!—'Abdu'l-Bahá

O Thou Almighty! I am a sinner, but Thou art the Forgiver! I am full of shortcomings, but Thou art the Compassionate! I am in the darkness of error, but Thou art the Light of Pardon!

Therefore, O Thou benevolent God, forgive my sins, grant thy bestowals, overlook my faults, provide for me a shelter, immerse me in the fountain of Thy patience and heal me of all sickness and disease.

Purify and sanctify me. Give me a portion from the outpouring of holiness, so that sorrow and sadness may vanish, joy and happiness descend, despondency and hopelessness be changed into cheerfulness and trustfulness, and courage take the place of fear.

Verily Thou art the Forgiver, the Compassionate, and Thou art the Generous, the Beloved!—'Abdu'l-Bahá.

O compassionate God! Thanks be to Thee for Thou has awakened and made me conscious. Thou hast given me a seeing eye and favored me with a hearing ear; hast led me to Thy Kingdom and guided me to Thy path. Thou hast shown me the right way and caused me to enter the Ark of deliverance. O God! Keep me steadfast and make me firm and staunch. Protect me from violent tests and preserve and shelter me in the strongly fortified fortress of Thy Covenant and Testament. Thou art the

Powerful! Thou art the Seeing! Thou art the Hearing! O Thou the compassionate God! Bestow upon me a heart which, like unto glass, may be illumined with the light of Thy love, and confer upon me a thought which may change this world into a rose garden through the spiritual bounty. Thou art the Compassionate, the Merciful! Thou art the great beneficent God!—'ABDU'L-BAHÁ.

Bahá'í prayer is not, however, confined to the use of prescribed forms, important as those are. Bahá'u'lláh teaches that one's whole life should be a prayer, that work done in the right spirit is worship, that every thought, word, and deed devoted to the glory of God and the good of one's fellows is prayer, in the truest sense of the word.[1]

---

[1] On the subject of Intercessory Prayer, see Chapter 11.

Health and Healing/7

Turning the face towards God brings healing to the body, the mind and the soul.—'ABDU'L-BAHÁ.

Body and Soul

According to the Bahá'í teaching the human body serves a temporary purpose in the development of the soul, and, when that purpose has been served, is laid aside; just as the eggshell serves a temporary purpose in the development of the chick, and, when that purpose has been served, is broken and discarded. 'Abdu'l-Bahá says that the physical body is incapable of immortality, for it is a composite thing, built up of atoms and molecules, and, like all things that are composed, must, in time, become decomposed.

The body should be the servant of the soul, never its master, but it should be a willing, obedient, and efficient servant, and should be treated with the consideration which a good servant deserves. If it is not properly treated, disease and disaster result, with injurious consequences to master as well as servant.

Oneness of All Life

The essential oneness of all the myriad forms and grades of life is one of the fundamental teachings of Bahá'u'lláh. Our physical health is so linked up with our mental, moral, and spiritual health, and also with the individual and social health of our fellowmen, nay, even with the life of the animals and plants, that each of these is affected by the others to a far greater extent than is usually realized.

There is no command of the Prophet, therefore, to whatever department of life it may primarily refer, which does not concern bodily health. Certain of the teachings, however, have a

101

more direct bearing on physical health than others, and these we may now proceed to examine.

Simple Life

'Abdu'l-Bahá says:—

Economy is the foundation of human prosperity. The spendthrift is always in trouble. Prodigality on the part of any person is an unpardonable sin. We must never live on others like a parasitic plant. Every person must have a profession, whether it be literary or manual, and must live a clean, manly, honest life, an example of purity to be imitated by others. It is more kingly to be satisfied with a crust of stale bread than to enjoy a sumptuous dinner of many courses, the money for which comes out of the pockets of others. The mind of a contented person is always peaceful and his heart at rest.—*Bahá'í Scriptures,* p. 453.

Animal food is not forbidden, but 'Abdu'l-Bahá says:— "The food of the future will be fruit and grains. The time will come when meat will no longer be eaten. Medical science is only in its infancy, yet it has shown that our natural food is that which grows out of the ground."—*Ten Days in the Light of 'Akká,* by Julia M. Grundy.

Alcohol and Narcotics

The use of narcotics and intoxicants of any kind, except as remedies in case of illness, is strictly forbidden by Bahá'u'lláh.

Enjoyments

The Bahá'í teaching is based on moderation, not on asceticism. Enjoyment of the good and beautiful things of life, both material and spiritual, is not only encouraged but enjoined. Bahá'u'lláh says: "Deprive not yourselves of that which has been created for you." Again He says: "It is incumbent upon

you that exultation and glad tidings be manifest in your faces."
'Abdu'l-Bahá says:—

All that has been created is for man, who is at the apex
of creation, and he must be thankful for the divine bestowals. All material things are for us, so that through our
gratitude we may learn to understand life as a divine benefit. If we are disgusted with life we are ingrates, for our
material and spiritual existence are the outward evidences
of the divine mercy. Therefore we must be happy and
spend our time in praises, appreciating all things.—*Divine Philosophy*.

Asked whether the Bahá'í prohibition of gambling applies
to games of every description, 'Abdu'l-Bahá replied:—

No, some games are innocent, and if pursued for pastime cause no harm; but there is danger that pastime may
degenerate into waste of time. Waste of time is not acceptable in the Cause of God, but recreation which may
improve the bodily powers, as exercise, is desirable.—*A
Heavenly Vista*, p. 9.

Cleanliness

Bahá'u'lláh says, in the *Book of Aqdas:*—

Be the essence of cleanliness among mankind . . . under all circumstances conform yourselves to refined man-
ners . . . let no trace of uncleanliness appear on your
clothes. . . . Immerse yourselves in pure water; a water
which hath been used is not allowable. . . . Verily We
have desired to see in you the manifestations of Paradise
on earth, so that there may be diffused from you that
whereat the hearts of the favored ones shall rejoice.

Mírzá Abu'l-Faḍl, in his book, *Bahá'í Proofs* (p. 89),
points out the extreme importance of these commands, more
especially in some parts of the East, where water of the foulest
description is often used for household purposes, for bathing

and even for drinking, and horribly insanitary conditions abound, causing a vast amount of preventable disease and misery. These conditions, often supposed to be sanctioned by the prevailing religion, can be changed, among Orientals, only by the commandment of one who is believed to have divine authority. In many parts of the Western Hemisphere, too, a wonderful transformation would result were cleanliness accepted not only as next to godliness, but as an essential part of godliness.

Effect of Obedience to Prophetic Commands

The bearing on health of these commands relating to the simple life, hygiene, abstinence from alcohol and opium, et cetera, is too obvious to call for much comment, although their vital importance is apt to be greatly underestimated. Were they to be generally observed, most of the infectious diseases and a good many others would soon vanish from among men. The amount of illness caused by neglect of simple hygienic precautions and by indulgence in alcohol and opium is prodigious. Moreover, obedience to these commands would not only affect health, but would have an enormous effect for good on character and conduct. Alcohol and opium affect a man's conscience long before they affect his gait or cause obvious bodily disease, so that the moral and spiritual gain from abstinence would be even greater than the physical. With regard to cleanliness, 'Abdu'l-Bahá says:—"External cleanliness, although it is but a physical thing, has great influence upon spirituality. . . . The fact of having a pure and spotless body exercises an influence upon the spirit of man."—*Tablets of 'Abdu'l-Bahá,* vol. iii, pp. 581-2.

Were the commands of the Prophets concerning chastity in sexual relations generally observed, another fertile cause of disease would be eliminated. The loathsome venereal diseases, which wreck the health of so many thousands today, innocent as well as guilty, babes as well as parents, would very soon be entirely a thing of the past.

Were the commands of the Prophets concerning justice, mutual aid, loving one's neighbor as oneself, carried out, how could overcrowding, sweated labor, and sordid poverty on the one hand, together with self-indulgence, idleness, and sordid luxury on the other, continue to work mental, moral, and physical ruin?

Simple obedience to the hygienic and moral commands of Moses, Buddha, Christ, Muḥammad, or Bahá'u'lláh would do more in the way of preventing disease than all the doctors and all the public health regulations in the world have been able to accomplish. In fact, it seems certain that were such obedience general, good health would also become general. Instead of lives being blighted by disease or cut off in infancy, youth, or prime, as so frequently happens now, men would live to a ripe old age, like sound fruits that mature and mellow ere they drop from the bough.

The Prophet as Physician

We live in a world, however, where from time immemorial obedience to the commands of the Prophets has been the exception rather than the rule; where love of self has been a more prevalent motive than love of God; where limited and party interests have taken precedence of the interests of humanity as a whole; where material possessions and sensual pleasures have been preferred to the social and spiritual welfare of mankind. Hence have arisen fierce competition and conflict, oppression, and tyranny, extremes of wealth and poverty—all those conditions which breed disease, mental and physical. As a consequence, the whole tree of humanity is sick, and every leaf on the tree shares in the general sickness. Even the purest and holiest have to suffer for the sins of others. Healing is needed —healing of humanity as a whole, of nations, and of individuals. So Bahá'u'lláh, like His inspired predecessors, not only shows how health is to be maintained, but also how it may be recovered when lost. He comes as the Great Physician, the Healer of the world's sicknesses, both of body and of mind.

Healing by Material Means

In the Western world of today there is evident a remarkable revival of belief in the efficacy of healing by mental and spiritual means. Indeed many, in their revolt against the materialistic ideas about disease and its treatment which prevailed in the nineteenth century, have gone to the opposite extreme of denying that material remedies or hygienic methods have any value whatever. Bahá'u'lláh recognizes the value of both material and spiritual remedies. He teaches that the science and art of healing must be developed, encouraged, and perfected, so that all means of healing may be used to the best advantage, each in its appropriate sphere. When members of Bahá'u'lláh's own family were sick, a professional physician was called in, and this practice is recommended to His followers. He says: "Should ye be attacked by illness or disease, consult skillful physicians" (*Kitáb-i-Aqdas*).

This is quite in accordance with the Bahá'í attitude towards science and art generally. All sciences and arts which are for the benefit of mankind, even in a material way, are to be esteemed and promoted. Through science man becomes the master of material things; through ignorance he remains their slave.

Bahá'u'lláh writes: —

Do not neglect medical treatment when it is necessary, but leave it off when health has been restored. Treat disease through diet, by preference, refraining from the use of drugs; and if you find what is required in a single herb, do not resort to a compounded medicament. . . . Abstain from drugs when the health is good, but administer them when necessary.—*Tablet to a Physician.*

In one of His Tablets 'Abdu'l-Bahá says: —

O seeker after truth! There are two ways of healing sickness, material means and spiritual means. The first way is through the use of material remedies. The second consists in praying to God and in turning to Him. Both means should be used and practiced. . . . Moreover, they are not incompatible, and you should accept the physical remedies as coming from the mercy and favor of God Who has revealed and made manifest medical knowledge, so that His servants may profit by this kind of treatment also.—*Tablets of 'Abdu'l-Bahá,* vol. iii, p. 587.

He teaches that, were our natural tastes and instincts not vitiated by foolish and unnatural modes of living, they would become reliable guides in the choice both of appropriate diet and of medicinal fruits, herbs, and other remedies, as is the case with wild animals. In an interesting talk on healing, recorded in *Some Answered Questions* (p. 298), He says in conclusion:—

It is therefore evident that it is possible to cure by foods, aliments, and fruits; but as today the science of medicine is imperfect, this fact is not yet fully grasped. When the science of medicine reaches perfection, treatment will be given by foods, aliments, fragrant fruits, and vegetables, and by various waters, hot and cold in temperature.

Even when the means of healing are material, the power that heals is really divine, for the attributes of the herb or mineral are from the divine bestowals. "All depends upon God. Medicine is merely an outward form or means by which we obtain heavenly healing."

Healing by Nonmaterial Means

He teaches that there are also many methods of healing without material means. There is a "contagion of health," as well as a contagion of disease, although the former is very slow and has a small effect, while the latter is often violent and rapid in its action.

Much more powerful effects result from the patient's own

mental states, and "suggestion" may play an important part in determining these states. Fear, anger, worry, et cetera, are very prejudicial to health, while hope, love, joy, et cetera, are correspondingly beneficial.

Thus Bahá'u'lláh says:—

Verily the most necessary thing is contentment under all circumstances; by this one is preserved from morbid conditions and from lassitude. Yield not to grief and sorrow: they cause the greatest misery. Jealousy consumeth the body and anger doth burn the liver: avoid these two as you would a lion.—*Tablet to a Physician.*

And 'Abdu'l-Bahá says:—"Joy gives us wings. In times of joy our strength is more vital, our intellect keener. . . . But when sadness visits us our strength leaves us."—*Wisdom of 'Abdu'l-Bahá, p. 100.*

Of another form of mental healing 'Abdu'l-Bahá writes that it results:—

from the entire concentration of the mind of a strong person upon a sick person, when the latter expects with all his concentrated faith that a cure will be effected from the spiritual power of the strong person, to such an extent that there will be a cordial connection between the strong person and the invalid. The strong person makes every effort to cure the sick patient, and the sick patient is then sure of receiving a cure. From the effect of these mental impressions an excitement of the nerves is produced, and this impression and this excitement of the nerves will become the cause of the recovery of the sick person.—*Some Answered Questions, p. 294.*

All these methods of healing, however, are limited in their effects, and may fail to effect a cure in severe maladies.

The Power of the Holy Spirit

The most potent means of healing is the power of the Holy Spirit.

This does not depend on contact, nor on sight, nor upon presence. . . . Whether the disease be light or severe, whether there be a contact of bodies or not, whether a personal connection be established between the sick person and the healer or not, this healing takes place through the power of the Holy Spirit.—*Some Answered Questions,* p. 295.

In a talk with Miss Ethel Rosenberg, in October 1904, 'Abdu'l-Bahá said:—

The healing that is by the power of the Holy Spirit needs no special concentration or contact. It is through the wish or desire and the prayer of the holy person. The one who is sick may be in the East and the healer in the West, and they may not have been acquainted with each other, but as soon as that holy person turns his heart to God and begins to pray, the sick one is healed. This is a gift belonging to the Holy Manifestations and those who are in the highest station.

Of this nature, apparently, were the works of healing performed by Christ and His apostles, and similar works of healing have been attributed to holy men in all ages. Both Bahá'u'lláh and 'Abdu'l-Bahá were gifted with this power, and similar powers are promised to Their faithful followers.

Attitude of the Patient

In order that the power of spiritual healing may be brought fully into operation certain requirements are necessary on the part of the patient, of the healer, of the patient's friends, and of the community at large.

On the part of the patient the prime requisite is, turning with all the heart to God, with implicit trust both in His power and in His will to do whatever is best. To an American lady, in August 1912, 'Abdu'l-Bahá said:—

All of these ailments will pass away and you will receive perfect physical and spiritual health. . . . Let your heart be confident and assured that through the bounty of Bahá'u'lláh, through the favor of Bahá'u'lláh, everything will become pleasant for you. . . . But you must turn your face wholly towards the Abhá (All-Glorious) Kingdom, giving perfect attention—the same attention that Mary Magdalene gave to His Holiness Christ—and I assure you that you will get physical health and spiritual health. You are worthy. I give you the glad tidings that you are worthy because your heart is pure. . . . Be confident! Be happy! Be rejoiced! Be hopeful!

Although in this particular case 'Abdu'l-Bahá guaranteed the attainment of sound physical health, He does not do so in every case, even where there is strong faith on the part of the individual. To a pilgrim at 'Akká He said:—

The prayers which were written for the purpose of healing are both for the spiritual and material healing. If healing is best for the patient, surely it will be granted. For some who are sick, healing would only be the cause of other ills. Thus it is that wisdom does not decree the answer to some prayers.

O handmaid of God! The power of the Holy Spirit heals both material and spiritual ills.—*Daily Lessons Received at 'Akká,* p. 95.

Again He writes to one who is ill:—

Verily the will of God acts sometimes in a way for which mankind is unable to find out the reason. The causes and reasons shall appear. Trust in God and confide in Him, and resign thyself to the will of God. Verily thy God is affectionate, compassionate and merciful . . . and will cause His mercy to descend upon thee."—*Star of the West,* vol. viii, p. 232.

He teaches that spiritual health is *conducive* to physical health, but physical health depends upon many factors, some of which are outside the control of the individual. Even the most exemplary spiritual attitude on the part of the individual, therefore, may not *ensure* physical health in every case. The holiest men and women sometimes suffer illness.

Nevertheless, the beneficent influence on bodily health which results from a right spiritual attitude is far more potent than is generally imagined, and is sufficient to banish ill-health in a large proportion of cases. 'Abdu'l-Bahá wrote to an English lady:—"You have written about the weakness of your body. I ask from the bounties of Bahá'u'lláh that your spirit may become strong, that through the strength of your spirit your body also may be healed."

Again He says:—

God hath bestowed upon man such wonderful powers, that he might ever look upward, and receive, among other gifts, healing from His divine bounty. But alas! man is not grateful for this supreme good, but sleeps the sleep of negligence, being careless of the great mercy which God has shown towards him, turning his face away from the Light and going on his way in darkness.—*Wisdom of 'Abdu'l-Bahá,* p. 16.

The Healer

The power of spiritual healing is doubtless common to all mankind in greater or less degree, but, just as some men are endowed with exceptional talent for mathematics or music, so others appear to be endowed with exceptional aptitude for healing. These are the people who ought to make the healing art their lifework. Unfortunately, so materialistic has the world become in recent centuries that the very possibility of spiritual healing has to a large extent been lost sight of. Like all other talents the gift of healing has to be recognized, trained, and educated in order that it may attain its highest development and power, and there are probably thousands in the world to-day, richly dowered with natural aptitude for healing, in whom this precious gift is lying dormant and inactive. When the potentialities of mental and spiritual treatment are more fully realized, the healing art will be transformed and ennobled and its efficacy immeasurably increased. And when this new knowledge and power in the healer are combined with lively faith and hope on the part of the patient, wonderful results may be looked for.

In God must be our trust. There is no God but Him, the Healer, the Knower, the Helper. . . . Nothing in earth or heaven is outside the grasp of God.

O physician! In treating the sick, first mention the Name of thy God, the Possessor of the Day of Judgment, and then use what God hath destined for the healing of His creatures. By My life! The physician who has drunk from the wine of My love, his visit is healing, and his breath is mercy and hope. Cling to him for the welfare of the constitution. He is confirmed by God in his treatment.

This knowledge (of the healing art) is the most important of all the sciences, for it is the greatest means from God, the Life-Giver to the dust, for preserving the bodies of all people, and He has put it in the forefront of all sciences and wisdoms. For this is the day when you must arise for My victory.

Thy Name is my healing, O my God, and remembrance of Thee is my remedy. Nearness to Thee is my hope, and love for Thee is my companion. Thy mercy to me is my healing and my succor in both this world and the world to come. Thou, verily, art the All-Bountiful, the All-Knowing, the All-Wise.—BAHÁ'U'LLÁH, *Tablet to a Physician.*

'Abdu'l-Bahá writes:—

He who is filled with love of Bahá, and forgets all things, the Holy Spirit will be heard from his lips and the spirit of life will fill his heart. . . . Words will issue from his lips in strands of pearls, and all sickness and disease will be healed by the laying on of the hands.—*Star of the West,* vol. viii, p. 233.

O thou pure and spiritual one! Turn thou toward God with thy heart beating with His love, devoted to His praise, gazing towards His Kingdom and seeking help from His Holy Spirit in a state of ecstasy, rapture, love, yearning, joy and fragrance. God will assist thee, through a spirit from His presence, to heal sickness and disease. Continue in healing hearts and bodies and seek healing for sick persons by turning unto the Supreme Kingdom and by setting the heart upon obtaining healing through the power of the Greatest Name and by the spirit of the love of God.—*Tablets of 'Abdu'l-Bahá,* vol. iii, pp. 628, 629.

How All Can Help

The work of healing the sick, however, is a matter that concerns not the patient and the practitioner only, but everyone. All must help, by sympathy and service, by right living and right thinking, and especially by prayer, for of all remedies prayer is the most potent. "Supplication and prayer on behalf of others," says 'Abdu'l-Bahá, "will surely be effective." The friends of the patient have a special responsibility, for their influence, either for good or ill, is most direct and powerful. In how many cases of sickness the issue depends *mainly* on the ministrations of parents, friends, or neighbors of the helpless sufferer!

Even the members of the community at large have an influence in every case of sickness. In individual cases that influence may not appear great, yet in the mass the effect is potent. Everyone is affected by the social "atmosphere" in which he lives, by the general prevalence of faith or materialism, of virtue or vice, of cheerfulness or depression; and each individual has his share in determining the state of that social "atmosphere." It may not be possible for everyone, in the present state of the world, to attain to perfect health, but it *is* possible for everyone to become a "willing channel" for the health-giving power of the Holy Spirit and thus to exert a healing, helpful influence both on his own body and on all with whom he comes in contact.

Few duties are impressed on Bahá'ís more repeatedly and

emphatically than that of healing the sick, and many beautiful prayers for healing have been revealed both by Bahá'u'lláh and 'Abdu'l-Bahá.

The Golden Age

Bahá'u'lláh gives the assurance that, through harmonious cooperation of patients, healers, and the community in general, and by appropriate use of the various means to health, material, mental, and spiritual, the Golden Age may be realized, when, by the power of God, "all sorrow will be turned into joy, and all disease into health." 'Abdu'l-Bahá says that "when the Divine Message is understood, all troubles will vanish." Again He says:—

> When the material world and the divine world are well correlated, when the hearts become heavenly and the aspirations pure, perfect connection shall take place. Then shall this power produce a perfect manifestation. Physical and spiritual diseases will then receive absolute healing.
> —*Tablets of 'Abdu'l-Bahá,* vol. ii, p. 309.

Right Use of Health

In concluding this chapter it will be well to recall 'Abdu'l-Bahá's teaching as to the right use of physical health. In one of His Tablets to the Bahá'ís of Washington He says:—

> If the health and well-being of the body be expended in the path of the Kingdom, this is very acceptable and praiseworthy; and if it be expended to the benefit of the human world in general—even though it be to their material (or bodily) benefit—and be a means of doing good, that is also acceptable. But if the health and welfare of man be spent in sensual desires, in a life on the animal plane, and in devilish pursuits—then disease were better than such health; nay, death itself were preferable to such a life. If thou art desirous of health, wish thou health for serving the Kingdom. I hope that thou mayest attain per-

fect insight, inflexible resolution, complete health, and spiritual and physical strength in order that thou mayest drink from the fountain of eternal life and be assisted by the spirit of divine confirmation.

Religious Unity/8

O ye people of the world! The virtue of this Most Great Manifestation is that We have effaced from the Book whatever was the cause of difference, corruption and discord, and recorded therein that which leads to unity, harmony and concord. Joy unto those who act in accordance therewith!— BAHÁ'U'LLÁH, *Tablet of the World.*

Sectarianism in the Nineteenth Century

Never, perhaps, did the world seem farther from religious unity than in the nineteenth century. For many centuries had the great religious communities—the Zoroastrian, Mosaic, Buddhist, Christian, Muḥammadan, and others—been existing side by side, but instead of blending together into a harmonious whole they had been at constant enmity and strife, each against the others. Not only so, but each had become split up, by division after division, into an increasing number of sects which were often bitterly opposed to each other. Yet Christ had said: "By this shall all men know that ye are My disciples, if ye have love one to another," and Muḥammad had said: "This your religion is the one religion. . . . To you hath God prescribed the faith which He commanded unto Noah, and which We have revealed unto thee, and which We commanded unto Abraham and Moses and Jesus saying: 'Observe this faith, and be not divided into sects therein!' " The Founder of every one of the great religious had called His followers to love and unity, but in every case the aim of the Founder was to a large extent lost sight of in a welter of intolerance and bigotry, formalism and hypocrisy, corruption and misrepresentation, schism and contention. The aggregate number of more or less hostile sects in the world was probably greater at the commencement of the Bahá'í Era than at any previous pe-

116

riod in human history. It seemed as if humanity at that time were experimenting with every possible kind of religious belief, with every possible sort of ritual and ceremonial observance, with every possible variety of moral code.

At the same time an increasing number of men were devoting their energies to fearless investigation and critical examination of the laws of nature and the foundations of belief. New scientific knowledge was being rapidly acquired and new solutions were being found for many of the problems of life. The development of inventions such as steamship and railway, postal system and press, greatly aided the diffusion of ideas and the fertilizing contact of widely different types of thought and life.

The so-called "conflict between religion and science" became a fierce battle. In the Christian world Biblical criticism combined with physical science to dispute, and to some extent to refute, the authority of the Bible, an authority that for centuries had been the generally accepted basis of belief. A rapidly increasing proportion of the population became skeptical about the teachings of the churches. A large number even of religious priests secretly or openly entertained doubts or reservations regarding the creeds adhered to by their respective denominations.

This ferment and flux of opinion, with increasing recognition of the inadequacy of the old orthodoxies and dogmas, and groping and striving after fuller knowledge and understanding, were not confined to Christian countries, but were manifest, more or less, and in different forms, among the people of all countries and religions.

The Message of Bahá'u'lláh

It was when this state of conflict and confusion was at its height, that Bahá'u'lláh sounded His great trumpet call to humanity:—

That all nations should become one in faith, and all men as brothers; that the bonds of affection and unity between the sons of men should be strengthened; that diversity of religion should cease, and differences of race be annulled. . . . These strifes and this bloodshed and discord must cease, and all men be as one kindred and one family (words spoken to Professor Browne).

It is a glorious message, but how are its proposals to be carried into effect? Prophets have preached, poets have sung, and saints have prayed about these things for thousands of years, but diversities of religion have not ceased nor have strife and bloodshed and discord been annulled. What is there to show that now the miracle is to be accomplished? Are there any new factors in the situation? Is not human nature the same as it ever was, and will it not continue to be the same while the world lasts? If two people want the same thing, or two nations, will they not fight for it in the future as they have done in the past? If Moses, Buddha, Christ, and Muḥammad failed to achieve world unity will Bahá'u'lláh succeed? If all previous faiths became corrupted and rent asunder into sects will not the Bahá'í Faith share the same fate? Let us see what answer the Bahá'í teachings give to these and similar questions.

Can Human Nature Change?

Education and religion are alike based on the assumption that it *is* possible to change human nature. In fact, it requires but little investigation to show that the one thing we can say with certainty about any living thing is that it cannot keep from changing. Without change there can be no life. Even the mineral cannot resist change, and the higher we go in the scale of being, the more varied, complex, and wonderful do the changes become. Moreover, in progress and development among creatures of all grades we find two kinds of change— one slow, gradual, often almost imperceptible; and the other rapid, sudden, and dramatic. The latter occur at what are called "critical stages" of development. In the case of minerals we find such critical stages at the melting and boiling points, for example, when the solid suddenly becomes a liquid or the liquid becomes a gas. In the case of plants we see such critical stages when the seed begins to germinate, or the bud bursts into leaf. In the animal world we see the same on every hand, as when the grub suddenly changes into a butterfly, the chick emerges from its shell, or the babe is born from its mother's womb. In the higher life of the soul we often see a similar transformation, when a man is "born again" and his whole being becomes radically changed in its aims, its character and activities. Such critical stages often affect a whole species or multitude of species simultaneously, as when vegetation of all kinds suddenly bursts into new life in springtime.

Bahá'u'lláh declares that just as lesser living things have times of sudden emergence into new and fuller life, so for mankind also a "critical stage," a time of "rebirth," is at hand. Then modes of life which have persisted from the dawn of history up till now will be quickly, irrevocably, altered, and humanity enter on a new phase of life as different from the old as the butterfly is different from the caterpillar, or the bird from the egg. Mankind as a whole, in the light of new Revelation, will attain to a new vision of truth; as a whole country is illumined when the sun rises, so that all men see clearly, where but an hour before everything was dark and dim. "This is a new cycle of human power," says 'Abdu'l-Bahá. "All the horizons of the world are luminous, and the world will become indeed as a rose garden and a paradise." The analogies of nature are all in favor of such a view; the Prophets of old have with one accord foretold the advent of such a glorious day; the signs of the times show clearly that profound and revolutionary changes in human ideas and institutions are even now in progress. What could be more futile and baseless, therefore, than the pessimistic argument that, although all things else change, human nature cannot change?

First Steps Toward Unity

As a means of promoting religious unity Bahá'u'lláh advocates the utmost charity and tolerance, and calls on His followers to "consort with the people of all religions with joy and gladness." In His last Will and Testament He says:—

Contention and conflict hath He strictly forbidden in His Book (*Kitáb-i-Aqdas*); such is the command of the Lord in this all-highest Revelation—a command which He hath exempted from all annulment and arrayed with the adorning of His confirmation.

O ye people of the world! The religion of God is for the sake of love and union; make it not the cause of enmity and conflict. . . . The hope is cherished, that the people of Bahá shall ever turn unto the hallowed Word: "Lo! All things are of God."—the all-glorious Word that, like unto water, quencheth the fire of hate and rancor which doth smolder in hearts and breasts. By this one Word shall the diverse sects of the world attain unto the light of real union; verily the truth He speaketh, and to the path He leadeth, and He is the Mighty, the Gracious, the Beauteous.

'Abdu'l Bahá says:—

All must abandon prejudices and must even go to each other's churches and mosques, for, in all of these worshiping places, the Name of God is mentioned. Since all gather to worship God, what difference is there? None of them worship Satan. The Muḥammadans must go to the churches of the Christians and the synagogues of the Jews, and *vice versa,* the others must go to the Muḥammadan mosques. They hold aloof from one another merely because of unfounded prejudices and dogmas. In America I went to the Jewish synagogues, which are similar to the Christian churches, and I saw them worshiping God everywhere.

In many of these places I spoke to them about the original foundations of the divine religions, and I explained to them the proofs of the validity of the divine Prophets and of the Holy Manifestations. I encouraged them to do away with blind imitations. All of the leaders must, likewise, go to each other's churches and speak of the foundation and of the fundamental principles of the divine religions. In the utmost unity and harmony they must worship God, in the worshiping places of one another, and must abandon fanaticism.—*Star of the West,* vol. ix, No. 3, p. 37.

Were even these first steps accomplished and a state of friendly mutual tolerance established between the various religious sects, what a wonderful change would be brought about in the world! In order that real unity may be achieved, however, something more than this is required. For the disease of sectarianism, tolerance is a valuable palliative, but it is not a radical cure. It does not remove the cause of the trouble.

The Problem of Authority

The different religious communities have failed to unite in the past, because the adherents of each have regarded the Founder of their own community as the one supreme authority, and His law as the divine law. Any Prophet Who proclaimed a different Message was, therefore, regarded as an enemy of the truth. The different sects of each community have separated for similar reasons. The adherents of each have accepted some subordinate authority and regarded some particular version or interpretation of the Founder's Message as the one true faith, and all others as wrong. It is obvious that while this state of matters exists no true unity is possible. Bahá'u'lláh, on the other hand, teaches that all the Prophets were bearers of authentic Messages from God; that each in His day gave the highest teachings that the people could then receive, and educated men so that they were able to receive further teachings from His successors. He calls on the adherents of each religion, not to deny the divine inspiration of their own Prophets, but to acknowledge the divine inspiration of all other Prophets, to see that the teachings of all are essentially in harmony, and are parts of a great plan for the education and the unification of humanity. He calls on the people of all denominations to show their reverence for their Prophets by devoting their lives to the accomplishment of that unity for which all the Prophets labored and suffered. In His letter to Queen Victoria He likens the world to a sick man whose malady is aggravated because he has fallen into the hands of unskilled physicians; and He tells how the remedy may be effected:—

> That which the Lord hath ordained as the sovereign remedy and mightiest instrument for the healing of all the world is the union of all its peoples in one universal Cause, one common Faith. This can in no wise be achieved except through the power of a skilled, an all-powerful and inspired Physician. This, verily, is the truth, and all else naught but error.—*Gleanings from the Writings of Bahá'u'lláh*, p. 255.

Progressive Revelation

A great stumbling block to many, in the way of religious unity, is the difference between the Revelations given by the different Prophets. What is commanded by one is forbidden by another; how then can both be right, how can both be proclaiming the Will of God? Surely the truth is one, and cannot change. Yes, the absolute truth is one and cannot change, but the absolute truth is infinitely beyond the present range of human understanding, and our conceptions of it must constantly change. Our earlier, imperfect ideas will be by the grace of God replaced, as time goes on, by more and more adequate conceptions. Bahá'u'lláh says, in a Tablet to some Bahá'ís of Persia:—

> O people! Words are revealed according to capacity so that the beginners may make progress. The milk must be given according to measure so that the babe of the world may enter into the Realm of Grandeur and be established in the Court of Unity.

It is milk that strengthens the babe so that it can digest more solid food later on. To say that because one Prophet is right in giving a certain teaching at a certain time, therefore another Prophet must be wrong Who gives a different teaching at a different time, is like saying that because milk is the best food for the newborn babe, therefore, milk and nothing but milk should be the food of the grown man also, and to give any other diet would be wrong! 'Abdu'l-Bahá says:—

Each divine Revelation is divided into two parts. The first part is essential and belongs to the eternal world. It is the exposition of divine truths and essential principles. It is the expression of the love of God. This is one in all the religions, unchangeable and immutable. The second part is not eternal; it deals with practical life, transactions and business, and changes according to the evolution of man and the requirements of the time of each Prophet. For example. . . . During the Mosaic period the hand of a person was cut off in punishment of a small theft; there was a law of an eye for an eye and a tooth for a tooth, but as these laws were not expedient in the time of Christ, they were abrogated. Likewise divorce had become so universal that there remained no fixed laws of marriage, therefore His Holiness Christ forbade divorce.

According to the exigencies of the time, His Holiness Moses revealed ten laws for capital punishment. It was impossible at that time to protect the community and to preserve social security without these severe measures, for the children of Israel lived in the wilderness of Tah, where there were no established courts of justice and no penitentiaries. But this code of conduct was not needed in the time of Christ. The history of the second part of religion is unimportant, because it relates to the customs of this life only; but the foundation of the religion of God is one, and His Holiness Bahá'u'lláh has renewed that foundation.—*Divine Philosophy.*

The religion of God is the one religion, and all the Prophets have taught it, but it is a living and a growing thing, not lifeless and unchanging. In the teaching of Moses we see the bud; in that of Christ the flower; in that of Bahá'u'lláh the fruit. The flower does not destroy the bud, nor does the fruit destroy the flower. It destroys not, but fulfills. The bud scales must fall in order that the flower may bloom, and the petals must fall that the fruit may grow and ripen. Were the bud scales and the petals wrong or useless, then, that they had to be discarded? Nay, both in their time were right and necessary; without them there could have been no fruit. So it is with the various prophetic teachings; their externals change from age to age, but each Revelation is the fulfillment of its predecessors; they are not separate nor incongruous, but different stages in the life history of the one religion, which has in turn been revealed as seed, as bud, and as flower, and now enters on the stage of fruition.

Infallibility of the Prophets

Bahá'u'lláh teaches that everyone endowed with the station of Prophethood is given sufficient proofs of His mission, is entitled to claim obedience from all men, and has authority to abrogate, alter, or add to the teachings of His predecessors. In the *Book of Íqán* we read:—

How far from the grace of the All-Bountiful and from His loving providence and tender mercies it is to single out a soul from amongst all men for the guidance of His creatures, and, on one hand, to withhold from Him the full measure of His divine testimony, and, on the other, inflict severe retribution on His people for having turned away from His chosen One! Nay, the manifold bounties of the Lord of all beings have, at all times, through the Manifestations of His divine Essence, encompassed the earth and all that dwell therein. . . .

And yet, is not the object of every Revelation to effect a transformation in the whole character of mankind, a transformation that shall manifest itself both outwardly and inwardly, that shall affect both its inner life and external conditions? For if the character of mankind be not changed, the futility of God's universal Manifestations would be apparent.—*Kitáb-i-Íqán*, pp. 14 and 240.

God is the one infallible Authority, and the Prophets are infallible because Their Message is the Message of God given to the world through Them. That Message remains valid until it is superseded by a later Message given by the same or another Prophet.

God is the Great Physician Who alone can rightly diagnose the world's sickness and prescribe the appropriate remedy. The remedy prescribed in one age is no longer suitable in a later age, when the condition of the patient is different. To cling to the old remedy when the physician has ordered new treatment is not to show faith in the physician, but infidelity. It may be a shock to the Jew to be told that some of the remedies for the world's sickness which Moses ordered over three thousand years ago are now out of date and unsuitable; the Christian may be equally shocked when told that Muḥammad had anything necessary or valuable to add to what Jesus prescribed; and so also the Muslim, when asked to admit that the Báb or Bahá'u'lláh had authority to alter the commands of Muḥammad; but according to the Bahá'í view, true devotion to God implies reverence to *all* His Prophets, and implicit obedience to His *latest* commands, as given by the Prophet for our own age. Only by such devotion can true unity be attained.

The Supreme Manifestation

Like all the other Prophets, Bahá'u'lláh states His own mission in the most unmistakable terms.

In the *Lawḥ-i-Aqdas,* a Tablet addressed especially to Christians, He says:—

> Surely the Father hath come and hath fulfilled that which you were promised in the Kingdom of God. This is the Word which the Son veiled when He said to those around Him that at that time they could not bear it. But when the stated time was ended, and the hour arrived, the Word shone forth from the horizon of the Will. Beware, O concourse of the Son (i.e. Christians)! Cast it not behind you, but hold thereunto. It is better for you than all that which is before you! . . . Verily, the Spirit of Truth is come, to guide you into all truth. Verily, He

speaketh not from Himself, nay, but rather from the All-Knowing and Wise. He is the One Whom the Son hath glorified. . . . Abandon that which is before you, O people of the earth, and take that which is commanded you by Him Who is the Powerful, the Faithful.

And in a letter to the Pope, written from Adrianople in 1867, He says:—

Beware lest celebration hinder you from the Celebrated and worship hinder you from the worshiped One! Behold the Lord, the Mighty, the All-Knowing! He hath come to minister to the life of the world, and for the uniting of whatever dwelleth therein. Come, O ye people, to the Dawning-Place of Revelation! Tarry not, even for an hour! Are ye learned in the Gospel, and yet are unable to see the Lord of Glory?

This beseemeth you not, O learned concourse! Say then, if ye deny this matter, by what proof do you believe in God? Produce your proof.

Just as in these letters to Christians He announces the fulfillment of the Gospel promises, so He proclaims also to Muḥammadan, Jews, Zoroastrians, and the people of other faiths the fulfillment of the promises of their Holy Books. He addresses all men as the sheep of God, who have hitherto been divided into different flocks and sheltered in different folds. His Message, He says, is the Voice of God, the Good Shepherd, Who has come in the fullness of time to gather His scattered sheep into one flock, removing the barriers between them, "that there may be one fold and one Shepherd."

A New Situation

The position of Bahá'u'lláh among the Prophets is unprecedented and unique, because the condition of the world at the time of His advent was unprecedented and unique. By a long and checkered process of development in religion, science, art, and civilization the world had become ripe for a teaching of unity. The barriers which in previous centuries had made a world unity impossible were ready to crumble when Bahá'u'lláh appeared, and since His birth, in 1817, and more especially since the promulgation of His teachings began, these barriers have been breaking down in most astonishing fashion. Be the explanation what it may, about the fact there can be no doubt. In the days of previous Prophets geographical barriers alone were amply sufficient to prevent world unity. Now that obstacle has been overcome. For the first time in human history men on opposite sides of the globe are able to communicate with each other quickly and easily. Things done in Europe yesterday are known in every continent of the world today, and a speech made in America today may be read in Europe, Asia, and Africa tomorrow.

Another great obstacle was the language difficulty. Thanks to the study and teaching of foreign languages, that difficulty has already been to a large extent overcome; and there is every reason to suppose that ere many years an international auxiliary language will be adopted and taught in all the schools of the world. Then this difficulty also will be completely removed.

The third great obstacle was religious prejudice and intolerance. That, too, is disappearing. Men's minds are becoming more open. The education of the people is passing more and more out of the hands of sectarian priests; and new and more liberal ideas can no longer be prevented from penetrating into even the most exclusive and conservative circles.

Bahá'u'lláh is thus the first of the great Prophets Whose Message has become known within a period of comparatively few years in every quarter of the globe. Within a short time the essential teachings of Bahá'u'lláh, translated from His own authentic Writings, will be directly accessible to every man, woman, and child in the world who is able to read.

Fullness of the Bahá'í Revelation

The Bahá'í Revelation is unprecedented and unique among the faiths of the world by reason of the fullness and completeness of its authentic records. The recorded words that can with certainty be attributed to Christ, to Moses, to Zoroaster, to Buddha, to Krishna, are very few, and leave many modern questions of great practical importance unanswered. Many of the teachings commonly attributed to these religious Founders are of doubtful authenticity, and some are evidently accretions of later date. The Muhammadans possess in the Qur'án, and in a large store of traditions, a much fuller record of the life and teachings of their Prophet, but Muhammad Himself, though inspired, was illiterate, as were most of His early followers. The methods employed for recording and spreading His teachings were in many respects unsatisfactory, and the authenticity of many of the traditions is very doubtful. As a result, differences of interpretation and conflicting opinions have caused divisions and dissensions in Islám, as in all previous religious communities.

On the other hand, both the Báb and Bahá'u'lláh wrote copiously and with great eloquence and power. As both were debarred from public speaking and spent most of Their lives (after the declaration of Their mission) in prison, They devoted a large proportion of Their time to writing, with the result that in richness of authentic scriptures the Bahá'í Revelation is unapproached by any of its predecessors. Clear and full expositions are given of many truths which were but dimly foreshadowed in previous Revelations, and the eternal principles of truth, which all the Prophets have taught, have been applied to the problems which are facing the world today— problems of the utmost complexity and difficulty, many of which had not arisen in the days of former Prophets. It is evident that this full record of authentic Revelation must have a powerful effect in preventing misunderstandings in the future and in clearing up those misunderstandings of the past which have kept the various sects asunder.

The Bahá'í Covenant

The Bahá'í Revelation is unprecedented and unique in still another way. Before the death of Bahá'u'lláh He repeatedly put in writing a Covenant appointing His eldest son 'Abdu'l-Bahá,

Whom He often refers to as "the Branch," or "the Most Great Branch," as the authorized interpreter of the teachings, and declaring that any explanations or interpretations given by Him are to be accepted as of equal validity with the words of Bahá'u'lláh Himself. In His Will and Testament He says:—

Reflect upon that which is revealed in My Book, the *Aqdas:* "When the ocean of My presence hath ebbed and the Book of My Revelation is ended, turn your faces toward Him Whom God hath purposed, Who hath branched from this Ancient Root." The reference in this blessed verse is to the Most Great Branch.

And in the *Tablet of the Branch,* in which He explains the station of 'Abdu'l-Bahá, He says:—

Render thanks unto God, O people, for His appearance; for verily He is the most great favor unto you, the most perfect bounty upon you; and through Him every moldering bone is quickened. Whoso turneth towards Him hath turned towards God, and whoso turneth away from Him hath turned away from My beauty, hath repudiated My proof, and transgressed against Me.

After the death of Bahá'u'lláh, 'Abdu'l-Bahá had abundant opportunities, both in His own own home and on His extensive travels, of meeting people from all parts of the world and of all shades of opinion. He heard all their questions, their difficulties and objections, and gave full explanations which were carefully recorded in writing. During a long series of years 'Abdu'l-Bahá continued this work of elucidating the teachings and showing their applications to the most varied problems of modern life. Differences of opinion which have arisen among believers have been referred to Him and authoritatively settled, and thus the risks of future misunderstandings have been further reduced.

Bahá'u'lláh further arranged that an International House of Justice representative of all Bahá'ís throughout the world should be elected to take charge of the affairs of the Cause, control and coordinate all its activities, prevent divisions and schisms, elucidate obscure matters, and preserve the teachings from corruption and misrepresentation. The fact that this supreme administrative body can not only initiate legislation on all matters not defined in the teachings, but also annul its own enactments when new conditions require different measures, enables the Faith to expand and adapt itself, like a living organism, to the needs and requirements of a changing society. Moreover, Bahá'u'lláh expressly forbade interpretation of the teachings by anyone but the authorized interpreter. In His *Will and Testament* 'Abdu'l-Bahá appointed Shoghi Effendi to be the Guardian of the Faith after Him and to be empowered to interpret the Writings.

In a thousand or more years another Manifestation will appear, under the shadow of Bahá'u'lláh, with clear proofs of His mission, but until then the words of Bahá'u'lláh, 'Abdu'l-Bahá, and the Guardian and the decisions of the International House of Justice constitute the authorities to which all believers must turn for guidance. No Bahá'í may found a school or sect based on any particular interpretation of the teachings or any supposed divine revelation. Anyone contravening these injunctions is considered a "Covenant-breaker." [1]

'Abdu'l-Bahá says:—

> One of the enemies of the Cause is he who endeavors to interpret the words of Bahá'u'lláh and thereby colors the meaning according to his capacity, and collects around him a following, forming a different sect, promoting his own station, and making a division in the Cause. —*Star of the West,* vol. iii, p. 8.

In another Tablet He writes:—

> These people (promoters of schism) are like the froth that gathers on the surface of the sea; a wave will surge from the ocean of the Covenant and through the power of the Abhá Kingdom will cast this foam ashore. . . . These corrupt thoughts that emanate from personal and

---

[1] See pp. 261-263 and 272-273 for further elucidations of the Guardianship and the Universal House of Justice.

evil intentions will all vanish, whereas the Covenant of God shall remain stable and secure.—*Star of the West,* vol. x, p. 95.

There is nothing to keep men from forsaking religion if they wish to do so. 'Abdu'l-Bahá says: "God Himself does not compel the soul to become spiritual. The exercise of the free human will is necessary." The spiritual Covenant, however, clearly makes sectarianism *within* the Bahá'í community quite impossible.

No Professional Priesthood

One other feature of the Bahá'í organization must be specially mentioned, and that is the absence of a professional priesthood. Voluntary contributions toward the expenses of teachers are permitted and many devote their whole time to work for the Cause, but all Bahá'ís are expected to share in the work of teaching, et cetera, according to their opportunity and ability, and there is no special class distinguished from their fellow believers by the exclusive exercise of priestly functions and prerogatives.

In former ages priesthoods were necessary, because people were illiterate and uneducated and were dependent on priests for their religious instruction, for the conduct of religious rites and ceremonies, for the administration of justice, et cetera. Now, however, times have changed. Education is fast becoming universal, and if the commands of Bahá'u'lláh are carried out, every boy and girl in the world will receive a sound education. Each individual will then be able to study the Scriptures for himself, to draw the Water of Life for himself, direct from the Fountainhead. Elaborate rites and ceremonies, requiring the services of a special profession or caste, have no place in the Bahá'í system; and the administration of justice is entrusted to the authorities instituted for that purpose.

For a child a teacher is necessary, but the aim of the true teacher is to fit his pupil to do without a teacher; to see things with his own eyes, hear with his own ears, and understand with his own mind. Just so, in the childhood of the race, the priest is necessary, but his real work is to enable men to do without him: to see things divine with their own eyes, hear them with their own ears and understand them with their own minds. Now the priest's work is all but accomplished, and the aim of the Bahá'í teaching is to complete that work, to make men independent of all save God, so that they can turn directly to Him, that is, to His Manifestation. When all turn to one Center, then there can be no cross-purposes or confusion and the nearer all draw to the Center, the nearer they will draw to each other.

True Civilization/9

O people of God! Be not occupied with yourselves. Be intent on the betterment of the world and the training of nations.— BAHÁ'U'LLÁH.

Religion the Basis of Civilization

According to the Bahá'í view, the problems of human life, individual and social, are so inconceivably complex that the ordinary human intellect is incapable of itself of solving them aright. Only the Omniscient fully knows the purpose of creation and how that purpose may be achieved. Through the Prophets He shows to mankind the true goal of human life and the right path of progress; and the building up of a true civilization depends upon faithful adherence to the guidance of prophetic Revelation. Bahá'u'lláh says:—

Religion is the greatest instrument for the order of the world and the tranquility of all existent beings. The weakening of the pillars of religion has encouraged the ignorant and rendered them audacious and arrogant. Truly, I say, whatever lowers the lofty station of religion will increase heedlessness in the wicked, and finally result in anarchy. . . .

Consider the civilization of the people of the Occident —how it has occasioned commotion and agitation to the people of the world. Infernal instruments have been devised, and such atrocity is displayed in the destruction of life as has not been seen by the eye of the world, nor heard by the ear of nations. It is impossible to reform these violent, overwhelming evils, except the peoples of the world become united upon a certain issue or under the shadow of one religion. . . .

O people of Bahá! Each one of the revealed commands is a mighty stronghold for the protection of the world.— *Words of Paradise.*

The present state of Europe and of the world in general eloquently confirms the truth of these words written so many years ago. Neglect of the prophetic commands and the prevalence of irreligion have been accompanied by disorder and destruction on the most terrible scale, and, without the change of heart and aim which is the essential characteristic of true religion, the reform of society seems an utter impossibility.

Justice

In the little book of *Hidden Words,* in which Bahá'u'lláh gives in brief the essence of the prophetic teachings, His first counsel refers to the individual life: "Possess a pure, kindly, and radiant heart." The next indicates the fundamental principle of true social life:—

O Son of Spirit!
The best beloved of all things in My sight is justice; turn not away therefrom if thou desirest Me, and neglect it not that I may confide in thee. By its aid thou shalt see with thine own eyes and not through the eyes of others, and shalt know of thine own knowledge and not through the knowledge of thy neighbor. Ponder this in thy heart; how it behooveth thee to be. Verily justice is My gift to thee and the sign of My loving-kindness. Set it then before thine eyes.

The first essential of social life is that individuals should become capable of discerning the true from the false and right from wrong, and of seeing things in their true proportions. The greatest cause of spiritual and social blindness, and the greatest foe of social progress, is selfishness. Bahá'u'lláh says:—

O ye sons of intelligence! The thin eyelid prevents the eye from seeing the world and what is contained therein. Then think of the result when the curtain of greed covers the sight of the heart!

O people! The darkness of greed and envy obscures the light of the soul as the cloud prevents the penetration of the sun's rays (Tablet to some Persian Zoroastrian Bahá'ís).

Long experience is at last convincing men of the truth of the prophetic teaching that selfish views and selfish actions inevitably bring social disaster, and that if humanity is not to perish ingloriously, each must look on the things of his neighbor as of equal importance with his own, and subordinate his own interests to those of humanity as a whole. In this way the interests of each and all will ultimately be best served. Bahá'u'-lláh says:—"O son of man! If thine eyes be turned towards mercy, forsake the things that profit thee, and cleave unto that which will profit mankind. And if thine eyes be turned towards justice, choose thou for thy neighbor that which thou choosest for thyself."—*Words of Paradise.*

Government

The teachings of Bahá'u'lláh contain two different types of reference to the question of true social order. One type is exemplified in the Tablets revealed to the kings, which deal with the problem of government as existing in the world during Bahá'u'lláh's life on earth; the other references are to the new order to be developed within the Bahá'í community itself.

Hence arises the sharp contrast between such passages as: "The one true God, exalted be His glory, hath ever regarded, and will continue to regard, the hearts of men as His own, His exclusive possession. All else, whether pertaining to land or sea, whether riches or glory, He hath bequeathed unto the kings and rulers of the earth"; and "It beseemeth all men, in this Day, to take firm hold on the Most Great Name, and to establish the unity of all mankind. There is no place to flee to, no refuge that any one can seek, except Him."—*Gleanings from the Writings of Bahá'u'lláh,* pp. 206, 203.

The apparent incompatibility of these two views is removed when we observe the distinction which Bahá'u'lláh makes between the "Lesser Peace" and the "Most Great Peace." In His

Tablets to the kings Bahá'u'lláh called upon them to assemble and take measures for the maintenance of political peace, the reduction of armaments and the removal of the burdens and insecurity of the poor. But His words make it perfectly clear that their failure to respond to the needs of the time would result in wars and revolutions leading to the overthrow of the old order. Therefore, on the one hand He said: "What mankind needeth in this day is obedience unto them that are in authority," and on the other, "Those men who, having amassed the vanities and ornaments of the earth, have turned away disdainfully from God—these have lost both this world and the world to come. Erelong, will God, with the hand of power, strip them of their possessions, and divest them of the robe of His bounty." "We have a fixed time for you, O peoples. If ye fail, at the appointed hour, to turn towards God, He, verily, will lay violent hold on you, and will cause grievous afflictions to assail you from every direction." "The signs of impending convulsions and chaos can now be discerned, inasmuch as the prevailing order appeareth to be lamentably defective." "We have pledged Ourselves to secure Thy triumph upon earth and to exalt Our Cause above all men, though no king be found who would turn his face towards Thee." *Gleanings from the Writings of Bahá'u'lláh,* pp. 207, 209, 214, 216, 248.

The Great Being, wishing to reveal the prerequisites of the peace and tranquillity of the world and the advancement of its peoples, hath written: The time must come when the imperative necessity for the holding of a vast, an all-embracing assemblage of men will be universally realized. The rulers and kings of the earth must needs attend it, and, participating in its deliberations, must consider such ways and means as will lay the foundations of the world's Great Peace amongst men. Such a peace demandeth that the Great Powers should resolve, for the sake of the tranquillity of the peoples of the earth, to be fully reconciled among themselves. Should any king take up arms against another, all should unitedly arise and prevent him.—*Gleanings from the Writings of Bahá'u'lláh,* p. 249.

By such counsel, Bahá'u'lláh revealed the conditions under which public responsibility must be discharged in this Day of God. Appealing for international solidarity on the one hand, He no less clearly warned the rulers that continuance of strife would destroy their power. Now modern history confirms this warning, in the rise of those coercive movements which in all civilized nations have attained such destructive energy, and in the development of warfare to the degree that victory is no longer attainable by any party. "Now that ye have refused the Most Great Peace, hold ye fast unto this, the Lesser Peace, that haply ye may in some degree better your own condition and that of your dependents." "That which the Lord hath ordained as the sovereign remedy and mightiest instrument for the healing of all the world is the union of all its peoples in one universal Cause, one common Faith. This can in no wise be achieved except through the power of a skilled, an all-powerful and inspired Physician."—*Gleanings from the Writings of Bahá'u'lláh,* pp. 254, 255.

By the Lesser Peace is meant a political unity of states, while the Most Great Peace is a unity embracing spiritual as well as political and economic factors. "Soon will the present-day order be rolled up, and a new one spread out in its stead."—*Gleanings from the Writings of Bahá'u'lláh,* p. 7.

In former ages, a government could concern itself with external matters and material affairs, but today the function of government demands a quality of leadership, of consecration, and of spiritual knowledge impossible save to those who have turned to God.

Political Freedom

Although advocating as the ideal condition a representative form of government, local, national, and international, Bahá'u'lláh teaches that this is possible only when men have attained a sufficiently high degree of individual and social development. Suddenly to grant full self-government to people without education, who are dominated by selfish desires and are inexperienced in the conduct of public affairs, would be disastrous. There is nothing more dangerous than freedom for those who are not fit to use it wisely. Bahá'u'lláh writes in the *Book of Aqdas:*—

> Consider the pettiness of men's minds. They ask for that which injureth them, and cast away the thing that profiteth them. They are, indeed, of those that are far astray. We find some men desiring liberty, and priding themselves therein. Such men are in the depths of ignorance.
>
> Liberty must, in the end, lead to sedition, whose flames none can quench. Thus warneth you He Who is the Reckoner, the All-Knowing. Know ye that the embodiment of liberty and its symbol is the animal. That which beseemeth man is submission unto such restraints as will protect him from his own ignorance, and guard him against the harm of the mischief-maker. Liberty causeth man to overstep the bounds of propriety, and to infringe on the dignity of his station. It debaseth him to the level of extreme depravity and wickedness.
>
> Regard men as a flock of sheep that need a shepherd for their protection. This, verily, is the truth, the certain truth. We approve of liberty in certain circumstances, and refuse to sanction it in others. We, verily, are the All-Knowing.
>
> Say: True liberty consisteth in man's submission unto My commandments, little as ye know it. Were men to observe that which We have sent down unto them from the heaven of Revelation, they would, of a certainty, attain unto perfect liberty. Happy is the man that hath apprehended the purpose of God in whatever He hath revealed from the heaven of His will, that pervadeth all created things. Say: The liberty that profiteth you is to be found nowhere except in complete servitude unto God, the Eternal Truth. Whoso hath tasted of its sweetness will refuse to barter it for all the dominion of earth and heaven.—*Kitáb-i-Aqdas.*

For improving the condition of backward races and nations, the divine teachings are the sovereign remedy. When both people and statesmen learn and adopt these teachings the nations will be freed from all their bonds.

Rulers and Subjects

Bahá'u'lláh forbids tyranny and oppression in the most emphatic terms. In *Hidden Words* He writes:—

O Oppressors on Earth!
Withdraw your hands from tyranny, for I have pledged Myself not to forgive any man's injustice. This is My covenant which I have irrevocably decreed in the preserved Tablet and sealed it with My seal of glory.

Those entrusted with the framing and administration of laws and regulations must "hold fast to the rope of consultation, and decide upon and execute that which is conducive to the people's security, affluence, welfare and tranquillity; for if matters be arranged otherwise, it will lead to discord and tumult."—*Tablet of the World.*

On the other hand, the people must be law-abiding and loyal to the just government. They must rely on educational methods and on the force of good example, not on violence, for bringing about a better state of affairs in the nation. Bahá'u'lláh says:—

In every country where any of this community reside, they must behave toward the government of that country with faithfulness, truthfulness and obedience.—*Glad Tidings.*

O people of God! Adorn your temples with the mantle of trustworthiness and integrity; then assist your Lord with the hosts of good deeds and good morals. Verily We have forbidden your sedition and strife, in My Books and Epistles, in My Writings and Tablets; and by this We have desired only your loftiness and exaltation.—*Tablet of Ishráqát.*

Appointment and Promotion

In making appointments, the only criterion must be fitness for the position. Before this paramount consideration, all others, such as seniority, social or financial status, family connection or personal friendship, must give way. Bahá'u'lláh says in the *Tablet of Ishráqát:*—

> The fifth Ishráq (Effulgence) is the knowledge by governments of the condition of the governed, and the conferring of ranks according to desert and merit. Regard to this matter is strictly enjoined upon every chief and ruler, that haply traitors may not usurp the positions of trustworthy men nor spoilers occupy the seats of guardians.

It needs but little consideration to show that when this principle becomes generally accepted and acted upon, the transformation in our social life will be astounding. When each individual is given the position for which his talents and capabilities specially fit him he will be able to put his heart into his work and become an artist in his profession, with incalculable benefit to himself and the rest of the world.

Economic Problems

The Bahá'í teachings insist in the strongest terms on the need for reform in the economic relations of rich and poor. 'Abdu'l-Bahá says:—

> The arrangements of the circumstances of the people must be such that poverty shall disappear, that everyone, as far as possible, according to his rank and position, shall share in comfort and well-being. We see among us men who are overburdened with riches on the one hand, and on the other those unfortunate ones who starve with nothing; those who possess several stately palaces, and those who have not where to lay their head. . . . This condition of affairs is wrong, and must be remedied. Now the remedy must be carefully undertaken. It cannot be done by bringing to pass absolute equality between men. Equality is a chimera! It is entirely impracticable. Even if equality could be achieved it could not continue; and if its existence were possible, the whole order of the world

would be destroyed. The law of order must always obtain in the world of humanity. Heaven has so decreed in the creation of man. . . . Humanity, like a great army, requires a general, captains, underofficers in their degree, and soldiers, each with their appointed duties. Degrees are absolutely necessary to ensure an orderly organization. An army could not be composed of generals alone, or of captains only, or of nothing but soldiers without anyone in authority.

Certainly, some being enormously rich and others lamentably poor, an organization is necessary to control and improve this state of affairs. It is important to limit riches, as it is also of importance to limit poverty. Either extreme is not good. . . . When we see poverty allowed to reach a condition of starvation, it is a sure sign that somewhere we shall find tyranny. Men must bestir themselves in this matter, and no longer delay in altering conditions which bring the misery of grinding poverty to a very large number of people.

The rich must give of their abundance; they must soften their hearts and cultivate a compassionate intelligence, taking thought for those sad ones who are suffering from lack of the very necessaries of life.

There must be special laws made, dealing with these extremes of riches and want. . . . The government of the countries should conform to the divine law which gives equal justice to all. . . . Not until this is done will the law of God be obeyed.—*Wisdom of 'Abdu'l-Bahá*, p. 140.

Public Finance

'Abdu'l-Bahá suggests that each town and village or district should be entrusted as far as possible with the administration of fiscal matters within its own area and should contribute its due proportion for the expenses of the general government. One of the principal sources of revenue should be a graduated income tax. If a man's income does not exceed his necessary expenditure he should not be required to pay any tax, but in all cases where income exceeds the necessary expenditure a tax should be levied, the percentage of tax increasing as the surplus of income over necessary expenditure increases. On the other hand, if a person, through illness, poor crops, or other cause for which he is not responsible, is unable to earn an income sufficient to meet his necessary expenses for the year, then what he lacks for the maintenance of himself and his family should be supplied out of public funds. There will also be other sources of public revenue, e.g. from interstate estates, mines, treasure trove, and voluntary contributions; while among the expenditures will be grants for the support of the infirm, of orphans, of schools, of the deaf and blind, and for the maintenance of public health. Thus the welfare and comfort of all will be provided for.[1]

Voluntary Sharing

In a letter to the Central Organization for a Durable Peace, written in 1919, 'Abdu'l-Bahá says:—

Among the teachings of Bahá'u'lláh is voluntary sharing of one's property with others among mankind. This voluntary sharing is greater than (legally imposed) equality, and consists in this, that one should not prefer oneself to others, but rather should sacrifice one's life and property for others. But this should not be introduced by coercion so that it becomes a law which man is compelled to follow. Nay, rather, man should voluntarily and of his own choice sacrifice his property and life for others, and spend willingly for the poor, just as is done in Persia among the Bahá'ís.

Work for All

One of the most important instructions of Bahá'u'lláh in regard to the economic question is that all must engage in

---

[1] For further particulars see 'Abdu'l-Bahá's published addresses, especially those given in the United States of America.

useful work. There must be no drones in the social hive, no able-bodied parasites on society. He says:—

It is enjoined on every one of you to engage in some occupation—some art, trade or the like. We have made this—your occupation—identical with the worship of God, the True One. Reflect, O people, upon the mercy of God and upon His favors, then thank Him in mornings and evenings.

Waste not your time in idleness and indolence, and occupy yourselves with that which will profit yourselves and others beside yourselves. Thus hath the matter been decreed in this Tablet, from the horizon of which the Sun of Wisdom and Divine Utterance is gleaming! The most despised of men before God is he who sits and begs. Cling unto the rope of means, relying upon God, the Causer of Causes.—*Glad Tidings.*

How much of the energy employed in the business world of today is expended simply in canceling and neutralizing the efforts of other people—in useless strife and competition! And how much in ways that are still more injurious! Were *all* to work, and were all work, whether of brain or hand, of a nature profitable to mankind, as Bahá'u'lláh commands, then the supplies of everything necessary for a healthy, comfortable, and noble life would amply suffice for all. There need be no slums, no starvation, no destitution, no industrial slavery, no health-destroying drudgery.

The Ethics of Wealth

According to the Bahá'í teachings, riches rightly acquired and rightly used are honorable and praiseworthy. Services rendered should be adequately rewarded. Bahá'u'lláh says in the *Tablet of Tarázát:*—"The people of Bahá must not refuse to discharge the due reward of anyone, and must respect possessors of talent. . . . One must speak with justice and recognize the worth of benefits."

With regard to interest on money, Bahá'u'lláh writes in the *Tablet of I<u>sh</u>ráqát* as follows:—

> Most of the people are found to be in need of this matter; for if no interest be allowed, affairs (business) will be trammeled and obstructed. . . . A person is rarely found who would lend money to anyone upon the principle of "Qarḍ-i-hasan" (literally "good loan," i.e. money advanced without interest and repaid at the pleasure of the borrower). Consequently, out of favor to the servants, We have appointed "profit on money" to be current, among other business transactions which are in force among people. That is . . . it is allowable, lawful and pure to charge interest on money . . . but this matter must be conducted with moderation and justice. The Pen of Glory has withheld itself from laying down its limits, as a wisdom from his presence and as a convenience for His servants. We exhort the friends of God to act with fairness and justice, and in such a way that the mercy of His beloved ones, and their compassion, may be manifested toward each other. . . .
>
> The execution of these matters has been placed in charge of the men of the House of Justice, in order that they may act in accordance with the exigencies of the time and with wisdom.

No Industrial Slavery

In the *Book of Aqdas* Bahá'u'lláh forbids slavery, and 'Abdu'l-Bahá has explained that not only chattel slavery, but also industrial slavery, is contrary to the law of God. When in the United States in 1912, He said to the American people:—

> Between 1860 and 1865 you did a wonderful thing; you abolished chattel slavery; but today you must do a much more wonderful thing: you must abolish industrial slavery. . . .
>
> The solution of economic questions will not be brought about by array of capital against labor, and labor against

capital, in strife and conflict, but by the voluntary attitude of goodwill on both sides. Then a real and lasting justness of conditions will be secured. . . .

Among the Bahá'ís there are no extortionate, mercenary and unjust practices, no rebellious demands, no revolutionary uprisings against existing governments. . . .

It will not be possible in the future for men to amass great fortunes by the labors of others. The rich will willingly divide. They will come to this gradually, naturally, by their own volition. It will never be accomplished by war and bloodshed.—*Star of the West,* vol. vii, No. 15, p. 147.

It is by friendly consultation and cooperation by just copartnership and profit-sharing, that the interests of both capital and labor will be best served. The harsh weapons of the strike and lockout are injurious, not only to the trades immediately affected, but to the community as a whole. It is, therefore, the business of the governments to devise means for preventing recourse to such barbarous methods of settling disputes. 'Abdu'l-Bahá said at Dublin, New Hampshire, in 1912:—

Now I want to tell you about the law of God. According to the divine law, employees should not be paid merely by wages. Nay, rather they should be partners in every work. The question of socialization is very difficult. It will not be solved by strikes for wages. All the governments of the world must be united, and organize an assembly, the members of which shall be elected from the parliaments and the noble ones of the nations. These must plan with wisdom and power, so that neither the capitalists suffer enormous losses, nor the laborers become needy. In the utmost moderation they should make the law, then announce to the public that the rights of the working people are to be effectively preserved; also the rights of the capitalists are to be protected. When such a general law is adopted, by the will of both sides, should a strike occur, all the governments of the world should collectively resist it. Otherwise the work will lead to much destruction, especially in Europe. Terrible things will take place. One of the several causes of a universal European war will be this question. The owners of properties, mines and factories, should share their incomes with their employees, and give a fairly certain percentage of their profits to their workingmen, in order that the employees should receive, besides their wages, some of the general income of the factory, so that the employee may strive with his soul in the work.—*Star of the West,* vol. viii, No. 1, p. 7.

Bequest and Inheritance

Bahá'u'lláh states that a person should be free to dispose of his possessions during his lifetime in any way he chooses, and it is incumbent on everyone to write a will stating how his property is to be disposed of after his death. When a person dies without leaving a will, the value of the property should be estimated and divided in certain stated proportions among seven classes of inheritors, namely, children, wife or husband, father, mother, brothers, sisters, and teachers, the share of each diminishing from the first to the last. In the absence of one or more of these classes, the share which would belong to them goes to the public treasury, to be expended on the poor, the fatherless, and the widows, or on useful public works. If the deceased has no heirs, then all his property goes to the public treasury.

There is nothing in the law of Bahá'u'lláh to prevent a man from leaving all his property to one individual if he pleases, but Bahá'ís will naturally be influenced, in making their wills, by the model Bahá'u'lláh has laid down for the case of intestate estates, which ensures distribution of the property among a considerable number of heirs.

Equality of Men and Women

One of the social principles to which Bahá'u'lláh attaches great importance is that women should be regarded as the equals of men and should enjoy equal rights and privileges, equal education, and equal opportunities.

The great means on which He relies for bringing about the emancipation of women is universal education. Girls are to receive as good an education as boys. In fact, the education of girls is even more important than that of boys, for in time these girls will become mothers, and, as mothers, they will be the first teachers of the next generation. Children are like green and tender branches; if the early training is right they grow straight, and if it is wrong they grow crooked; and to the end of their lives they are affected by the training of their earliest years. How important, then, that girls should be well and wisely educated!

During His Western tours, 'Abdu'l-Bahá had frequent occasion to explain the Bahá'í teaching on this subject. At a meeting of the Women's Freedom League in London in January 1913, He said:—

Humanity is like a bird with its two wings—the one is male, the other female. Unless both wings are strong and impelled by some common force, the bird cannot fly heavenwards. According to the spirit of this age, women must advance and fulfill their mission in all departments of life, becoming equal to men. They must be on the same level as men and enjoy equal rights. This is my earnest prayer and it is one of the fundamental principles of Bahá'u'lláh.

Some scientists have declared that the brains of men weigh more than those of women, and claim this as a proof of man's superiority. Yet when we look around us we see people with small heads, whose brains must weigh little, who show the greatest intelligence and great powers of understanding; and others with big heads, whose brains must be heavy, and yet they are witless. Therefore the avoirdupois of the brain is no true measure of intelligence or superiority.

When men bring forward as a second proof of their superiority the assertion that women have not achieved as much as men, they use poor arguments which leave history out of consideration. If they kept themselves more fully informed historically, they would know that great women have lived and achieved great things in the past, and that there are many living and achieving great things today.

Here 'Abdu'l-Bahá described the achievements of Zenobia and other great women of the past, concluding with an eloquent tribute to the fearless Mary Magdalene, whose faith remained firm while that of the apostles was shaken. He continued:—

Amongst the women of our own time is Qurratu'l-'Ayn, the daughter of a Muḥammadan priest. At the time of the appearance of the Báb she showed such tremendous courage and power that all who heard her were astonished. She threw aside her veil despite the immemorial custom of the women of Persia, and although it was considered impolite to speak with men, this heroic woman carried on controversies with the most learned men, and in every meeting she vanquished them. The Persian Government took her prisoner; she was stoned in the streets, anathematized, exiled from town to town, threatened with death, but she never failed in her determination to work for the freedom of her sisters. She bore persecution and suffering with the greatest heroism; even in prison she gained converts. To a Minister of Persia, in whose house she was imprisoned, she said: "You can kill me as soon as you like but you cannot stop the emancipation of women." At last the end of her tragic life came; she was carried into a garden and strangled. She put on, however, her choicest robes as if she were going to join a bridal party. With such magnanimity and courage she gave her life, startling and thrilling all who saw her. She was truly a great heroine. Today in Persia, among the Bahá'ís, there are women who also show unflinching courage, and who are endowed with great poetic insight. They are most eloquent, and speak before large gatherings of people.

Women must go on advancing; they must extend their knowledge of science, literature, history, for the perfection of humanity. Erelong they will receive their rights. Men will see women in earnest, bearing themselves with dignity, improving the civil and political life, opposed to warfare, demanding suffrage and equal opportunities. I expect to see you advance in all phases of life; then will your brows be crowned with the diadem of eternal glory.

Women and the New Age

When woman's point of view receives due consideration and woman's will is allowed adequate expression in the arrangement of social affairs, we may expect great advancement in matters which have often been grievously neglected under the old regime of male dominance—such matters as health, temperance, peace, and regard for the value of the individual life. Improvements in these respects will have very far-reaching and beneficent effects. 'Abdu'l-Bahá says:—

The world in the past has been ruled by force, and man has dominated over woman by reason of his more forceful and aggressive qualities both of body and mind. But the balance is already shifting; force is losing its dominance, and mental alertness, intuition, and the spiritual qualities of love and service, in which woman is strong, are gaining ascendancy. Hence the new age will be an age less masculine and more permeated with the feminine ideals, or, to speak more exactly, will be an age in which the masculine and feminine elements of civilization will be more evenly balanced.—*Star of the West*, viii, No. 3, p. 4.

Methods of Violence Discarded

In bringing about the emancipation of women as in other matters, Bahá'u'lláh counsels His followers to avoid methods of violence. An excellent illustration of the Bahá'í method of social reform has been given by the Bahá'í women in Persia,

Egypt, and Syria. In these countries it is customary for Muhammadan women outside their homes to wear a veil covering the face. The Báb indicated that in the new Dispensation women would be relieved from this irksome restraint, but Bahá'u'lláh counsels His followers, where no important question of morality is involved, to defer to established customs until people become enlightened, rather than scandalize those amongst whom they live, and arouse needless antagonism. The Bahá'í women, therefore, although well aware that the antiquated custom of wearing the veil is, for enlightened people, unnecessary and inconvenient, yet quietly put up with the inconvenience, rather than rouse a storm of fanatical hatred and rancorous opposition by uncovering their faces in public. This conformity to custom is in no way due to fear, but to an assured confidence in the power of education and in the transforming and life-giving effect of true religion. Bahá'ís in these regions are devoting their energies to the education of their children, especially their girls, and to the diffusion and promotion of the Bahá'í ideals, well knowing that as the new spiritual life grows and spreads among the people, antiquated customs and prejudices will by and by be shed, as naturally and inevitably as bud scales are shed in spring when the leaves and flowers expand in the sunshine.

Education

Education—the instruction and guidance of men and the development and training of their innate faculties—has been the supreme aim of all the Holy Prophets since the world began, and in the Bahá'í teachings the fundamental importance and limitless possibilities of education are proclaimed in the clearest terms. The teacher is the most potent factor in civilization and his work is the highest to which men can aspire. Education begins in the mother's womb and is as unending as the life of the individual. It is a perennial necessity of right living and the foundation of both individual and social welfare. When education on right lines becomes general, humanity will be transformed and the world will become a paradise.

At present a really well educated man is the rarest of phenomena, for nearly everyone has false prejudices, wrong ideals, erroneous conceptions, and bad habits drilled into him from babyhood. How few are taught from their earliest childhood to love God with all their hearts and dedicate their lives to Him; to regard service to humanity as the highest aim of life; to develop their powers to the best advantage for the general good of all! Yet surely these are the essential elements of a good education. Mere cramming of the memory with facts about arithmetic, grammar, geography, languages, etc., has comparatively little effect in producing noble and useful lives.

Bahá'u'lláh says that education must be universal:—

It is decreed that every father must educate his sons and daughters in learning and in writing and also in that which hath been ordained in the Tablet. He who neglects that which hath been commanded (in this matter), if he be rich, it is incumbent on the trustees of the House of Justice to recover from him the amount required for the education of his children; otherwise (i.e. if the parent be not capable) the matter shall devolve upon the House of Justice. Verily We have made it (the House of Justice) an asylum for the poor and needy.

He who educates his son, or any other children, it is as though he hath educated one of My children.—*Tablet of Ishráqát.*

Men and women must place a part of what they earn by trade, agriculture or other business, in charge of a trustworthy person, to be spent in the education and instruction of the children. That deposit must be invested in the education of the children, under the advice of the trustees (or members) of the House of Justice.—*Tablet of the World.*

Innate Differences of Nature

In the Bahá'í view the child's nature is not like so much wax that can be molded indifferently to any shape according to the will of the teacher. Nay, each from the first has his own God-given character and individuality which can develop to the best advantage only in a particular way; and that way in each case is unique. No two people have exactly the same capabilities and talents, and the true educator will never attempt to force two natures into the same mold. In fact, he will never attempt to force any nature into any mold. Rather he will reverently tend the developing powers of the young nature, encourage and protect them, and supply the nourishment and assistance which they need. His work is like that of a gardener tending different plants. One plant likes the bright sunshine, another the cool shade; one loves the water's edge and another the dry knoll; one thrives best on sandy soil and another on rich loam. Each must have its needs appropriately supplied, else its perfections can never be fully revealed. 'Abdu'l-Bahá says:—

> The Prophets acknowledge that education hath a great effect upon the human race, but They declare that minds and comprehensions are originally different. We see that certain children of the same age, nativity and race, nay, from the same household, under the tutorship of the same teacher, differ in minds and comprehensions. No matter how the shell is educated (or polished) it can never become the radiant pearl. The black stone will not become the world-illuminating gem. The thorny cactus can never by training and development become the blessed tree. That is to say, training doth not change the essential nature of the human gem, but it produceth a marvelous effect. By this effective power all that is latent, of virtues and capacities in the human reality, will be revealed.— *Tablets of 'Abdu'l-Bahá,* vol. iii, p. 577.

Character Training

The thing of paramount importance in education is character training. With regard to this, example is more effective than precept, and the lives and characters of the child's parents, teachers, and habitual associates are factors of the utmost importance.

The Prophets of God are the great Educators of mankind, and Their counsels and the story of Their lives should be instilled into the child's mind as soon as it is able to grasp them. Especially important are the words of the supreme Teacher, Bahá'u'lláh, Who reveals the root principles on which the civilization of the future must be built up. He says:—

Teach your children what hath been revealed through the Pen of Glory. Instruct them in what hath descended from the heaven of greatness and power. Let them memorize the Tablets of the Merciful and chant them with the most melodious voices in the halls of the Mashriqu'l-Adhkár.—*Star of the West,* vol. ix, No. 7, p. 81.

Arts, Sciences, and Crafts

Training in arts, sciences, crafts, and useful professions is regarded as important and necessary. Bahá'u'lláh says:—

Knowledge is like unto wings for the being (of man), and is like a ladder for ascending. To acquire knowledge is incumbent upon all, but of those sciences which may profit the people of the earth, and not such sciences as begin in mere words, and end in mere words. The possessors of sciences and arts have a great right among the people of the world. Indeed, the real treasury of man is his knowledge. Knowledge is the means of honor, prosperity, joy, gladness, happiness and exultation.—*Tablet of Tajallíyát.*

Treatment of Criminals

In a talk on the right method of treating criminals, 'Abdu'l-Bahá spoke as follows:—

. . . The most essential thing is that the people must be educated in such a way . . . that they will avoid and shrink from perpetrating crimes, so that the crime itself will appear to them as the greatest chastisement, the utmost condemnation and torment. Therefore no crimes which require punishment will be committed. . . .

. . . If someone oppresses, injures, and wrongs another, and the wronged man retaliates, this is vengeance, and is censurable. . . . If 'Amru dishonors Zaid, the latter has not the right to dishonor 'Amru; if he does so, this is vengeance, and it is very reprehensible. No, rather he must return good for evil, and not only forgive, but also, if possible, be of service to his oppressor. This conduct is worthy of man: for what advantage does he gain by vengeance? The two actions are equivalent; if one action is reprehensible, both are reprehensible. The only difference is that one was committed first, the other later.

But the community has the right of defense and self-protection; moreover, the community has no hatred nor animosity for the murderer: it imprisons or punishes him merely for the protection and security of others. . . .

Thus when Christ said: "Whosoever shall smite thee on the right cheek, turn to him the left one also," it was for the purpose of teaching men not to take personal revenge. He did not mean that if a wolf should fall upon a flock of sheep and wish to destroy it, that the wolf should be encouraged to do so. No, if Christ had known that a wolf had entered the fold and was about to destroy the sheep, most certainly He would have prevented it. . . .

. . . The constitution of the communities depends upon justice. . . . Then what Christ meant by forgiveness and pardon is not that, when nations attack you, burn your homes, plunder your goods, assault your wives, children, and relatives and violate your honor, you should be submissive in the presence of these tyrannical foes, and allow them to perform all their cruelties and oppressions. No, the words of Christ refer to the conduct of two individuals towards each other: if one person assaults another, the injured one should forgive him. But the communities must protect the rights of man.

. . . One thing remains to be said: it is that the communities are day and night occupied in making penal laws, and in preparing and organizing instruments and means of punishment. They build prisons, make chains and fetters, arrange places of exile and banishment, and different kinds of hardships and tortures, and think by these means to discipline criminals; whereas, in reality, they are causing destruction of morals and perversion of characters. The community, on the contrary, ought day and night to strive and endeavor with the utmost zeal and effort to accomplish the education of men, to cause them day by day to progress and to increase in science and knowledge, to acquire virtues, to gain good morals and to avoid vices, so that crimes may not occur.—*Some Answered Questions,* pp. 307-311.

Influence of the Press

The importance of the press as a means of diffusing knowledge and educating the people, and its power as a civilizing force, when rightly directed, are fully recognized by Bahá'u'- lláh. He writes:—

In this day the mysteries of this earth are unfolded and visible before the eyes, and the pages of swiftly appearing newspapers are indeed the mirror of the world; they display the doings and actions of the different nations; they both illustrate them and cause them to be heard. Newspapers are as a mirror endowed with hearing, sight and speech; they are a wonderful phenomenon and a great matter.

But it behooves the writers and editors thereof to be sanctified from the prejudice of egotism and desire, and to be adorned with the ornament of equity and justice. They must inquire into matters as fully as possible, in order that they may be informed of the real facts, and commit the same to writing. Concerning this wronged One, what the newspapers have published has for the most part been devoid of truth. Good speech and truthfulness are, in loftiness of position and rank, like the sun which has risen from the horizon of the heaven of knowledge.—*Tablet of Tarázát.*

The Way to Peace/10

*Today, this Servant has assuredly come to vivify the world
and to bring into unity all who are on the face of the earth.
That which God willeth shall come to pass and thou shalt see
the earth even as the Abhá (Most Glorious) Paradise.—*
BAHÁ'U'LLÁH, *Tablet to Ra'ís.*

Conflict versus Concord

During the past century scientists have devoted an immense
amount of study to the struggle for existence in the plant and
animal world, and, amid the perplexities of social life, many
have turned for guidance to the principles which have been
found to hold good in the lower world of nature. In this way
they have come to regard rivalry and conflict as necessities of
life, and the ruthless killing out of the weaker members of
society as a legitimate or even necessary means of improving
the race. Bahá'u'lláh tells us, on the other hand, that, if we
wish to ascend the scale of progress, instead of looking backward to the animal world, we must direct our gaze forward
and upward, and must take not the beasts, but the Prophets
as our guides. The principles of unity, concord, and compassion taught by the Prophets are the very antithesis of those
dominating the animal struggle for self-preservation, and we
must choose between them, for they cannot be reconciled.
'Abdu'l-Bahá says:—

> In the world of nature the dominant note is the struggle
> for existence—the result of which is the survival of the
> fittest. The law of the survival of the fittest is the origin
> of all difficulties. It is the cause of war and strife, hatred
> and animosity, between human beings. In the world of
> nature there is tyranny, egoism, aggression, overbearance,
> usurpation of the rights of others and other blameworthy

156

attributes which are defects of the animal world. Therefore, so long as the requirements of the natural world play paramount part among the children of men, success and prosperity are impossible. Nature is warlike, nature is bloodthirsty, nature is tyrannical, for nature is unaware of God the Almighty. That is why these cruel qualities are natural to the animal world.

Therefore the Lord of mankind, having great love and mercy, has caused the appearance of the Prophets and the revelation of the Holy Books, so that through divine education humanity may be released from the corruption of nature and the darkness of ignorance, be confirmed with ideal virtues and spiritual attributes, and become the dawning-place of merciful emotions. . . .

A hundred thousand times, alas! that ignorant prejudice, unnatural differences and antagonistic principles are yet displayed by the nations of the world toward one another, thus causing the retardation of general progress. This retrogression comes from the fact that the principles of divine civilization are completely abandoned, and the teachings of the Prophets are forgotten.—*Star of the West,* vol. viii, p. 15.

The Most Great Peace

In all ages the Prophets of God have foretold the coming of an era of "peace on earth, goodwill among men." As we have already seen Bahá'u'lláh, in the most glowing and confident terms, confirms these prophecies and declares that their fulfillment is at hand. 'Abdu'l-Bahá says:—

. . . In this marvelous cycle, the earth will be transformed, and the world of humanity arrayed in tranquillity and beauty. Disputes, quarrels, and murders will be replaced by peace, truth, and concord; among the nations, peoples, races, and countries, love and amity will appear. Cooperation and union will be established, and finally war will be entirely suppressed. . . . Universal peace will raise its tent in the center of the earth, and the blessed Tree of Life will grow and spread to such an extent that it will overshadow the East and the West. Strong and weak, rich and poor, antagonistic sects and hostile nations—which are like the wolf and the lamb, the leopard and the kid, the lion and the calf—will act towards each other with the most complete love, friendship, justice, and equity. The world will be filled with science, with the knowledge of the reality of the mysteries of beings, and with the knowledge of God.—*Some Answered Questions,* pp. 74-75.

Religious Prejudices

In order to see clearly how the Most Great Peace may be established, let us first examine the principal causes that have let to war in the past and see how Bahá'u'lláh proposes to deal with each.

One of the most fertile causes of war has been religious prejudice. With regard to this the Bahá'í teachings show clearly that animosity and conflict between people of different religions and sects have always been due, not to true religion, but to the want of it, and to its replacement by false prejudices, imitations, and misrepresentations.

In one of His talks in Paris, 'Abdu'l-Bahá said:—

Religion should unite all hearts and cause wars and disputes to vanish from the face of the earth; it should give birth to spirituality, and bring light and life to every soul. If religion becomes a cause of dislike, hatred and division it would be better to be without it, and to withdraw from such a religion would be a truly religious act. For it is clear that the purpose of a remedy is to cure, but if the remedy only aggravates the complaint, it had better be left alone. Any religion which is not a cause of love and unity is no religion.—*Wisdom of 'Abdu'l-Bahá.*

Again He says:—

From the beginning of human history down to the present time various religions of the world have anathe-

matized one another and accused one another of falsity.
. . . They have shunned one another most rigidly, exercising mutual animosity and rancor. Consider the history
of religious warfare. . . . One of the greatest religious
wars, the Crusades, extended over a period of 200 years.
. . . Sometimes the Crusaders were successful, killing,
pillaging and taking captive the Muḥammadan people;
sometimes the Mussulmans were victorious, inflicting
bloodshed and ruin in turn upon the invaders.

So they continued for two centuries, alternately fighting
with fury and relaxing with weakness until the European
religionists withdrew from the East, leaving ashes of desolation behind them and finding their own nations in a condition of turbulence and upheaval. . . . Yet this was only
one of the "holy wars."

Religious wars have been many. Nine hundred thousand martyrs of the Protestant cause was the record of
conflict and difference between that sect of Christians and
the Catholics. . . . How many languished in prisons!
How merciless the treatment of captives! All in the name
of religion!

The Christians and Muḥammadans considered the
Jews as satanic and the enemies of God. Therefore they
cursed and persecuted them. Great numbers of Jews
were killed, their houses burnt and pillaged, their children
carried into captivity. The Jews in turn regarded the
Christians as infidels, and the Muḥammadans as enemies
and destroyers of the laws of Moses; therefore they called
down vengeance upon them and curse them even to this
day.

When the light of Bahá'u'lláh dawned from the East,
He proclaimed the promise of the oneness of humanity.
He addressed all mankind saying: "Ye are all fruits of
one tree. There are not two trees, one a tree of divine
mercy, the other the tree of Satan." . . . Therefore we
must exercise the utmost love toward one another. We
must not consider any people the people of Satan, but
know and recognize all as servants of one God. At most

it is this: some do not know, they must be guided and trained. . . . Some are ignorant, they must be informed. Some are as children, they must be helped to reach maturity. Some are ailing, their moral condition is bad, they must be treated until their morals are purified. But the sick man is not to be hated because he is sick; the child must not be shunned because he is a child, the ignorant one is not to be despised because he lacks knowledge. They must be treated, educated, trained and assisted in love. Everything must be done in order that all humanity may live under the shadow of God in the utmost security, in happiness of the highest type.—*Star of the West,* vol. viii, p. 76.

Racial and Patriotic Prejudices

The Bahá'í doctrine of the unity of mankind strikes at the root of another cause of war, namely, racial prejudice. Certain races have assumed themselves to be superior to others and have taken for granted, on the principle of "survival of the fittest," that this superiority gives them the right to exploit for their own advantage, or even to exterminate, weaker races. Many of the blackest pages in the world's history are examples of the pitiless application of this principle. According to the Bahá'í view people of every race are of equal value in the sight of God. All have wonderful innate capacities which only require suitable education for their development, and each can play a part, which, instead of impoverishing, will enrich and complete the life of all the other members of the body of humanity. 'Abdu'l-Bahá says:—

Concerning the prejudice of race; it is an illusion, a superstition pure and simple, for God created us all of one race. . . . In the beginning also there were no limits and boundaries between the different lands; no part of the earth belonged more to one people than to another. In the sight of God there is no difference between the various races. Why should man invent such a prejudice? How can we uphold war caused by such an illusion? God has not created men that they should destroy one another. All races, tribes, sects and classes share equally in the bounty of their heavenly Father.

The only real difference lies in the degree of faithfulness, of obedience to the laws of God. There are some who are as lighted torches; there are others who shine as stars in the sky of humanity.

The lovers of mankind, these are the superior men, of whatever nation, creed or color they may be.—*Wisdom of 'Abdu'l-Bahá,* p. 137.

Equally mischievous with racial prejudice is political or patriotic prejudice. The time has now come when narrow national patriotisms should be merged in the wider patriotism whose country is the world. Bahá'u'lláh says:—

Of old it hath been revealed: "Love of one's country is an element of the Faith of God." . . . The Tongue of Grandeur hath . . . in the day of His manifestation proclaimed: "It is not his to boast who loveth his country, but it is his who loveth the world." Through the power released by these exalted words He hath lent a fresh impulse, and set a new direction, to the birds of men's hearts, and hath obliterated every trace of restriction and limitation from God's Holy Book.—*Tablet of the World.*

Territorial Ambitions

Many are the wars which have been fought over pieces of territory whose possession has been coveted by two or more rival nations. The greed of possession has been as fertile a cause of strife among nations as among individuals. According to the Bahá'í view, land rightly belongs not to individual men or individual nations but to humanity as a whole; nay, rather, it belongs to God alone, and all men are but tenants.

On the occasion of the Battle of Benghazi,[1] 'Abdu'l-Bahá said:—

The news of the Battle of Benghazi grieves my heart. I wonder at the human savagery that still exists in the world: How is it possible for men to fight from morning till night, killing each other, shedding the blood of their fellowmen? And for what object? To gain possession of a part of the earth! Even the animals when they fight have an immediate and more reasonable cause for their attacks. How terrible is it that men who are of the higher kingdom can descend to slaying and bringing misery to their fellow beings for the possession of a tract of land— the highest of created beings fighting to obtain the lowest form of matter, earth.

Land belongs not to one people but to all people. The earth is not man's home but his tomb.

However great the conqueror, however many countries he may reduce to slavery, he is unable to retain any part of these devastated lands but one tiny portion—his tomb.

If more land is required for the improvement of the condition of the people, for the spread of civilization . . . surely it would be possible to acquire peaceably the necessary extension of territory. But war is made for the satisfaction of men's ambition. For the sake of worldly gain to the few terrible misery is brought to numberless homes, breaking the hearts of hundreds of men and women. . . .

I charge you all that each one of you concentrate all the thoughts of his heart on love and unity. When a thought of war comes, oppose it by a stronger thought of peace. A thought of hatred must be destroyed by a more powerful thought of love. When soldiers of the world draw their swords to kill, soldiers of God clasp each other's hands. So may all the savagery of men disappear by the mercy of God, working through the pure in heart and the

---

[1] A battle of the Italo-Turkish War which broke out on September 29, 1911.

sincere of soul. Do not think the peace of the world
an ideal impossible to attain. Nothing is impossible to the
divine benevolence of God. If you desire with all your
heart friendship with every race on earth, your thought,
spiritual and positive, will spread; it will become the
desire of others, growing stronger until it reaches the
minds of all men.—*Wisdom of 'Abdu'l-Bahá*, p. 23.

Universal Language

Having glanced at the principal causes of war and how they
may be avoided, we may now proceed to examine certain
constructive proposals made by Bahá'u'lláh with a view to
achieving the Most Great Peace.

The first deals with the establishment of a universal auxiliary
language. Bahá'u'lláh refers to this matter in the *Book of
Aqdas* and in many of His Tablets. Thus in the *Tablet of
Ishráqát* He says:—

> The Sixth Ishráq (Effulgence) is concord and union
> amongst men. Through the radiance of Union have the
> regions of the world at all times been illumined, and the
> greatest of all means thereunto is the understanding of
> one another's writing and speech. Ere this, in Our epis-
> tles, have We commanded the Trustees of the House of
> Justice, either to choose one of the existing tongues, or to
> originate a new one, and in like manner to adopt a com-
> mon script, teaching these to the children in all the
> schools of the world, that the world may become even
> as one land and one home.

About the time when this proposal of Bahá'u'lláh was first
given to the world, there was born in Poland a boy named
Ludovic Zamenhof, who was destined to play a leading part
in carrying it into effect. Almost from his infancy, the ideal
of a universal language became a dominant motive in Zamenhof's life, and the result of his devoted labors was the inven-
tion and widespread adoption of the language known as
Esperanto, which has now stood the test of many years and

has proved to be a very satisfactory medium of international intercourse. It has the great advantage that it can be mastered in about a twentieth part of the time required to master such languages as English, French, or German. At an Esperanto banquet given in Paris in February 1913, 'Abdu'l-Bahá said:—

Today one of the chief causes of the differences in Europe is the diversity of languages. We say this man is a German, the other is an Italian, then we meet an Englishman and then again a Frenchman. Although they belong to the same race, yet language is the greatest barrier between them. Were a universal auxiliary language in operation they would all be considered as one.

His Holiness Bahá'u'lláh wrote about this international language more than forty years ago. He says that as long as an international language is not adopted, complete union between the various sections of the world will be unrealized, for we observe that misunderstandings keep people from mutual association, and these misunderstandings will not be dispelled except through an international auxiliary language.

Generally speaking, the whole people of the Orient are not fully informed of events in the West, neither can the Westerners put themselves in sympathetic touch with the Easterners; their thoughts are enclosed in a casket —the international language will be the master key to open it. Were we in possession of a universal language, the Western books could easily be translated into that language, and the Eastern peoples be informed of their contents. In the same way the books of the East could be translated into that language for the benefit of the people in the West. The greatest means of progress towards the union of East and West will be a common language. It will make the whole world one home and become the strongest impulse for human advancement. It will upraise the standard of the oneness of humanity. It will make the earth one universal commonwealth. It will be the cause of love between the children of men. It will cause good fellowship between the various races.

Now, praise be to God that Dr. Zamenhof [1] has invented the Esperanto language. It has all the potential qualities of becoming the international means of communication. All of us must be grateful and thankful to him for this noble effort; for in this way he has served his fellowmen well. With untiring effort and self-sacrifice on the part of its devotees Esperanto will become universal. Therefore every one of us must study this language and spread it as far as possible so that day by day it may receive a broader recognition, be accepted by all nations and governments of the world, and become a part of the curriculum in all the public schools. I hope that Esperanto will be adopted as the language of all the future international conferences and congresses, so that all people need acquire only two languages—one their own tongue and the other the international language. Then perfect union will be established between all the people of the world. Consider how difficult it is today to communicate with various nations. If one studies fifty languages one may yet travel through a country and not know the language. Therefore I hope that you will make the utmost effort, so that this language of Esperanto may be widely spread.

While these allusions to Esperanto are specific and encouraging, it remains true that until the House of Justice has acted on the matter in accordance with Bahá'u'lláh's instruction, the Bahá'í Faith is not committed to Esperanto nor to any other living or artificial tongue. 'Abdu'l-Bahá Himself said: "The love and effort put into Esperanto will not be lost, but no one person can construct a universal language."—*'Abdu'l-Bahá in London,* p. 95.

Which language to adopt, and whether it is to be a natural

---

[1] It is of interest that Zamenhof's daughter, Lydia, became an active Bahá'í.

or constructed one, is a decision which the nations of the world will have to make.

Universal League of Nations

Another proposal frequently and powerfully advocated by Bahá'u'lláh was that a universal League of Nations should be formed for the maintenance of international peace. In a letter to Queen Victoria, written while He was still a prisoner in the barracks of 'Akká,[1] He said:—

> O rulers of the earth! Be reconciled among yourselves, that ye may need no more armaments save in a measure to safeguard your territories and dominions. . . . Be united, O kings of the earth, for thereby will the tempest of discord be stilled amongst you, and your people find rest. . . . Should any one among you take up arms against another, rise ye all against him, for this is naught but manifest justice.

In 1875, 'Abdu'l-Bahá gave a forecast of the establishment of a universal League of Nations, which is especially interesting at the present time [2] in view of the strenuous attempts now being made to establish such a league. He wrote:—

> True civilization will unfurl its banner in the midmost heart of the world whenever a certain number of its distinguished and high-minded sovereigns—the shining exemplars of devotion and determination—shall, for the good and happiness of all mankind, arise, with firm resolve and clear vision, to establish the Cause of Universal Peace. They must make the Cause of Peace the object of general consultation, and seek by every means in their power to establish a union of the nations of the world. They must conclude a binding treaty and establish a covenant, the provisions of which shall be sound, inviolable, and definite. They must proclaim it to all the world and obtain for it the sanction of all the human race.

---

[1] 1868 to 1870.
[2] The author wrote this passage in 1919–1920.

This supreme and noble undertaking—the real source of the peace and well-being of all the world—should be regarded as sacred by all that dwell on earth. All the forces of humanity must be mobilized to ensure the stability and permanence of this Most Great Covenant. In this all-embracing pact the limits and frontiers of each and every nation should be clearly fixed, the principles underlying the relations of governments towards one another definitely laid down, and all international agreements and obligations ascertained. In like manner, the size of the armaments of every government should be strictly limited, for if the preparations for war and the military forces of any nation should be allowed to increase, they will arouse the suspicion of others. The fundamental principle underlying this solemn pact should be so fixed that if any government later violate any one of its provisions, all the governments on earth should arise to reduce it to utter submission, nay the human race as a whole should resolve, with every power at its disposal, to destroy that government. Should this greatest of all remedies be applied to the sick body of the world, it will assuredly recover from its ills and will remain eternally safe and secure.—*The Secret of Divine Civilization,* pp. 64-65.

Bahá'ís see grave deficiencies in the structure of the League of Nations [1] which falls short of the type of institution which Bahá'u'lláh described as essential to the establishment of world peace.

At present universal peace is a matter of great importance, but unity of conscience is essential, so that the foundation of this matter may become secure, its establishment firm and its edifice strong. . . . Although the League of Nations has been brought into existence, yet it is incapable of establishing universal peace. But the Supreme Tribunal which His Holiness Bahá'u'lláh has de-

---

[1] The same considerations apply to the United Nations Organization.

scribed will fulfill this sacred task with the utmost might and power.

International Arbitration

Bahá'u'lláh also advocated the establishment of an international court of arbitration, so that differences arising between nations might be settled in accordance with justice and reason, instead of by appeal to the ordeal of battle. In a letter to the Secretary of the Mohonk Conference on International Arbitration, in August 1911, 'Abdu'l-Bahá said:—

About fifty years ago in the *Book of Aqdas,* Bahá'u'lláh commanded people to establish universal peace and summoned all the nations to the divine banquet of international arbitration, so that the questions of boundaries, of national honor and property, and of vital interests between nations might be settled by an arbitral court of justice, and that no nation would dare to refuse to abide by the decisions thus arrived at. If any quarrel arise between two nations it must be adjudicated by this international court and be arbitrated and decided upon like the judgment rendered by the judge between two individuals. If at any time any nation dares to break such a decision, all the other nations must arise to put down this rebellion.

Again, in one of His Paris talks in 1911, He said:—

A Supreme Tribunal shall be established by the peoples and governments of every nation, composed of members elected from each country and government. The members of this great council shall assemble in unity. All disputes of an international character shall be submitted to this court, its work being to arrange by arbitration everything which otherwise would be a cause of war. The mission of this tribunal would be to prevent war.—*Wisdom of 'Abdu'l-Bahá,* p. 145.

During the quarter of a century preceding the establishment of the League of Nations a permanent Court of Arbitration was established at The Hague (1900), and many arbitration treaties were signed, but most of these fell far short of the comprehensive proposals of Bahá'u'lláh. No arbitration treaty was made between two Great Powers in which all matters of dispute were included. Differences affecting "vital interests," "honor," and "independence" were specifically excepted. Not only so, but effective guarantees that nations would abide by the terms of the treaties into which they had entered were lacking. In the Bahá'í proposals, on the other hand, questions of boundaries, of national honor, and of vital interest are expressly included, and agreements will have the supreme guarantee of the world League of Nations behind them. Only when these proposals are completely carried out will international arbitration attain the full scope of its beneficent possibilities and the curse of war be finally banished from the world.

Limitation of Armaments

'Abdu'l-Bahá says:—

By a general agreement all the governments of the world must disarm simultaneously. It will not do if one lays down its arms and the others refuse to do so. The nations of the world must concur with each other concerning this supremely important subject, so that they may abandon together the deadly weapons of human slaughter. As long as one nation increases her military and naval budget other nations will be forced into this crazed competition through their natural and supposed interests.
—*Diary of Mírzá Aḥmad Sohrab,* May 11-14, 1914.

Nonresistance

As a religious body, Bahá'ís have, at the express command of Bahá'u'lláh, entirely abandoned the use of armed force in their own interests, even for strictly defensive purposes. In Persia many, many thousands of the Bábís and Bahá'ís have suffered cruel deaths because of their faith. In the early days of the Cause the Bábís on various occasions defended themselves and their families by the sword, with great courage and bravery. Bahá'u'lláh, however, forbade this. 'Abdu'l-Bahá writes:—

When Bahá'u'lláh appeared, He declared that the promulgation of the truth by such means must on no account be allowed, even for purposes of self-defense. He abrogated the rule of the sword and annulled the ordinance of "Holy War." "If ye be slain," said He, "it is better for you than to slay. It is through the firmness and assurance of the faithful that the Cause of the Lord must be diffused. As the faithful, fearless and undaunted, arise with absolute detachment to exalt the Word of God, and, with eyes averted from the things of this world, engaged in service for the Lord's sake and by His power, thereby will they cause the Word of truth to triumph. These blessed souls bear witness by their lifeblood to the truth of the Cause and attest it by the sincerity of their faith, their devotion and their constancy. The Lord can avail to diffuse His Cause and to defeat the froward. We desire no defender but Him, and with our lives in our hands face the foe and welcome martyrdom" (written by 'Abdu'l-Bahá for this book).

Bahá'u'lláh wrote to one of the persecutors of His Cause:—

Gracious God! This people need no weapons of destruction, inasmuch as they have girded themselves to reconstruct the world. Their hosts are the hosts of goodly deeds, and their arms the arms of upright conduct, and their commander the fear of God. Blessed that one that judgeth with fairness. By the righteousness of God! Such hath been the patience, the calm, the resignation and contentment of this people that they have become the exponents of justice, and so great hath been their forbearance, that they have suffered themselves to be killed rather than kill, and this notwithstanding that these whom the world hath wronged have endured tribulations the like of which the history of the world hath never recorded, nor the eyes of any nation witnessed. What is it that could have induced them to reconcile themselves to these grievous trials, and to refuse to put forth a hand to repel them? What could have caused such resignation and serenity? The true cause is to be found in the ban which the Pen of Glory hath, day and night, chosen to impose, and in Our assumption of the reins of authority, through the power and might of Him Who is the Lord of all mankind.— *Epistle to the Son of the Wolf*, pp. 74-75.

The soundness of Bahá'u'lláh's nonresistance policy has already been proved by results. For every believer martyred in Persia, the Bahá'í Faith has received a hundred new believers into its fold, and the glad and dauntless way in which these martyrs cast the crowns of their lives at the feet of their Lord has furnished to the world the clearest proof that they had found a new life for which death has no terrors, a life of ineffable fullness and joy, compared with which the pleasures of earth are but as dust in the balance, and the most fiendish physical tortures but trifles light as air.

Righteous Warfare

Although Bahá'u'lláh, like Christ, counsels His followers as individuals and as a religious body to adopt an attitude of nonresistance and forgiveness toward their enemies, He teaches that it is the duty of the community to prevent injustice and oppression. If individuals are persecuted and injured it is right for them to forgive and abstain from retaliation, but it is wrong for a community to allow pillage and murder to continue unchecked within its borders. It is the duty of a good government to prevent wrongdoing and to punish offenders.[1] So also with the community of nations. If one nation oppresses or injures another, it is the duty of all other nations to unite to prevent such oppression. 'Abdu'l-Bahá writes:—"It may happen that at a given time warlike and savage tribes may furiously

---

[1] See also section on Treatment of Criminals, pp. 153-155.

attack the body politic with the intention of carrying on a wholesale slaughter of its members; under such a circumstance defense is necessary."—*Wisdom of 'Abdu'l-Bahá,* p. 170.

Hitherto the usual practice of mankind has been that if one nation attacked another, the rest of the nations of the world remained neutral, and accepted no responsibility in the matter unless their own interests were directly affected or threatened. The whole burden of defense was left to the nation attacked, however weak and helpless it might be. The teaching of Bahá'u'lláh reverses this position and throws the responsibility of defense not specially on the nation attacked, but on *all* the others, individually and collectively. As the whole of mankind is one community, an attack on any one nation is an attack on the community, and ought to be dealt with by the community. Were this doctrine generally recognized and acted on, any nation contemplating an aggression on another would know in advance that it would have to reckon with the opposition not of that other nation only, but of the whole of the rest of the world. This knowledge alone would be sufficient to deter even the boldest and most bellicose of nations. When a sufficiently strong league of peace-loving nations is established war will, therefore, become a thing of the past. During the period of transition from the old state of international anarchy to the new state of international solidarity, aggressive wars will still be possible, and in these circumstances, military or other coercive action in the cause of international justice, unity, and peace may be a positive duty. 'Abdu'l-Bahá writes that in such case:—

A conquest can be a praiseworthy thing, and there are times when war becomes the powerful basis of peace, and ruin the very means of reconstruction. If, for example, a high-minded sovereign marshals his troops to block the onset of the insurgent and the aggressor, or again, if he takes the field and distinguishes himself in a struggle to unify a divided state and people, if, in brief, he is waging war for a righteous purpose, then this seeming wrath is mercy itself, and this apparent tyranny the very substance

of justice and this warfare the cornerstone of peace. Today, the task befitting great rulers is to establish universal
peace, for in this lies the freedom of all peoples.—*The
Secret of Divine Civilization,* pp. 70-71.

Unity of East and West

Another factor which will help in bringing about universal
peace is the linking together of the East and the West. The
Most Great Peace is no mere cessation of hostilities, but a fertilizing union and cordial cooperation of the hitherto sundered
peoples of the earth which will bear much precious fruit. In
one of His talks in Paris, 'Abdu'l-Bahá said:—

> In the past, as in the present, the spiritual Sun of Truth
> has always shone from the horizon of the East. In the East
> Moses arose to lead and teach the people. On the Eastern
> horizon arose the Lord Christ. Muḥammad was sent to an
> Eastern nation. The Báb arose in the Eastern land of Per-
> sia. Bahá'u'lláh lived and taught in the East. All the great
> spiritual Teachers arose in the Eastern world.
>
> But although the Sun of Christ dawned in the East, the
> radiance thereof was apparent in the West, where the
> effulgence of its glory was more clearly seen. The divine
> light of His teaching shone with a greater force in the
> Western world, where it has made more rapid headway
> than in the land of its birth.
>
> In these days the East is in need of material progress
> and the West is in need of a spiritual ideal. It would be
> well for the West to turn to the East for illumination, and
> to give in exchange its scientific knowledge. There must
> be this interchange of gifts. The East and the West must
> unite to give to each other what is lacking. This union will
> bring about true civilization where the spiritual is ex-
> pressed and carried out in the material. Receiving thus,
> the one from the other, the greatest harmony will prevail,
> all people will be united, a state of great perfection will be
> attained, there will be a firm cementing, and this world

will become a shining mirror for the reflection of the attributes of God.

We all, the Eastern and the Western nations, must strive day and night, with heart and soul, to achieve this high ideal, to cement the unity between all the nations of the earth. Every heart will then be refreshed, all eyes will be opened, the most wonderful power will be given, the happiness of humanity will be assured. . . . This will be the Paradise which is to come on earth, when all mankind will be gathered together under the Tent of Unity in the Kingdom of Glory.—*Wisdom of 'Abdu'l-Bahá,* p. 17.

Various Ordinances and Teachings/11

Know thou that in every age and dispensation all divine ordinances are changed and transformed according to the requirement of the time, except the law of love, which, like a fountain, always flows and is never overtaken by change.—
BAHÁ'U'LLÁH.

Monastic Life

Bahá'u'lláh, like Muḥammad, forbids His followers to lead lives of monastic seclusion.

In the Tablet to Napoleon III we read:—

O concourse of monks! Seclude not yourselves in churches and cloisters. Come forth by My leave, and occupy yourselves with that which will profit your souls and the souls of men. . . . Enter ye into wedlock, that after you someone may fill your place. We have forbidden you perfidious acts, and not that which will demonstrate fidelity. Have ye clung to the standards fixed by your own selves, and cast the standards of God behind your backs? Fear God, and be not of the foolish. But for man, who would make mention of Me on My earth, and how could My attributes and My Name have been revealed? Ponder ye, and be not of them that are veiled and fast asleep. He that wedded not (Jesus) found no place wherein to dwell or lay His head, by reason of that which the hands of the treacherous had wrought. His sanctity consisteth not in that which ye believe or fancy, but rather in the things We possess. Ask, that ye may apprehend His station

175

which hath been exalted above the imaginings of all that
dwell on earth. Blessed are they who perceive it.

Does it not seem strange that Christian sects should have instituted the monastic life and celibacy for the clergy, in view of
the facts that Christ chose married men for His disciples, and
both He Himself and His apostles lived lives of active benefi-
cence, in close association and familiar intercourse with the
people?

In the Muḥammadan Qur'án we read:—

> To Jesus the son of Mary We gave the Gospel, and We
> put into the hearts of those who followed Him kindness
> and compassion: but as to the monastic life, they in-
> vented it themselves. The desire only of pleasing God did
> We prescribe to them, and this they observed not as it
> ought to have been observed.—Qur'án, s. lvii. 27.

Whatever justification there may have been for the monastic
life in ancient times and bygone circumstances, Bahá'u'lláh
declares that such justification no longer exists; and, indeed, it
seems obvious that the withdrawal of a large number of the
most pious and God-fearing of the population from association with their fellows, and from the duties and responsibilities
of parenthood, must result in the spiritual impoverishment of
the race.

Marriage

The Bahá'í teachings enjoin monogamy, and Bahá'u'lláh
makes marriage conditional on the consent of both parties and
of their parents. He says in the *Book of Aqdas:*—

> Verily in the *Book of Bayán* (the Báb's Revelation)
> the matter is restricted to the consent of both (bride and
> bridegroom). As We desired to bring about love and
> friendship and the unity of the people, therefore We made

it conditional upon the consent of the parents also, that enmity and ill-feeling might be avoided.—*Kitáb-i-Aqdas.*

On this point 'Abdu'l-Bahá wrote to an inquirer:—"As to the question of marriage, according to the law of God: First you must select one, and then it depends on the consent of the father and mother. Before your selection they have no right of interference."—*Tablets of 'Abdu'l-Bahá,* vol. iii, p. 563.

'Abdu'l-Bahá says that as a result of this precaution of Bahá'u'lláh's the strained relations between relatives-in-law which have become proverbial in Christian and Muḥammadan countries are almost unknown among the Bahá':s, and divorce is also of very rare occurrence. He writes on the subject of matrimony:—

Bahá'í marriage is union and cordial affection between the two parties. They must, however, exercise the utmost care and become acquainted with each other's character. This eternal bond should be made secure by a firm covenant, and the intention should be to foster harmony, fellowship and unity and to attain everlasting life. . . .

"In a true Bahá'í marriage the two parties must become fully united both spiritually and physically, so that they may attain eternal union throughout all the worlds of God, and improve the spiritual life of each other. This is Bahá'í matrimony.—*Tablets of 'Abdu'l-Bahá.*

The Bahá'í marriage ceremony is very simple, the only requirement being that the groom and the bride, in the presence of at least two witnesses, each says, "We will all, verily, abide by the will of God."

Divorce

In the matter of divorce, as in that of marriage, the instructions of the Prophets have varied in accordance with the circumstances of the times. 'Abdu'l-Bahá states the Bahá'í teaching, with regard to divorce, thus:—

The friends (Bahá'ís) must strictly refrain from divorce unless something arises which compels them to separate because of their aversion for each other; in that case, with the knowledge of the Spiritual Assembly, they may decide to separate. They must then be patient and wait one complete year. If during this year harmony is not reestablished between them, then their divorce may be realized. . . . The foundation of the Kingdom of God is based upon harmony and love, oneness, relationship and union, not upon differences, especially between husband and wife. If one of these two become the cause of divorce, that one will unquestionably fall into great difficulties, will become the victim of formidable calamities and experience deep remorse (Tablet to the Bahá'ís of America).

In the matter of divorce, as in other matters, Bahá'ís will, of course, be bound not only by the Bahá'í teaching, but also by the laws of the country in which they live.

The Bahá'í Calendar

Among different peoples and at different times many different methods have been adopted for the measurement of time and fixing of dates, and several different calendars are still in daily use, e.g., the Gregorian in Western Europe, the Julian in many countries of Eastern Europe, the Hebrew among the Jews, and the Muḥammadan in Muslim communities.

The Báb signalized the importance of the Dispensation which He came to herald by inaugurating a new calendar. In this, as in the Gregorian Calendar, the lunar month is abandoned and the solar year is adopted.

The Bahá'í year consists of 19 months of 19 days each (i.e. 361 days), with the addition of certain "Intercalary Days" (four in ordinary and five in leap years) between the eighteenth and nineteenth months in order to adjust the calendar to the solar year. The Báb named the months after the attributes of God. The Bahá'í New Year, like the ancient Persian New Year, is astronomically fixed, commencing at the March equinox (usually March 21), and the Bahá'í Era commences with the year of the Báb's declaration (i.e. A.D. 1844, A.H. 1260).

In the not far distant future it will be necessary that all peoples in the world agree on a common calendar.

It seems, therefore, fitting that the new age of unity should have a new calendar free from the objections and associations which make each of the older calendars unacceptable to large sections of the world's population, and it is difficult to see how any other arrangement could exceed in simplicity and convenience that proposed by the Báb.

The months in the Bahá'í Calendar are as follows:—

	Arabic-Name	Translation	First Days
1st	Bahá	Splendor	March 21
2nd	Jalál	Glory	April 9
3rd	Jamál	Beauty	April 28
4th	'Azamat	Grandeur	May 17
5th	Núr	Light	June 5
6th	Rahmat	Mercy	June 24
7th	Kalimát	Words	July 13
8th	Kamál	Perfection	Aug. 1
9th	Asmá'	Names	Aug. 20
10th	'Izzat	Might	Sept. 8
11th	Mashíyyat	Will	Sept. 27
12th	'Ilm	Knowledge	Oct. 16
13th	Qudrat	Power	Nov. 4
14th	Qawl	Speech	Nov. 23
15th	Masá'il	Questions	Dec. 12
16th	Sharaf	Honor	Dec. 31
17th	Sultán	Sovereignty	Jan. 19
18th	Mulk	Dominion	Feb. 7
	Intercalary Days	Feb. 26 to March 1,	inclusive.
19th	'Alá'	Loftiness	March 2

Spiritual Assemblies

Before 'Abdu'l-Bahá completed His earthly mission, He had laid a basis for the development of the administrative order established in Bahá'u'lláh's Writings. To show the high importance to be attributed to the institution of the spiritual assembly, 'Abdu'l-Bahá in a Tablet declared that a certain translation must be approved by the Spiritual Assembly of Cairo before publication, even though He Himself had reviewed and corrected the text.

By spiritual assembly is meant the administrative body of nine persons, elected annually by each local Bahá'í community, in which is vested the authority of decision on all matters of mutual action on the part of the community. This designation is temporary, since in future the spiritual assemblies will be termed Houses of Justice.

Unlike the organization of churches, these Bahá'í bodies are social rather than ecclesiastical institutions. That is, they apply the law of consultation to all questions and difficulties arising between Bahá'ís, who are called upon not to carry them to the civil court, and seek to promote unity as well as justice throughout the community. The spiritual assembly is in no wise equivalent to the priest or clergy, but is responsible for upholding the teachings, stimulating active service, conducting meetings, maintaining unity, holding Bahá'í property in trust for the community, and representing it in its relations to the public and to other Bahá'í communities.

The nature of the spiritual assembly, local and national, is described more fully in the section devoted to the Will and Testament of 'Abdu'l-Bahá in the final chapter, but its general functions have been defined by Shoghi Effendi as follows:—

The matter of teaching, its direction, its ways and means, its extension, its consolidation, essential as they are to the interests of the Cause, constitute by no means the only issue which should receive the full attention of these assemblies. A careful study of Bahá'u'lláh's and 'Abdu'l-Bahá's Tablets will reveal that other duties, no less vital to the interests of the Cause, devolve upon the elected representatives of the friends in every locality.

It is incumbent upon them to be vigilant and cautious, discreet and watchful, and protect at all times the Temple of the Cause from the dart of the mischief-maker and the onslaught of the enemy.

They must endeavor to promote amity and concord amongst the friends, efface every lingering trace of distrust, coolness and estrangement from every heart, and secure in its stead an active and wholehearted cooperation for the service of the Cause.

They must do their utmost to extend at all times the helping hand to the poor, the sick, the disabled, the orphan, the widow, irrespective of color, caste and creed.

They must promote by every means in their power the material as well as spiritual enlightenment of youth, the means for the education of children, institute, whenever possible, Bahá'í educational institutions, organize and supervise their work and provide the best means for their progress and development. . . .

They must undertake the arrangement of the regular meetings of the friends, the feasts and anniversaries, as well as the special gatherings designed to serve and promote the social, intellectual and spiritual interests of their fellowmen.

They must supervise in these days when the Cause is still in its infancy all Bahá'í publications and translations, and provide in general for a dignified and accurate presentation of all Bahá'í literature and its distribution to the general public.

The possibilities inherent in Bahá'í institutions can only be estimated when one realizes how rapidly modern civilization is disintegrating for lack of that spiritual power which can alone supply the necessary attitude of responsibility and humility to the leaders and the requisite loyalty to the individual members of society.

Bahá'í Feasts, Anniversaries, and Days of Fasting

Feast of Naw-Rúz (Bahá'í New Year), March 21.
Feast of Riḍván (Declaration of Bahá'u'lláh), April 21– May 2.

Declaration of the Báb, May 23.[1]
Ascension of Bahá'u'lláh, May 29.
Martyrdom of the Báb, July 9.
Birth of the Báb, October 20.
Birth of Bahá'u'lláh, November 12.
Day of the Covenant, November 26.
Ascension of 'Abdu'l-Bahá, November 28.
Period of the Fast, nineteen days beginning March 2.

Feasts

The essential joyousness of the Bahá'í religion finds expression in numerous feasts and holidays throughout the year. In a talk on the Feast of Naw-Rúz, in Alexandria, Egypt, in 1912, 'Abdu'l-Bahá said:—

In the sacred laws of God, in every cycle and dispensation there are blessed feasts, holidays and workless days. On such days all kinds of occupations, commerce, industry, agriculture, et cetera, should be suspended.

All should rejoice together, hold general meetings, become as one assembly, so that the national oneness, unity and harmony may be demonstrated in the eyes of all.

As it is a blessed day it should not be neglected, nor deprived of results by making it a day devoted to the pursuit of mere pleasure.

During such days institutions should be founded that may be of permanent benefit and value to the people. . . .

Today there is no result or fruit greater than guiding the people. Undoubtedly the friends of God, upon such a day, must leave tangible philanthropic or ideal traces that should reach all mankind and not pertain only to the Bahá'ís. In this wonderful Dispensation, philanthropic affairs are for all humanity without exception, because it is the manifestation of the mercifulness of God. Therefore,

---

[1] This date coincides with the birth of 'Abdu'l-Bahá.

My hope is that the friends of God, every one of them, may become as the mercy of God to all mankind.

The Feasts of Naw-Rúz (New Year) and Riḍván, the anniversaries of the birth of the Báb and Bahá'u'lláh, and of the Báb's Declaration (which is also the birthday of 'Abdu'l-Bahá), are the great joy-days of the year for Bahá'ís. In Persia they are celebrated by picnics or festal gatherings at which music, the chanting of verses and tablets, and short addresses suitable to the occasion are contributed by those present. The intercalary days between the eighteenth and nineteenth months (that is, February 26 to March 1 inclusive) are specially devoted to hospitality to friends, the giving of presents, ministering to the poor and sick, et cetera.

The anniversaries of the martyrdom of the Báb and the departure of Bahá'u'lláh and 'Abdu'l-Bahá are celebrated with solemnity by appropriate meetings and discourses, the chanting of prayers and tablets.

Fast

The nineteenth month, following immediately on the hospitality of the intercalary days, is the month of the fast. During nineteen days the fast is observed by abstaining from both food and drink from sunrise to sunset. As the month of the fast ends at the March equinox, the fast always falls in the same season, namely, spring in the Northern, and autumn in the Southern, Hemisphere; never in the extreme heat of summer nor in the extreme cold of winter, when hardship would be likely to result. At that season, moreover, the interval between sunrise and sunset is approximately the same all over the habitable portion of the globe, namely, from about 6 A.M. to 6 P.M. The fast is not binding on children and invalids, on travelers, or on those who are too old or too weak (including women who are with child or have babes at the breast).

There is much evidence to show that a periodical fast such as is enjoined by the Bahá'í teachings is beneficial as a measure of physical hygiene, but just as the reality of the Bahá'í feast does not lie in the consumption of physical food, but in the commemoration of God, which is our spiritual food, so the reality of the Bahá'í fast does not consist in abstention from physical food, although that may help in the purification of the body, but in the abstention from the desires and lusts of the flesh, and in severance from all save God. 'Abdu'l-Bahá says:—

Fasting is a symbol. Fasting signifies abstinence from lust. Physical fasting is a symbol of that abstinence, and is a reminder; that is, just as a person abstains from physical appetites, he is to abstain from self-appetites and self-desires. But mere abstention from food has no effect on the spirit. It is only a symbol, a reminder. Otherwise it is of no importance. Fasting for this purpose does not mean entire abstinence from food. The golden rule as to food is, do not take too much or too little. Moderation is necessary. There is a sect in India who practice extreme abstinence, and gradually reduce their food until they exist on almost nothing. But their intelligence suffers. A man is not fit to do service for God with brain or body if he is weakened by lack of food. He cannot see clearly (quoted by Miss E. S. Stevens in *Fortnightly Review,* June 1911).

Meetings

'Abdu'l-Bahá attaches the greatest importance to regular meetings of the believers for united worship, for the exposition and study of the teachings, and for consultation regarding the progress of the Movement. In one of His Tablets He says:—

It hath been decided by the Desire of God that union and harmony may day by day increase among the friends of God and the handmaids of the Merciful. Not until this is realized will the affairs advance by any means whatever! And the greatest means for the union and harmony of all are spiritual meetings. This matter is very impor-

tant and is as a magnet to attract divine confirmation.—
Tablets of 'Abdu'l-Bahá, vol. i, pp. 124-25.

In the spiritual meetings of Bahá'ís contentious argument
and the discussion of political or worldly affairs must be
avoided; *the sole aim of the believers should be to teach and
learn divine truth,* to have their hearts filled with divine love,
to attain more perfect obedience to the divine will, and to promote the coming of the Kingdom of God. In an address given
at New York in 1912, 'Abdu'l-Bahá said:—

The Bahá'í meeting must be the meeting of the Celestial Concourse. It must be illumined by the lights of the
Celestial Concourse. The hearts must be as mirrors
wherein the lights of the Sun of Truth shall be revealed.
Every bosom must be as a telegraph station: one terminal
of the wire shall be in the bosom of the soul, the other in
the Celestial Concourse, so that messages may be ex-
changed between them. In this way from the Abhá Kingdom inspiration shall flow and in all discussions harmony
shall prevail. . . . The more agreement, unity and love
prevail among you, the more shall the confirmations of
God assist you, and the help and aid of the Blessed
Beauty, Bahá'u'lláh, support you.

In one of His Tablets He said:—

In these meetings outside conversation must be entirely
avoided, and the gathering must be confined to chanting
the verses and reading the words, and to matters which
concern the Cause of God, such as explaining proofs, ad-
ducing clear and manifest evidences, and tracing the
signs of the Beloved One of the creatures. Those who attend the meeting must, before entering, be arrayed with
the utmost cleanliness and turn to the Abhá Kingdom,
and then enter the meeting with all meekness and hum-
bleness; and while the Tablets are being read, must be
quiet and silent; and if one wishes to speak he must do so

with all courtesy, with the satisfaction and permission of those present, and do it with eloquence and fluency.

The Nineteen Day Feast

With the development of the Bahá'í Administrative Order since the ascension of 'Abdu'l-Bahá, the Nineteen Day Feast, observed on the first day of each Bahá'í month, has assumed a very special importance, providing as it does not only for community prayer and reading from the Holy Books, but also for general consultation on all current Bahá'í affairs and for the association of the friends together. This Feast is the occasion when the spiritual assembly makes its reports to the community and invites both discussion of plans and suggestions for new and better methods of service.

Mashriqu'l-Adhkár [1]

Bahá'u'lláh left instructions that temples of worship should be built by his followers in every country and city. To these temples He gave the name of "Mashriqu'l-Adhkár," which means "Dawning-Place of God's Praise." The Mashriqu'l-Adhkár is to be a nine-sided building surmounted by a dome, and as beautiful as possible in design and workmanship. It is to stand in a large garden adorned with fountains, trees, and flowers, surrounded by a number of accessory buildings devoted to educational, charitable, and social purposes, so that the worship of God in the temple may always be closely associated with reverent delight in the beauties of nature and of art, and with practical work for the amelioration of social conditions.[2]

---

[1] (Pronounced Azkar).

[2] In connection with the Mashriqu'l-Adhkár it is interesting to recall Tennyson's lines:—

> "I dreamed
> That stone by stone I reared a sacred fane,
> A temple, neither Pagod, Mosque nor Church,
> But loftier, simpler, always open-doored
> To every breath from heaven, and Truth and Peace
> And Love and Justice came and dwelt therein."
>
> *Akbar's Dream*, 1892

In Persia, up till the present, Bahá'ís have been debarred from building temples for public worship, and so the first great Mashriqu'l-Adhkár was built in 'Ishqábád,[1] Russia. 'Abdu'l-Bahá dedicated the site of the second Bahá'í House of Worship, to stand on the shore of Lake Michigan a few miles north of Chicago, during His visit to America in 1912.[2] In Tablets referring to this "Mother Temple" of the West, 'Abdu'l-Bahá writes as follows:—

> Praise be to God, that, at this moment, from every country in the world, according to their various means, contributions are continually being sent toward the fund of the Mashriqu'l-Adhkár in America. . . . From the day of Adam until now, such a thing has never been witnessed by man, that from the furthermost country of Asia contributions were forwarded to America. This is through the power of the Covenant of God. Verily this is a cause of astonishment for the people of perception. It is hoped that the believers of God may show magnanimity and raise a great sum for the building. . . . I want everyone left free to act as he wills. If anyone wishes to put money into other things, let him do so. Do not interfere with him in any way, but be assured the most important thing at this time is the building of the Mashriqu'l-Adhkár.
>
> The mystery of the edifice is great, and cannot be unveiled yet, but its erection is the most important undertaking of this day. The Mashriqu'l-Adhkár has important accessories, which are accounted of the basic foundations. These are: school for orphan children, hospital and dispensary for the poor, home for the incapable, college for the higher scientific education, and hospice. In every city a great Mashriqu'l-Adhkár must be founded after this or-

---

[1] This first House of Worship was seriously damaged in an earthquake in 1948 and had to be demolished some years later.

[2] This temple was completed in 1953. Since then other Bahá'í temples have been constructed in Kampala, Uganda; Sydney, Australia; Frankfurt, Germany; and one is under construction near the city of Panama. At the present time, 1969, sites for fifty others have been purchased. (See Epilogue)

der. In the Ma<u>sh</u>riqu'l-A<u>dh</u>kár services will be held every morning. There will be no organ in the temple. In buildings nearby, festivals, services, conventions, public meetings and spiritual gatherings will be held, but in the temple the chanting and singing will be unaccompanied. Open ye the gates of the temple to all mankind.

When these institutions, college, hospital, hospice and establishment for the incurables, university for the study of higher sciences, giving post-graduate courses, and other philanthropic buildings are built, the doors will be opened to all the nations and religions. There will be absolutely no line of demarcation drawn. Its charities will be dispensed irrespective of color or race. Its gates will be flung wide open to mankind; prejudice towards none, love for all. The central building will be devoted to the purpose of prayer and worship. Thus . . . religion will become harmonized with science, and science will be the handmaid of religion, both showering their material and spiritual gifts on all humanity.

Life After Death

Bahá'u'lláh tells us that the life in the flesh is but the embryonic stage of our existence, and that escape from the body is like a new birth through which the human spirit enters on a fuller, freer life. He writes:—

Know thou of a truth that the soul, after its separation from the body, will continue to progress until it attaineth the presence of God, in a state and condition which neither the revolution of ages and centuries, nor the changes and chances of this world, can alter. It will endure as long as the Kingdom of God, His sovereignty, His dominion and power will endure. It will manifest the signs of God and His attributes, and will reveal His loving-kindness and bounty. The movement of My pen is stilled when it attempteth to befittingly describe the loftiness and glory of so exalted a station. The honor with which the Hand of

Mercy will invest the soul is such as no tongue can adequately reveal, nor any other earthly agency describe. Blessed is the soul which, at the hour of its separation from the body, is sanctified from the vain imaginings of the peoples of the world. Such a soul liveth and moveth in accordance with the will of its Creator, and entereth the all-highest Paradise. The Maids of Heaven, inmates of the loftiest mansions, will circle around it, and the Prophets of God and His chosen ones will seek its companionship. With them that soul will freely converse, and will recount unto them that which it hath been made to endure in the path of God, the Lord of all worlds. If any man be told that which hath been ordained for such a soul in the worlds of God, the Lord of the throne on high and of earth below, his whole being will instantly blaze out in his great longing to attain that most exalted, that sanctified and resplendent station. . . . The nature of the soul after death can never be described, nor is it meet and permissible to reveal its whole character to the eyes of men. The Prophets and Messengers of God have been sent down for the sole purpose of guiding mankind to the straight path of truth. The purpose underlying Their Revelation hath been to educate all men, that they may, at the hour of death, ascend, in the utmost purity and sanctity and with absolute detachment, to the throne of the Most High. The light which these souls radiate is responsible for the progress of the world and the advancement of its peoples. They are like unto leaven which leaveneth the world of being, and constitute the animating force through which the arts and wonders of the world are made manifest. Through them the clouds rain their bounty upon men, and the earth bringeth forth its fruits. All things must needs have a cause, a motive power, an animating principle. These souls and symbols of detachment have provided, and will continue to provide, the supreme moving impulse in the world of being. The world beyond is as different from this world as this world is different from that of the child while still in the womb of

its mother.—*Gleanings from the Writings of Bahá'u'lláh,*
pp. 155-157.

Similarly 'Abdu'l-Bahá writes:—

The mysteries of which man is heedless in the earthly
world, those will he discover in the heavenly world, and
there will he be informed of the secrets of the truth; how
much more will he recognize or discover persons with
whom he has been associated. Undoubtedly the holy souls
who find a pure eye and are favored with insight will, in
the kingdom of lights, be acquainted with all mysteries,
and will seek the bounty of witnessing the reality of every
great soul. They will even manifestly behold the Beauty
of God in that world. Likewise will they find all the
friends of God, both those of the former and recent times,
present in the heavenly assemblage.

The difference and distinction between men will naturally become realized after their departure from this mortal world. But this distinction is not in respect to place,
but in respect to the soul and conscience. For the Kingdom of God is sanctified (or free) from time and place;
it is another world and another universe. And know
thou for a certainty that in the divine worlds the spiritual
beloved ones will recognize one another, and will seek
union with each other, but a spiritual union. Likewise a
love that one may have entertained for anyone will not be
forgotten in the world of the Kingdom, nor wilt thou forget there the life that thou hadst in the material world.—
Tablets of 'Abdu'l-Bahá, vol. i, p. 205.

Heaven and Hell

Bahá'u'lláh and 'Abdu'l-Bahá regard the descriptions of
heaven and hell given in some of the older religious writings
as symbolic, like the Biblical story of the Creation, and not as
literally true. According to Them, heaven is the state of perfection, and hell that of imperfection; heaven is harmony with
God's will and with our fellows, and hell is the want of such

harmony; heaven is the condition of spiritual life, and hell that of spiritual death. A man may be either in heaven or in hell while still in the body. The joys of heaven are spiritual joys, and the pains of hell consist in the deprivation of these joys. 'Abdu'l-Bahá says:—

When they (men) are delivered through the light of faith from the darkness of these vices, and become illuminated with the radiance of the sun of reality, and ennobled with all the virtues, they esteem this the greatest reward, and they know it to be the true paradise. In the same way they consider that the spiritual punishment . . . is to be subjected to the world of nature, to be veiled from God, to be brutal and ignorant, to fall into carnal lusts, to be absorbed in animal frailties, to be characterized with dark qualities . . . these are the greatest punishments and tortures. . . .

The rewards of the other world are the perfections and the peace obtained in the spiritual worlds after leaving this world . . . the spiritual graces, the various spiritual gifts in the Kingdom of God, the gaining of the desires of the heart and the soul, and the meeting of God in the world of eternity. In the same way, the punishments of the other world . . . consist in being deprived of the special divine blessings and the absolute bounties, and falling into the lowest degrees of existence. He who is deprived of these divine favors, although he continues after death, is considered as dead by the people of truth.

The wealth of the other world is nearness to God. Consequently it is certain that those who are near the Divine Court are allowed to intercede, and this intercession is approved by God. . . .

It is even possible that the condition of those who have died in sin and unbelief may become changed; that is to say, they may become the object of pardon through the bounty of God, not through His justice; for bounty is giving without desert, and justice is giving what is deserved. As we have power to pray for these souls here, so likewise we shall possess the same power in the other world, which is the Kingdom of God. . . . Therefore in that world also they can make progress. As here they can receive light by their supplications, there also they can plead for forgiveness, and receive light through entreaties and supplications.

Both before and after putting off this material form, there is progress in perfection, but not in state. . . . There is no other being higher than a perfect man. But man when he has reached this state can still make progress in perfections but not in state, because there is no state higher than that of a perfect man to which he can transfer himself. He only progresses in the state of humanity, for the human perfections are infinite. Thus, however learned a man may be, we can imagine one more learned.

Hence, as the perfections of humanity are endless, man can also make progress in perfections after leaving this world. *Some Answered Questions,* pp. 260, 261, 268, 269, 274.

Oneness of the Two Worlds

The unity of humanity as taught by Bahá'u'lláh refers not only to men still in the flesh, but to all human beings, whether embodied or disembodied. Not only all men now living on the earth, but all in the spiritual world as well, are parts of one and the same organism and these two parts are intimately dependent, one on the other. Spiritual communion one with the other, far from being impossible or unnatural, is constant and inevitable. Those whose spiritual faculties are as yet undeveloped are unconscious of this vital connection, but as one's faculties develop, communications with those beyond the veil gradually becomes more conscious and definite. To the Prophets and saints this spiritual communion is as familiar and real as are ordinary vision and conversation to the rest of mankind.

'Abdu'l-Bahá says:—

The visions of the Prophets are not dreams; no, they are spiritual discoveries and have reality. They say, for example: "I saw a person in a certain form, and I said such a thing, and he gave such an answer." This vision is in the world of wakefulness, and not in that of sleep. Nay, it is a spiritual discovery. . . .

Among spiritual souls there are spiritual understandings, discoveries, a communion which is purified from imagination and fancy, an association which is sanctified from time and place. So it is written in the Gospel that on Mount Tabor, Moses and Elias came to Christ, and it is evident that this was not a material meeting. It was a spiritual condition. . . .

[Communications such as] these are real, and produce wonderful effects in the minds and thoughts of men, and cause their hearts to be attracted.—*Some Answered Questions,* pp. 290, 291, 292.

While admitting the reality of "supernormal" psychic faculties, He deprecates attempts to force their development prematurely. These faculties will unfold naturally when the right time comes, if we only follow the path of spiritual progress which the Prophets have traced for us. He says:—

To tamper with psychic forces while in this world interferes with the condition of the soul in the world to come. These forces are real, but, normally, are not active on this plane. The child in the womb has its eyes, ears, hands, feet, etc., but they are not in activity. The whole purpose of life in the material world is the coming forth into the world of reality, where those forces will become active. They belong to that world (from Miss Buckton's notes, revised by 'Abdu'l-Bahá).

Intercourse with spirits of the departed ought not to be sought for its own sake, nor in order to gratify idle curiosity. It is both a privilege and duty, however, for those on one side of the veil to love and help and pray for those on the other. Prayers for the dead are enjoined on Bahá'ís. 'Abdu'l-Bahá said to Miss E. J. Rosenberg in 1904: The grace of effective intercession is one of the perfections belonging to advanced souls, as well as to the Manifestations of God. Jesus Christ had the power of interceding for the forgiveness of His enemies when on earth, and He certainly has this power now. 'Abdu'l-Bahá never mentions the name of a dead person without saying "May God forgive him!" or words to that effect. Followers of the Prophets have also this power of praying for the forgiveness of souls. Therefore we may not think that any souls are condemned to a stationary condition of suffering or loss arising from absolute ignorance of God. The power of effective intercession for them always exists.

The rich in the other world can help the poor, as the rich can help the poor here. In every world all are the creatures of God. They are always dependent on Him. They are not independent and can never be so. While they are needful of God, the more they supplicate, the richer they become. What is their merchandise, their wealth? In the other world what is help and assistance? It is intercession. Undeveloped souls must gain progress at first through the supplications of the spiritually rich; afterwards they can progress through their own supplications.

Again He says:—"Those who have ascended have different attributes from those who are still on earth, yet there is no real separation. In prayer there is a mingling of station, a mingling of condition. Pray for them as they pray for you."—*'Abdu'l-Bahá in London,* p. 97.

Asked whether it was possible through faith and love to bring the new Revelation to the knowledge of those who have departed from this life without hearing of it, 'Abdu'l-Bahá replied:—"Yes, surely! since sincere prayer always has its effect, and it has a great influence in the other world. We are never cut off from those who are there. The real and genuine influence is not in this world but in that other."—*Notes of Mary Hanford Ford:* Paris, 1911.

On the other hand, Bahá'u'lláh writes:—

He who lives according to what was ordained for him —the Celestial Concourse, and the people of the Supreme

Paradise, and those who are dwelling in the Dome of Greatness will pray for him, by a command from God, the Dearest and the Praiseworthy (Tablet translated by 'Alí Kulí Khán).

When 'Abdu'l-Bahá was asked how it was that the heart often turns with instinctive appeal to some friend who has passed into the next life, He answered:—"It is a law of God's creation that the weak should lean upon the strong. Those to whom you turn may be mediators of God's power to you, even as when on earth, but it is the one Holy Spirit which strengthens all men."—*'Abdu'l-Bahá in London,* p. 97.

The Nonexistence of Evil

According to Bahá'í philosophy it follows from the doctrine of the unity of God that there can be no such thing as positive evil. There can only be one Infinite. If there were any other power in the universe outside of or opposed to the One, then the One would not be infinite. Just as darkness is but the absence or lesser degree of light, so evil is but the absence or lesser degree of good—the undeveloped state. A bad man is a man with the higher side of his nature still undeveloped. If he is selfish, the evil is not in his love of self—all love, even self-love, is good, is divine. The evil is that he has such a poor, inadequate, misguided love of self and such a lack of love for others and for God. He looks upon himself as only a superior sort of animal, and foolishly pampers his lower nature as he might pamper a pet dog—with worse results in his own case than in that of the dog.

In one of His letters 'Abdu'l-Bahá says:—

As to thy remark, that 'Abdu'l-Bahá hath said to some of the believers that evil never exists, nay rather, it is a nonexistent thing, this is but truth, inasmuch as the greatest evil is man's going astray and being veiled from truth. Error is lack of guidance; darkness is absence of light; ignorance is lack of knowledge; falsehood is lack of truthfulness; blindness is lack of sight; and deafness is lack of hearing. Therefore, error, blindness, deafness and ignorance are nonexistent things.

Again He says:—

In creation there is no evil; all is good. Certain qualities and natures innate in some men and apparently blameworthy are not so in reality. For example, from the beginning of his life you can see in a nursing child the signs of desire, of anger, and of temper. Then, it may be said, good and evil are innate in the reality of man, and this is contrary to the pure goodness of nature and creation. The answer to this is that desire, which is to ask for something more, is a praiseworthy quality provided that it is used suitably. So, if a man has the desire to acquire science and knowledge, or to become compassionate, generous, and just, it is most praiseworthy. If he exercises his anger and wrath against the bloodthirsty tyrants who are like ferocious beasts, it is very praiseworthy; but if he does not use these qualities in a right way, they are blameworthy. . . .

It is the same with all the natural qualities of man, which constitute the capital of life; if they be used and displayed in an unlawful way, they become blameworthy. Therefore it is clear that creation is purely good.—*Some Answered Questions*, pp. 250, 251.

Evil is always lack of life. If the lower side of man's nature is disproportionately developed, the remedy is not less life for that side, but *more* life for the higher side, so that the balance may be restored. "I am come," said Christ, "that ye may have life and that ye may have it more abundantly." That is what we all need—life, more life, the life that is life indeed! Bahá'u'lláh's Message is the same as Christ's. "Today," He says, "this Servant has assuredly come to vivify the world" (*Tablet to Ra'ís*), and to His followers He says: "Come ye after Me, that We may make you to become quickeners of mankind." (*Tablet to the Pope.*)

Religion and Science/12

'Alí, the son-in-law of Muhammad, said: "That which is in conformity with science is also in conformity with religion." Whatever the intelligence of man cannot understand, religion ought not to accept. Religion and science walk hand in hand, and any religion contrary to science is not the truth.—'ABDU'L-BAHÁ, *Wisdom of 'Abdu'l-Bahá.*

Conflict Due to Error

One of the fundamental teachings of Bahá'u'lláh is that true science and true religion must always be in harmony. Truth is one, and whenever conflict appears it is due, not to truth, but to error. Between so-called science and so-called religion there have been fierce conflicts all down the ages, but looking back on these conflicts in the light of fuller truth we can trace them every time to ignorance, prejudice, vanity, greed, narrow-mindedness, intolerance, obstinacy, or something of the kind— something foreign to the true spirit of both science and religion, for the spirit of both is one. As Huxley tells us, "The great deeds of philosophers have been less the fruit of their intellect than the direction of that intellect by an eminently religious tone of mind. Truth has yielded herself rather to their patience, their love, their single-heartedness and self-denial than to their logical acumen." Boole, the mathematician, assures us that "geometric induction is essentially a process of prayer—an appeal from the finite mind to the Infinite for light on finite concerns." The great prophets of religion and science have never denounced each other. It is the unworthy followers of these great world teachers—worshipers of the letter but not of the spirit of their teaching—who have always been the persecutors of the later prophets and the bitterest opponents of progress. They have studied the light of the particular revela-

197

tion which they hold sacred, and have defined its properties and peculiarities as seen by their limited vision, with the utmost care and precision. That is for them the one true light. If God in His infinite bounty sends fuller light from another quarter, and the torch of inspiration burns brighter than before from a new torchholder, instead of welcoming the new light and worshiping with renewed gratitude the Father of all lights they are angry and alarmed. This new light does not correspond with their definitions. It has not the orthodox color, and does not shine from the orthodox place, therefore it must at all costs be extinguished lest it lead men astray into the paths of heresy! Many enemies of the Prophets are of this type—blind leaders of the blind, who oppose new and fuller truth in the supposed interests of what they believe to be *the* truth. Others are of baser sort and are moved by selfish interests to fight against truth, or else block the path of progress by reason of spiritual deadness and inertia.

Persecution of Prophets

The great Prophets of religion have always been, at Their coming, despised and rejected of men. Both They and Their early followers have given their backs to the smiters and sacrificed their possessions and their lives in the path of God. Even in our own times this has been so. Since A.D. 1844, many thousands of Bábís and Bahá'ís in Persia have suffered cruel deaths for their faith, and many more have borne imprisonment, exile, poverty, and degradation. The latest of the great religions has been "baptized in blood" more than its predecessors, and martyrdoms have continued down to the present day. With the prophets of science the same thing has happened. Giordano Bruno was burned as a heretic in A.D. 1600 for teaching, amongst other things, that the earth moved around the sun. A few years later the veteran philosopher Galileo had to abjure the same doctrine on his knees in order to escape a similar fate. In later times, Darwin and the pioneers of modern geology were vehemently denounced for daring to dispute the teaching of Holy Writ that the world was made in six days, and less than six thousand years ago! The opposition to new scientific truth has not all come from the Church, however. The orthodox in science have been just as hostile to progress as the orthodox in religion. Columbus was laughed to scorn by the so-called scientists of his day, who proved to their own satisfaction that if ships did succeed in getting down to the Antipodes over the side of the globe, it would be absolutely impossible for them to get up again! Galvani, the pioneer of electrical science, was scoffed at by his learned colleagues, and called the "frogs' dancing master." Harvey, who discovered the circulation of the blood, was ridiculed and persecuted by his professional brethren on account of his heresy and driven from his lecture chair. When Stephenson invented his locomotive engine, European mathematicians of the time, instead of opening their eyes and studying the facts, continued for years to prove to their own satisfaction that an engine on smooth rails could never pull a load, as the wheels would simply slip round and the train make no progress. To examples like these one might add indefinitely, both from ancient and modern history, and even from our own times. Dr. Zamenhof, the inventor of Esperanto, had to battle for his wonderful international language against the same sort of ridicule, contempt, and stupid opposition which greeted Columbus, Galvani, and Stephenson. Even Esperanto, which was given to the world so recently as 1887, has had its martyrs.

The Dawn of Reconciliation

In the last half century or so, however, a change has come over the spirit of the times, a new Light of Truth has arisen which has already made the controversies of last century seem strangely out of date. Where are now the boastful materialists and dogmatic atheists who, only a few short years ago, were threatening to drive religion out of the world? And where are the preachers who so confidently consigned those who did not accept their dogmas to the fires of hell and the tortures of the damned? Echoes of their clamor we may still hear, but their day is fast declining and their doctrines are being discredited.

We can see now that the doctrines around which their controversies waxed most bitter were neither true science nor true
religion. What scientist in the light of modern psychical research could still maintain that "brain secretes thought as the
liver secretes bile"? Or that decay of the body is necessarily
accompanied by decay of the soul? We now see that thought
to be really free must soar to the realms of psychical and
spiritual phenomena and not be confined to the material only.
We realize that what we now know about nature is but as a
drop in the ocean compared with what remains to be discovered. We therefore freely admit the possibility of miracles,
not indeed in the sense of the breaking of nature's laws, but as
manifestations of the operation of subtle forces which are still
unknown to us, as electricity and X rays were to our ancestors.
On the other hand, who amongst our leading religious teachers
would still declare it is necessary to salvation to believe that
the world was made in six days, or that the description of the
plagues of Egypt as given in the Book of Exodus is literally
true, or that the sun stood still in the heavens (that is, that the
earth stopped its rotation) to let Joshua pursue his enemies,
or that if a man accept not the creed of St. Athanasius, "without doubt he shall perish everlastingly"? Such beliefs may still
be repeated in form, but who accepts them in their literal
sense and without reservation? Their hold on people's hearts
and minds has gone or is fast going. The religious world owes
a debt of gratitude to the men of science who helped to tear
such worn-out creeds and dogmas to tatters and allowed the
truth to step forth free. But the scientific world owes an even
heavier debt to the real saints and mystics who, through good
report and ill, held to the vital truths of spiritual experience
and demonstrated to an incredulous world that the life is more
than meat and the unseen greater than the seen. These scientists and saints were like the mountain peaks which caught the
first rays of the rising sun and reflected them to the lower world,
but now the sun has risen and its rays are illuminating the
world. In the teachings of Bahá'u'lláh we have a glorious
Revelation of truth which satisfies both heart and mind, in
which religion and science are at one.

Search after Truth

Complete harmony with science is evident in the Bahá'í teachings regarding the way in which we must seek the truth. Man must cut himself free from all prejudice so that he may search after truth unhindered.

'Abdu'l-Bahá says:—

In order to find truth we must give up our prejudices, our own small trivial notions; an open receptive mind is essential. If our chalice is full of self, there is no room in it for the Water of Life. The fact that we imagine ourselves to be right and everybody else wrong is the greatest of all obstacles in the path towards unity, and unity is essential if we would reach truth, for truth is one. . . .

No one truth can contradict another truth. Light is good in whatsoever lamp it is burning! A rose is beautiful in whatsoever garden it may bloom! A star has the same radiance if it shines from the East or from the West! Be free from prejudice; so will you love the Sun of Truth from whatever point in the horizon it may arise. You will realize that if the divine light of truth shone in Jesus Christ, it also shone in Moses and Buddha. This is what is meant by the search after truth.

It also means that we must be willing to clear away all that we have previously learned, all that would clog our steps on the way to truth; we must not shrink, if necessary, from beginning our education all over again. We must not allow our love for any one religion or any one personality so to blind our eyes that we become fettered by superstition. When we are freed from all these bonds, seeking with liberated minds, then shall we be able to arrive at our goal.—*Wisdom of 'Abdu'l-Bahá,* p. 127.

True Agnosticism

The Bahá'í teaching is at one with science and philosophy in declaring the essential nature of God to be entirely beyond human comprehension. As emphatically as Thomas Huxley and Herbert Spencer teach that the nature of the Great First Cause is unknowable, does Bahá'u'lláh teach that "God comprehends all; He cannot be comprehended." To knowledge of the Divine Essence "the way is barred and the road is impassable," for how can the finite comprehend the Infinite; how can a drop contain the ocean or a mote dancing in the sunbeam embrace the universe? Yet the whole universe is eloquent of God. In each drop of water are hidden oceans of meaning, and in each mote is concealed a whole universe of significances, reaching far beyond the ken of the most learned scientist. The chemist and physicist pursuing their researches into the nature of matter have passed from masses to molecules, from molecules to atoms, from atoms to electrons and ether, but at every step the difficulties of the research increase till the most profound intellect can penetrate no farther, and can but bow in silent awe before the unknown Infinite which remains ever shrouded in inscrutable mystery.

> Flower in the crannied wall,
>   I pluck you out of the crannies.
> I hold you here, root and all, in my hand,
>   Little flower—but *if* I could understand
> What you are, root and all, and all in all,
>   I should know what God and man is.—TENNYSON.

If the flower in the crannied wall, if even a single atom of matter, presents mysteries which the most profound intellect cannot solve, how is it possible for man to comprehend the universe? How dare he pretend to define or describe the Infinite Cause of all things? All theological speculations about the nature of God's essence are thus swept aside as foolish and futile.

Knowledge of God

But if the Essence is unknowable, the manifestations of its bounty are everywhere apparent. If the First Cause cannot be conceived, its effects appeal to our every faculty. Just as knowledge of a painter's pictures gives to the connoisseur a true knowledge of the artist, so knowledge of the universe in any of its aspects—knowledge of nature or of human nature, of things visible or of things invisible—is knowledge of God's handiwork, and gives to the seeker for divine truth a real knowledge of His glory. "The heavens declare the glory of God; and the firmament showeth his handiwork. Day unto day uttereth speech, and night unto night showeth knowledge."— Ps. xix, 1-2.

The Divine Manifestations

All things manifest the bounty of God with greater or less clearness, as all material objects exposed to the sun reflect its light in greater or less degree. A heap of soot reflects a little, a stone reflects more, a piece of chalk more still, but in none of these reflections can we trace the form and color of the glorious orb. A perfect mirror, however, reflects the sun's very form and color, so that looking into it is like looking at the sun itself. So it is with the way in which things speak to us of God. The stone can tell us something of the divine attributes, the flower can tell us more, the animal with its marvelous senses, instincts, and power of movement, more still. In the lowest of our fellowmen we can trace wonderful faculties which tell of a wonderful Creator. In the poet, the saint, the genius, we find a higher revelation still, but the great Prophets and Founders of religions are the perfect mirrors by which the love and wisdom of God are reflected to the rest of mankind. Other men's mirrors are dulled by the stains and the dust of selfishness and prejudice, but these are pure and without blemish—wholly devoted to the will of God. Thus They become the greatest educators of mankind. The divine teachings and the power of the Holy Spirit proceeding through Them have been and are the cause of the progress of humanity, for God helps men through other men. Each man who is higher in the ascent of life is the means of helping those who are lower, and those who are the highest of all are the helpers of all mankind. It is as if all men were connected together by elastic cords. If a man rises a little above the general level of his fellows, the cords tighten. His former companions tend to draw him back, but with an equal force he draws them upwards. The higher he gets, the more he feels the weight of the whole world pulling him back, and the more dependent he is on the divine support, which reaches him through the few who are still above him. Highest of all are the great Prophets and Saviors, the Divine "Manifestations"— those perfect men Who were each, in Their day, without peer or companion, and bore the burden of the whole world, supported by God alone. "The burden of our sins was upon Him" was true of each of Them. Each was the "Way, the Truth, and the Life" to His followers. Each was the channel of God's bounty to every heart that would receive it. Each had His part to play in the great divine plan for the upliftment of humanity.

Creation

Bahá'u'lláh teaches that the universe is without beginning in time. It is a perpetual emanation from the Great First Cause. The Creator always had His creation and always will have. Worlds and systems may come and go, but the universe remains. All things that undergo composition, in time undergo decomposition, but the component elements remain. The creation of a world, a daisy, or a human body is not "making something out of nothing"; it is rather a bringing together of elements which before were scattered, a making visible of something which before was hidden. By and by the elements will again be scattered, the form will disappear, but nothing is really lost or annihilated; ever new combinations and forms arise from the ruins of the old. Bahá'u'lláh confirms the scientists who claim, not six thousand, but millions and billions of years for the history of the earth's creation. The evolution theory does not deny creative power. It only tries to describe the method of its manifestation; and the wonderful story of the material universe which the astronomer, the geologist, the physicist, and the biologist are gradually unfolding to our gaze is, rightly appreciated, far more capable of evoking the deepest reverence and worship than the crude and bald account of creation given in the Hebrew Scriptures. The old account in the Book of Genesis had, however, the advantage of indicating by a few bold strokes of symbolism the essential spiritual meanings of the story, as a master painter may, by a few strokes of the brush, convey expressions which the mere plodder with the most laborious attention to details may utterly fail to portray. If the material details blind us to the spiritual meaning, then we should be better without them; but if we have once firmly grasped the essential meaning of the whole scheme, then knowledge of the details will give our conception a wonderful added richness and splendor and make it a magnificent picture instead of a mere sketch plan.

'Abdu'l-Bahá says:—

Know that it is one of the most abstruse spiritual truths that the world of existence, that is to say this endless universe, has no beginning. . . .

Know that . . . a creator without a creature is impossible, a provider without those provided for cannot be conceived; for all the divine names and attributes demand the existence of beings. If we could imagine a time when no beings existed, this imagination would be the denial of the divinity of God. Moreover, absolute nonexistence cannot become existence. If the beings were absolutely nonexistent, existence would not have come into being. Therefore, as the Essence of Unity, that is the existence of God, is everlasting and eternal—that is to say it has neither beginning nor end—it is certain that this world of existence . . . has neither beginning nor end . . . it may be that one of the parts of the universe, one of the globes, for example, may come into existence, or may be disintegrated, but the other endless globes are still existing. . . . As each globe has a beginning, necessarily it has an end, because every composition, collective or particular, must of necessity become decomposed; the only difference is that some are quickly decomposed, and others more slowly, but it is impossible that a composed thing should not eventually be decomposed.—*Some Answered Questions,* pp. 209-210.

The Evolution of Man

Bahá'u'lláh also confirms the biologist who finds for the body of man a history reaching back in the development of the species through millions of years. Starting from a very simple, apparently insignificant form, the human body is pictured as developing stage by stage, in the course of untold generations, becoming more and more complex, and better and better organized until the man of the present day is reached. Each individual human body develops through such a series of stages, from a tiny round speck of jelly-like matter to the fully developed man. If this is true of the individual, as nobody denies, why should we consider it derogatory to human dignity to admit a similar development for the species? *This is a very different thing from claiming that man is descended from a monkey.* The human embryo may at one time resemble a fish with gill-slits and tail, but it is not a fish. It is a human embryo. So the human species [1] may at various stages of its long development have resembled to the outward eye various species of lower animals, but it was still the human species, possessing the mysterious latent power of developing into man as we know him today, nay more, of developing in the future, we trust, into something far higher still.

'Abdu'l-Bahá says:—

It is clear that this terrestrial globe in its present form did not come into existence all at once; but . . . gradually passed through different phases until it became adorned with its present perfection. . . .

Man, in the beginning of his existence and in the womb of the earth, like the embryo in the womb of the mother, gradually grew and developed, and passed from one form to another . . . until he appeared with this beauty and perfection, this force and this power. It is certain that in the beginning he had not this loveliness and grace and

---

[1] The word "species" is used here to explain the distinction which has always existed between men and animals, despite outward appearances. It should not be read with its current specialized biological meaning.

elegance, and that he only by degrees attained this shape, this form, this beauty, and this grace. . . .

Man's existence on this earth, from the beginning until it reaches this state, form, and condition, necessarily lasts a long time. . . . But from the beginning of man's existence he is a distinct species. . . . Admitting that the traces of organs which have disappeared actually exist [in the human body], this is not a proof of the impermanence and the nonoriginality of the species. At the most it proves that the form, and fashion, and the organs of man have progressed. Man was always a distinct species, a man, not an animal.—*Some Answered Questions,* pp. 211, 212, 213, 214.

Of the story of Adam and Eve He says:—

If we take this story in its apparent meaning, according to the interpretation of the masses, it is indeed extraordinary. The intelligence cannot accept it, affirm it, or imagine it; for such arrangements, such details, such speeches and reproaches are far from being those of an intelligent man, how much less of the Divinity—that Divinity Who has organized this infinite universe in the most perfect form, and its innumerable inhabitants with absolute system, strength, and perfection. . . .

Therefore this story of Adam and Eve who ate from the tree, and their expulsion from Paradise, must be thought of simply as a symbol. It contains divine mysteries and universal meanings, and it is capable of marvelous explanations.—*Some Answered Questions,* p. 140.

Body and Soul

The Bahá'í teachings with regard to body and soul, and the life after death, are quite in harmony with the results of psychical research. They teach, as we have seen, that death is but a new birth—the escape from the prison of the body into a larger life, and that progress in the afterlife is limitless.

A large body of scientific evidence has gradually been accumulating which in the opinion of impartial but highly critical investigators is amply sufficient to establish beyond all question the fact of a life after death—of the continued life and activity of the conscious "soul" after the dissolution of the material body. As F. W. H. Myers says in his *Human Personality*, a work which summarizes many of the investigations of the Psychical Research Society:—

Observation, experiment, inference, have led many inquirers, of whom I am one, to a belief in direct or telepathic intercommunication, not between the minds of men still on earth only, but between minds or spirits still on earth and spirits departed. Such a discovery opens the door also to revelation. . . .

We have shown that amid much deception and self-deception, fraud and illusion, veritable manifestations do reach us from beyond the grave. . . .

By discovery and by revelation certain theses have been provisionally established with regard to such departed souls as we have been able to encounter. First and chiefly, I, at least, see ground to believe that their state is one of endless evolution in wisdom and in love. Their loves of earth persist, and most of all, those highest loves which find their outlet in adoration and worship. . . . Evil to them seems less a terrible than a slavish thing. It is embodied in no mighty potentate; rather it forms an isolating madness from which higher spirits strive to free the distorted soul. There needs no chastisement of fire; self-knowledge is man's punishment and his reward; self-knowledge and the nearness or the aloofness of companion souls. For in that world love is actually self-preservation; the communion of saints not only adorns but constitutes the life everlasting. Nay, from the laws of telepathy it follows that that communion is valid to us here and now. Even now the love of souls departed makes answer to our invocations. Even now our loving memory —love is itself a prayer—supports and strengthens those delivered spirits upon their upward way.

The measure of agreement between this view, which is founded on careful scientific research, and that of the Bahá'í teachings, is truly remarkable.

Unity of Mankind

"Ye are all fruits of one tree, the leaves of one branch, the flowers of one garden." That is one of the most characteristic sayings of Bahá'u'lláh, and another is like it: "Glory is not his who loves his own country, but glory is his who loves his kind." Unity—unity of mankind, and of all created beings in God—is the main theme of His teaching. Here again the harmony between true religion and science is evident. With every advance in science the oneness of the universe and the interdependence of its parts has become more clearly evident. The astronomer's domain is inseparably bound up with the physicist's, and the physicist's with the chemist's, the chemist's with the biologist's, the biologist's with the psychologist's, and so on. Every new discovery in one field of research throws new light on other fields. Just as physical science has shown that every particle of matter in the universe attracts and influences every other particle, no matter how minute or how distant, so psychical science is finding that every soul in the universe affects and influences every other soul. Prince Kropotkin, in his book on *Mutual Aid,* shows most clearly that even among the lower animals, mutual aid is absolutely necessary to continued life, while in the case of man, the progress of civilization depends on the increasing substitution of mutual aid for mutual enmity. "Each for all and all for each" is the only principle on which a community can prosper.

The Era of Unity

All the signs of the times indicate that we are at the dawn of a new era in the history of mankind. Hitherto the young eagle of humanity has clung to the old aerie in the solid rock of selfishness and materialism. Its attempts to use its wings have been timid and tentative. It has had restless longings for something still unattained. More and more it has been chafing in the confinement of the old dogmas and orthodoxies. But now the era of confinement is at an end, and it can launch on the wings of faith and reason into the higher realms of spiritual love and truth. It will no longer be earthbound as it was before its wings had grown, but will soar at will to the regions of wide outlook and glorious freedom. One thing is necessary, however, if its flight is to be sure and steady. Its wings must not only be strong, but they must act in perfect harmony and coordination. As 'Abdu'l-Bahá says:—"It cannot fly with one wing alone. If it tries to fly with the wing of religion alone it will land in the slough of superstition, and if it tries to fly with the wing of science alone it will end in the dreary bog of materialism."—*Wisdom of 'Abdu'l-Bahá,* p. 132.

Perfect harmony between religion and science is the *sine qua non* of the higher life for humanity. When that is achieved, and every child is trained not only in the study of the sciences and arts, but equally in love to all mankind and in radiant acquiescence to the will of God as revealed in the progress of evolution and the teachings of the Prophets, then and not till then, shall the Kingdom of God come and His will be done on earth as it is in heaven; then and not till then shall the Most Great Peace shed its blessings on the world.

"When religion," says 'Abdu'l-Bahá, "shorn of its superstitions, traditions and unintelligent dogmas, shows its conformity with science, then there will be a great unifying, cleansing force in the world, which will sweep before it all wars, disagreements, discords and struggles, and then will mankind be united in the power of the love of God."—*Wisdom of 'Abdu'l-Bahá,* p. 135.

Prophecies Fulfilled by the Bahá'í Movement/13

As to the Manifestation of the Greatest Name (Bahá'u'lláh): This is He Whom God promised in all His Books and Scriptures, such as the Bible, the Gospels and the Qur'an.—'ABDU'L-BAHÁ.

Interpretation of Prophecy

The interpretation of prophecy is notoriously difficult, and on no subject do the opinions of the learned differ more widely. This is not to be wondered at, for, according to the revealed writings themselves, many of the prophecies were given in such a form that they could not be fully understood until the fulfillment came, and even then, only by those who were pure in heart and free from prejudice. Thus at the end of Daniel's visions the seer was told:—

> But thou, O Daniel, shut up the words, and seal the book, even to the time of the end: many shall run to and fro, and knowledge shall be increased. . . . And I heard, but I understood not: then said I, "O my Lord, what shall be the end of these things?" And he said, "Go thy way, Daniel: for the words are closed up and sealed till the time of the end."—Daniel xii, 4-9.

If God sealed up the prophecies until the appointed time, and did not fully reveal the interpretation even to the prophets who uttered them, we may expect that none but the appointed Messenger of God will be able to break the seal and disclose the meanings concealed in the casket of the prophetic parables. Reflection on the history of prophecies and their misinterpretation in previous ages and dispensations, combined with the

211

solemn warnings of the prophets themselves, should render us very chary of accepting the speculations of theologians as to the real meaning of these utterances and the manner of their fulfillment. On the other hand, when someone appears who claims to fulfill the prophecies, it is important that we examine his claim with open, unprejudiced minds. Should he be an impostor, the fraud will soon be discovered and no harm will be done, but woe to all who carelessly turn God's Messenger from the door because He comes in an unexpected form or time.

The life and utterances of Bahá'u'lláh testify that He is the Promised One of all the Holy Books, Who has power to break the seals of the prophecies and to pour forth the "sealed choice wine" of the divine mysteries. Let us hasten, then, to hear His explanations and to reexamine in their light the familiar but often mysterious words spoken by the Prophets of old.

The Coming of the Lord

The "coming of the Lord" in the "last days" is the one "far-off divine event" to which all the Prophets look forward, about which Their most glorious songs are sung. Now what is meant by the "coming of the Lord"? Surely God is at all times with His creatures, in all, through all, and over all; "Closer is He than breathing, nearer than hands and feet." Yes, but men cannot see or hear God immanent and transcendent, cannot realize His presence, until He reveals Himself through a visible form and talks to them in human language. For the revelation of His higher attributes, God has always made use of a human instrument. Each of the Prophets was a mediator through whom God visited and spoke to His people. Jesus was such a mediator, and the Christians have rightly regarded His appearance as a coming of God. In Him they saw the face of God and through His lips they heard the voice of God. Bahá'u'lláh tells us that the "coming" of the Lord of Hosts, the everlasting Father, the Maker and Redeemer of the world, which, according to all the Prophets, is to take place at "the time of the end," means no other than His manifestation in a human temple, as He manifested through the temple of Jesus of Nazareth, only this time with a fuller and more glorious Revelation, for which Jesus and all the former Prophets came to prepare men's hearts and minds.

Prophecies about Christ

Through failing to understand the meaning of the prophecies about the dominion of the Messiah, the Jews rejected Christ. 'Abdu'l-Bahá says:—

The Jews still await the coming of the Messiah, and pray to God day and night to hasten His advent. When Jesus came they denounced and slew Him, saying: "This is not the One for Whom we wait. Behold, when the Messiah shall come, signs and wonders shall testify that He is in truth the Christ. The Messiah will arise out of an unknown city. He shall sit upon the throne of David, and behold, He shall come with a sword of steel, and with a scepter of iron shall He rule. He shall fulfill the law of the Prophets. He shall conquer the East and the West, and shall glorify His chosen people the Jews. He shall bring with Him a reign of peace during which even the animals shall cease to be at enmity with man. For behold, the wolf and the lamb shall drink from the same spring . . . and all God's creatures shall be at rest. . . ."

Thus the Jews thought and spoke, for they did not understand the Scriptures nor the glorious truths that were contained in them. The letter they knew by heart, but of the life-giving Spirit they understood not a word.

Hearken, and I will show you the meaning thereof: Although Christ came from Nazareth, which was a known place, He came also from heaven. His body was born of Mary, but His spirit came from heaven. The sword He carried was the sword of His tongue, with which He divided the good from the evil, the true from the false, the faithful from the unfaithful, and the light from the darkness. His Word was indeed a sharp sword! The throne

upon which He sat is the eternal throne from which
Christ reigns forever, a heavenly throne, not an earthly
one, for the things of earth pass away but heavenly things
pass not away. He reinterpreted and completed the laws
of Moses and fulfilled the law of the Prophets. His Word
conquered the East and the West. His Kingdom is everlasting. He exalted those Jews who recognized Him. They
were men and women of humble birth, but contact with
Him made them great and gave them everlasting dignity.
The animals who were to live with one another signified
the different sects and races, who, once having been at
war, were now to dwell in love and charity, drinking
together the Water of Life from Christ the eternal Spring.
—*Wisdom of 'Abdu'l-Bahá*, p. 48.

Most Christians accept these interpretations of Messianic
prophecies as applied to Christ; but with regard to similar
prophecies about the latter-day Messiah, many of them take
up the same attitude as the Jews, expecting a miraculous display on the material plane which will fulfill the very letter of
the prophecies.

Prophecies about the Báb and Bahá'u'lláh

According to the Bahá'í interpretations, the prophecies
which speak of "the time of the end," the "last days," the coming of the "Lord of hosts," of the "everlasting Father," refer
especially, not to the advent of Jesus Christ, but to that of
Bahá'u'lláh. Take, for instance, the well-known prophecy in
Isaiah:—

The people that walked in darkness have seen a great
light: they that dwell in the land of the shadow of death,
upon them hath the light shined. . . . For thou hast
broken the yoke of his burden, and the staff of his shoulder, the rod of his oppressor, as in the day of Midian. For
every battle of the warrior is with confused noise, and
garments rolled in blood; but this shall be with burning
and fuel of fire. For unto us a child is born, unto us a son

is given: and the government shall be upon his shoulder: and his name shall be called Wonderful, Counsellor, the mighty God, the everlasting Father, the Prince of Peace. Of the increase of his government and peace there shall be no end, upon the throne of David, and upon his kingdom, to order it, and to establish it with judgment and with justice from henceforth even for ever. The zeal of the Lord of hosts will perform this.—Isa. ix, 2-7.

This is one of the prophecies that has often been regarded as referring to Christ, and much of it may quite fairly be thus applied, but a little examination will show how much more fully and aptly it applies to Bahá'u'lláh. Christ has, indeed, been a light-bringer and Savior, but for nearly two thousand years since His advent the great majority of the people of the earth have continued to walk in darkness, and the children of Israel and many others of God's children have continued to groan under the rod of the oppressor. On the other hand, during the first few decades of the Bahá'í Era, the light of truth has illumined the East and the West, the gospel of the Fatherhood of God and the brotherhood of man has been carried into all countries of the world, the great military autocracies have been overthrown, and a consciousness of world unity has been born which brings hope of eventual relief to all the downtrodden and oppressed nationalities of the world. The great war which from 1914 to 1918 convulsed the world, with its unprecedented use of firearms, liquid fire, incendiary bombs, and fuel for engines, has indeed been "with burning and fuel of fire." [1] Bahá'u'lláh, by dealing at great length in His Writings with questions of government and administration, and showing how they may best be solved, has "taken the government upon His shoulders" in a way that Christ never did. With regard to the titles "everlasting Father," "Prince of Peace," Bahá'u'lláh repeatedly refers to Himself as the Manifestation of the Father, of Whom Christ and Isaiah spoke, whereas Christ always referred to Himself as the Son; and Bahá'u'lláh declares

---

[1] The Second World War further demonstrated the fulfillment of this prophecy, culminating in the use of the atomic bomb.

that His mission is to establish peace on earth, while Christ said: "I came not to send peace but a sword," and as a matter of fact during the whole of the Christian Era wars and sectarian strifes have abounded.

The Glory of God

The title "Bahá'u'lláh" is the Arabic for "Glory of God," and this very title is frequently used by the Hebrew prophets for the Promised One Who is to appear in the last days. Thus in the 40th chapter of Isaiah we read:—

Comfort ye, comfort ye my people, saith your God. Speak ye comfortably to Jerusalem, and cry unto her, that her warfare is accomplished, that her iniquity is pardoned: for she hath received of the Lord's hand double for all her sins. The voice of him that crieth in the wilderness, "Prepare ye the way of the Lord, make straight in the desert a highway for our God. Every valley shall be exalted, and every mountain and hill shall be made low: and the crooked shall be made straight, and the rough places plain: And the glory of the Lord shall be revealed, and all flesh shall see it together." Isa. xl, 1-5.

Like the former prophecy, this has also been partly fulfilled in the advent of Christ and His forerunner, John the Baptist; but only partly, for in the days of Christ the warfare of Jerusalem was not accomplished; many centuries of bitter trial and humiliation were yet in store for her. With the advent of the Báb and Bahá'u'lláh, however, the more complete fulfillment is beginning to appear, for even already brighter days have dawned for Jerusalem, and her prospects of a peaceful and glorious future seem now to be reasonably assured.

Other prophecies speak of the Redeemer of Israel, the Glory of the Lord, as coming to the Holy Land from the East, from the rising of the sun. Now Bahá'u'lláh appeared in Persia, which is eastward from Palestine, towards the rising of the sun, and He came to the Holy Land, where He spent the last twenty-four years of His life. Had He come there as a free man, people might have said that it was the trick of an impostor in order to conform to the prophecies; but He came as an exile and prisoner. He was sent there by the S͟háh of Persia and the Sultán of Turkey, who can hardly be suspected of any design to furnish arguments in favor of Bahá'u'lláh's claim to be the "Glory of God" Whose coming the Prophets foretold.

The Branch

In the prophecies of Isaiah, Jeremiah, Ezekiel, and Zechariah are several references to a man called the Branch. These have often been taken by Christians as applying to Christ, but are regarded by Bahá'ís as referring especially to Bahá'u'lláh.

The longest Bible prophecy about the Branch is in the 11th chapter of Isaiah:—

And there shall come forth a rod out of the stem of Jesse and a Branch shall grow out of his roots: And the spirit of the Lord shall rest upon him, the spirit of wisdom and understanding, the spirit of counsel and might, the spirit of knowledge and of the fear of the Lord . . . righteousness shall be the girdle of his loins, and faithfulness the girdle of his reins. The wolf also shall dwell with the lamb, and the leopard . . . with the kid; and the calf and the young lion and the fatling together; and a little child shall lead them. . . . They shall not hurt nor destroy in all my holy mountain: for the earth shall be full of the knowledge of the Lord, as the waters cover the sea. . . . And it shall come to pass in that day, that the Lord shall set his hand again the second time to recover the remnant of his people, which shall be left, from Assyria, and from Egypt, and from Pathros, and from Cush, and from Elam, and from Shinar, and from Hamath, and from the islands of the sea. And he shall set up an ensign for the nations, and shall assemble the outcasts of Israel, and gather together the dispersed of Judah from the four corners of the earth.—Isa. xi, 1-12.

'Abdu'l-Bahá remarks about this and other prophecies of the Branch:—

One of the great events which is to occur in the day of the manifestation of that incomparable Branch, is the hoisting of the standard of God among all nations; meaning that all the nations and tribes will come under the shadow of this divine banner, which is no other than the lordly Branch itself, and will become a single nation. The antagonism of faiths and religions, the hostilities of races and peoples, and the national differences, will be eradicated from amongst them. All will become one religion, one faith, one race, and one single people, and will dwell in one native land, which is the terrestrial globe. Universal peace and concord will be realized between all the nations, and that incomparable Branch will gather together all Israel: signifying that in this cycle Israel will be gathered in the Holy Land, and that the Jewish people who are scattered to the East and West, South and North, will be assembled together.

Now see: these events did not take place in the Christian cycle, for the nations did not come under the one standard which is the divine Branch. But in this cycle of the Lord of Hosts all the nations and peoples will enter under the shadow of this flag. In the same way, Israel, scattered all over the world, was not reassembled in the Holy Land in the Christian cycle; but in the beginning of the cycle of Bahá'u'lláh this divine promise, as is clearly stated in all the Books of the Prophets, has begun to be manifest. You can see that from all the parts of the world tribes of Jews are coming to the Holy Land; they live in villages and lands which they make their own, and day by day they are increasing to such an extent that all Palestine will become their home.—*Some Answered Questions,* p. 75-76.

The Day of God

The word "Day" in such phrases as "Day of God" and "Last Day" is interpreted as meaning "Dispensation." Each of the great religion Founders has His "Day." Each is like a sun. His teachings have their dawn, their truth gradually illumines more and more the minds and hearts of the people until they attain the zenith of their influence. Then they gradually become obscured, misrepresented, and corrupted, and darkness overshadows the earth until the Sun of a new Day arises. The day of the supreme Manifestation of God is the Last Day, because it is a day that shall never end, and shall not be overtaken by night. His sun shall never set, but shall illumine the souls of men both in this world and in the world to come. In reality none of the spiritual suns ever set. The suns of Moses, of Christ, of Muḥammad, and all the other Prophets are still shining in heaven with undiminished luster. But earthborn clouds have concealed their radiance from the people of earth. The supreme sun of Bahá'u'lláh will finally disperse these dark clouds, so that the people of all religions will rejoice in the light of all the Prophets, and with one accord worship the one God Whose light all the Prophets have mirrored forth.

The Day of Judgment

Christ spoke much in parables about a great Day of Judgment, when "the Son of man shall come in the glory of his Father . . . and . . . shall reward every man according to his works" (Matt. xvi, 27). He compares this Day to the time of harvest, when the tares are burned and the wheat gathered into barns:—

> So shall it be in the end of this world [consummation of the age]. The Son of man shall send forth his angels, and they shall gather out of his kingdom all things that offend, and them which do iniquity; And shall cast them into a furnace of fire: there shall be wailing and gnashing of teeth. Then shall the righteous shine forth as the sun in the kingdom of their Father.—Matt. xiii, 40-43.

The phrase "end of the world" used in the Authorized Version of the Bible in this and similar passages has led many to suppose that when the Day of Judgment comes, the earth will suddenly be destroyed, but this is evidently a mistake. The true translation of the phrase appears to be "the consummation or end of the age." Christ teaches that the Kingdom of the Father is to be established on earth, as well as in heaven. He teaches us to pray: "Thy Kingdom come; Thy will be done on earth as it is in heaven." In the parable of the Vineyard, when the Father, the Lord of the Vineyard, comes to destroy the wicked husbandmen, He does not destroy the vineyard (the world) also, but lets it out to other husbandmen, who will render Him the fruits in their season. The earth is not to be destroyed, but to be renewed and regenerated. Christ speaks of that day on another occasion as "the regeneration, when the Son of man shall sit on the throne of his glory." St. Peter speaks of it as "the times of refreshing," "the times of restitution of all things, which God hath spoken by the mouth of all His Holy Prophets since the world began." The Day of Judgment of which Christ speaks is evidently identical with the coming of the Lord of Hosts, the Father, which was prophesied by Isaiah and the other Old Testament prophets; a time of terrible punishment for the wicked, but a time in which justice shall be established and righteousness rule, on earth as in heaven.

In the Bahá'í interpretation, the coming of each Manifestation of God is a Day of Judgment, but the coming of the supreme Manifestation of Bahá'u'lláh is the great Day of Judgment for the world cycle in which we are living. The trumpet blast of which Christ and Muḥammad and many other prophets speak is the call of the Manifestation, which is sounded for all who are in heaven and on earth—the embodied and the disembodied. The meeting with God, through His Manifestation, is, for those who desire to meet Him, the gateway to the paradise of knowing and loving Him, and living in love with all His creatures. Those, on the other hand, who prefer their own way to God's way, as revealed by the Manifestation, thereby consign themselves to the hell of selfishness, error, and enmity.

The Great Resurrection

The Day of Judgment is also the Day of Resurrection, of the raising of the dead. St. Paul in his First Epistle to the Corinthians says:—

Behold, I show you a mystery; we shall not all sleep, but we shall all be changed, in a moment, in the twinkling of an eye, at the last trump: for the trumpet shall sound, and the dead shall be raised incorruptible, and we shall be changed. For this corruptible must put on incorruption, and this mortal must put on immortality.—I Cor. xv, 51-53.

As to the meaning of these passages about the raising of the dead, Bahá'u'lláh writes in the *Book of Íqán:*—

By the terms "life" and "death," spoken of in the Scriptures, is intended the life of faith and the death of unbelief. The generality of the people, owing to their failure to grasp the meaning of these words, rejected and despised the person of the Manifestation, deprived themselves of the light of His divine guidance, and refused to follow the example of that immortal Beauty. . . .

Even as Jesus said: "Ye must be born again" [John iii, 7]. Again He saith: "Except a man be born of water and of the Spirit, he cannot enter into the kingdom of God. That which is born of the flesh is flesh; and that which is born of the Spirit is spirit" [John iii, 5-6]. The purport of these words is that whosoever in every Dispensation is born of the Spirit and is quickened by the breath of the Manifestation of holiness, he verily is of those that have attained unto "life" and "resurrection" and have entered into the "paradise" of the love of God. And whosoever is not of them is condemned to "death" and "deprivation," to the "fire" of unbelief, and to the "wrath" of God. . . .

In every age and century, the purpose of the Prophets of God and Their chosen ones hath been no other but to affirm the spiritual significance of the terms "life," "resurrection," and "judgment." . . . Wert thou to attain to but a dewdrop of the crystal waters of divine knowledge, thou wouldst readily realize that true life is not the life of the flesh but the life of the spirit. For the life of the flesh is common to both men and animals, whereas the life of the spirit is possessed only by the pure in heart who have quaffed from the ocean of faith and partaken of the fruit of certitude. This life knoweth no death, and this existence is crowned by immortality. Even as it hath been said: "He who is a true believer liveth both in this world and in the world to come." If by "life" be meant this earthly life, it is evident that death must needs overtake it.— *Kitáb-i-Íqán*, pp. 114, 118, 120.

According to the Bahá'í teaching the resurrection has nothing to do with the gross physical body. That body, once dead, is done with. It becomes decomposed and its atoms will never be recomposed into the same body.

Resurrection is the birth of the individual to spiritual life, through the gift of the Holy Spirit bestowed through the Manifestation of God. The grave from which he arises is the grave of ignorance and negligence of God. The sleep from which he awakens is the dormant spiritual condition in which many await the dawn of the Day of God. This dawn illumines all who have lived on the face of the earth, whether they are in the body or out of the body, but those who are spiritually blind cannot perceive it. The Day of Resurrection is not a day of twenty-four hours, but an era which has now begun and will last as long as the present world cycle continues. It will continue when all traces of the present civilization will have been wiped off the surface of the globe.

Return of Christ

In many of His conversations Christ speaks of the future Manifestation of God in the third person, but in others the first person is used. He says: "I go to prepare a place for you. And if I go and prepare a place for you, I will come again, and receive you unto myself" (John xiv, 2-3). In the first chapter of Acts we read that the disciples were told, at the ascension of Jesus: "This same Jesus, which is taken up from you into heaven, shall so come in like manner as ye have seen him go into heaven." Because of these and similar sayings, many

Christians expect that when the Son of Man comes "in the clouds of heaven and with great glory" they shall see in bodily form the very Jesus Who walked the streets of Jerusalem two thousand years ago, and bled and suffered on the cross. They expect to be able to thrust their fingers into the prints of the nails on His hands and feet, and their hands into the spear wound in His side. But surely a little reflection on Christ's own words would dissipate such an idea. The Jews of Christ's time had just such ideas about the return of Elias, but Jesus explained their error, showing that the prophecy that "Elias must first come" was fulfilled, not by the return of the person and body of the former Elias, but in the person of John the Baptist, who came "in the spirit and power of Elias." "And if ye will receive it," said Christ, "this is Elias, which was for to come. He that hath ears to hear, let him hear." The "return" of Elias, therefore, meant the appearance of another person, born of other parents, but inspired by God with the same spirit and power. These words of Jesus may surely be taken to imply that the return of Christ will, in like manner, be accomplished by the appearance of another person, born of another mother, but showing forth the spirit and power of God even as Christ did. Bahá'u'lláh explains that the "coming again" of Christ was fulfilled in the advent of the Báb and in His own coming. He says:—

Consider the sun. Were it to say now, "I am the sun of yesterday," it would speak the truth. And should it, bearing the sequence of time in mind, claim to be other than that sun, it still would speak the truth. In like manner, if it be said that all the days are but one and the same, it is correct and true. And if it be said, with respect to their particular names and designations, that they differ, that again is true. For though they are the same, yet one doth recognize in each a separate designation, a specific attribute, a particular character. Conceive accordingly the distinction, variation, and unity characteristic of the various Manifestations of holiness, that thou mayest comprehend the allusions made by the Creator of all names and attributes to the mysteries of distinction and unity, and discover the answer to thy question as to why that everlasting Beauty should have, at sundry times, called Himself by different names and titles.—*Kitáb-i-Íqán*, 21-22.

'Abdu'l-Bahá says:—

Know that the return of Christ for a second time doth not mean what the people believe, but rather signifieth the One promised to come after Him. He shall come with the Kingdom of God and His power which hath surrounded the world. This dominion is in the world of hearts and spirits, and not in that of matter; for the material world is not comparable to a single wing of a fly, in the sight of the Lord, wert thou of those who know! Verily, Christ came with His Kingdom from the beginning which hath no beginning, and will come with His Kingdom to the eternity of eternities, inasmuch as in this sense "Christ" is an expression of the Divine Reality, the simple Essence and heavenly Entity, which hath no beginning nor ending. It hath appearance, arising, manifestation and setting in each of the cycles.—*Tablets of 'Abdu'l-Bahá*, vol. i, p. 138.

The Time of the End

Christ and His apostles mentioned many signs which would distinguish the times of the "Return" of the Son of Man in the glory of the Father. Christ said:—

And when ye shall see Jerusalem compassed with armies, then know that the desolation thereof is nigh. . . . For these be the days of vengeance, that all things which are written may be fulfilled. . . . for there shall be great distress in the land, and wrath upon this people. And they shall fall by the edge of the sword, and shall be led away captive into all nations: and Jerusalem shall be trodden down of the Gentiles, until the times of the Gentiles shall be fulfilled.—Luke xxi, 20-24.

Again He said:—

> Take heed that no man deceive you. For many shall
> come in my name, saying, "I am Christ"; and shall de-
> ceive many. And ye shall hear of wars and rumors of
> wars: see that ye be not troubled: for all these things must
> come to pass, but the end is not yet. For nation shall rise
> against nation, and kingdom against kingdom: and there
> shall be famines, and pestilences, and earthquakes, in
> divers places. All these are the beginning of sorrows.
> Then shall they deliver you up to be afflicted, and shall kill
> you: and ye shall be hated of all nations for my name's
> sake. And then shall many be offended, and shall betray
> one another, and shall hate one another. And many false
> prophets shall rise, and shall deceive many. And because
> iniquity shall abound, the love of many shall wax cold.
> But he that shall endure unto the end, the same shall be
> saved. And this gospel of the Kingdom shall be preached
> in all the world for a witness unto all nations; and then
> shall the end come.—Matt. xxiv, 4-14.

In these two passages Christ foretold in plain terms, without
veil or covering, the things that must come to pass *before* the
coming of the Son of Man. During the centuries that have
elapsed since Christ spoke, every one of these signs has been
fulfilled. In the last part of each passage He mentions an event
that shall mark the time of the coming—in one case the ending
of the Jewish exile and the restoration of Jerusalem, and in the
other the preaching of the Gospel in all the world. It is startling to find that both of these signs are being literally fulfilled
in our own times. If these parts of the prophecy are as true as
the rest, it follows that we must be living now in the "time of
the end" of which Christ spoke.

Muḥammad also mentions certain signs which will persist
until the Day of Resurrection. In the Qur'án we read:—

> When Alláh said: "O Jesus! Verily I will cause thee
> to die, and exalt thee towards me, and clear thee of the
> charges of those who disbelieve, and will place those who

follow thee [that is, Christians] above those who disbelieve [Jews and others], until the day of resurrection; then to me shall be your return, so I will decide between you concerning that in which you differed."—Súra iii, 54.

"The hand of God," say the Jews, "is chained up." Their own hands shall be chained up—and for that which they have said shall they be cursed. Nay! outstretched are both His hands! At His own pleasure doth He bestow gifts. That which hath been sent down to thee from thy Lord will surely increase the rebellion and unbelief of many of them; and we have put enmity and hatred between them that shall last till the day of Resurrection. Oft as they kindle a beacon fire for war shall God quench it.—Súra v, 69.

And of those who say, "We are Christians," have we accepted the covenant. But they too have forgotten a part of what they were taught; wherefore we have stirred up enmity and hatred among them that shall last till the day of Resurrection; and in the end will God tell them of their doings.—Súra v, 17.

These words also have been literally fulfilled in the subjection of the Jews to Christian (and Muslim) peoples, and in the sectarianism and strife which have divided both Jews and Christians among themselves during all the centuries since Muḥammad spoke. Only since the commencement of the Bahá'í Era (the Day of Resurrection) have signs of the approaching end of these conditions made their appearance.

Signs in Heaven and Earth

In the Hebrew, Christian, Muḥammadan, and many other Scriptures, there is a remarkable similarity in the description of the signs which are to accompany the coming of the Promised One.

In the Book of Joel we read:—

And I will show wonders in the heavens and in the earth, blood, and fire, and pillars of smoke. The sun shall be turned into darkness, and the moon into blood, before the great and the terrible day of the Lord come. . . . For behold, in those days . . . when I shall bring again the captivity of Judah and Jerusalem, I will also gather all nations, and will bring them down into the valley of Jehoshaphat [Jehovah judgeth], and will plead with them there. . . . Multitudes, multitudes in the valley of decision: for the day of the Lord is near in the valley of decision. The sun and the moon shall be darkened, and the stars shall withdraw their shining. The Lord also shall roar out of Zion, and utter his voice from Jerusalem; and the heavens and the earth shall shake: but the Lord will be the hope of his people.—Joel ii, 30-31; iii, 1-2, 14-16.

Christ says:—

Immediately after the tribulation of those days shall the sun be darkened, and the moon shall not give her light, and the stars shall fall from heaven, and the powers of the heavens shall be shaken: And then shall appear the sign of the Son of man in heaven: and then shall all the tribes of the earth mourn, and they shall see the Son of man coming in the clouds of heaven with power and great glory.—Matt. xxiv, 29-30.

In the Qur'án we read:—

When the sun shall be shrouded,
And when the stars shall fall,
And when the mountains are made to pass away . . .
And when the leaves of the Book shall be unrolled,
And when the Heaven shall be uncovered,
And when Hell shall be made to blaze.—Súra lxxxi.

In the *Book of Íqán* Bahá'u'lláh explains that these prophecies about the sun, moon, and stars, the heavens and the earth, are symbolical and are not to be understood merely in the literal sense. The Prophets were primarily concerned with spiritual, not with material, things; with spiritual, not with physical, light. When They mention the sun, in connection with the

Day of Judgment, They refer to the Sun of Righteousness. The sun is the supreme source of light, so Moses was a Sun for the Hebrews, Christ for the Christians, and Muḥammad for the Muslims. When the Prophets speak of the sun being darkened, what is meant is that the pure teachings of these spirtual Suns have become obscured by misrepresentation, misunderstanding, and prejudice, so that the people are in spiritual darkness. The moon and stars are the lesser sources of illumination, the religious leaders and teachers, who should guide and inspire the people. When it is said that the moon shall not give her light or shall be turned into blood, and the stars shall fall from heaven, it is indicated that the leaders of the churches shall become debased, engaging in strife and contention, and the priests shall become worldy minded, concerned about earthly instead of heavenly things.

The meaning of these prophecies is not exhausted by one explanation, however, and there are other senses in which these symbols can be interpreted. Bahá'u'lláh says that in another sense the words "sun," "moon," and "stars" are applied to the ordinances and instructions enacted in every religion. As in every subsequent Manifestation the ceremonies, forms, customs, and instructions of the preceding Manifestations are changed in accordance with the requirements of the times, so, in this sense the sun and moon are changed and the stars dispersed.

In many cases the literal fulfillment of these prophecies in the outward sense would be absurd or impossible; for example, the moon being turned into blood or the stars falling upon the earth. The least of the visible stars is many thousand times larger than the earth, and were one to fall on the earth there would be no earth left for another to fall on! In other cases, however, there is a material as well as a spiritual fulfillment. For example, the Holy Land did literally become desert and desolate during many centuries, as foretold by the prophets, but already, in the Day of Resurrection, it is beginning to "rejoice and blossom as the rose," as Isaiah foretold. Prosperous colonies are being started, the land is being irrigated and cultivated, and vineyards, olive groves, and gardens are flourishing where half a century ago there was only sandy waste. Doubtless when men beat their swords into plough-shares and their spears into pruning hooks, wildernesses and deserts in all parts of the world will be reclaimed; the scorching winds and sandstorms that blow from these deserts, and make life in their neighborhood well-nigh intolerable, will be things of the past; the climate of the whole earth will become milder and more equable; cities will no longer defile the air with smoke and poisonous fumes, and even in the outward, material sense there will be "new heavens and a new earth."

Manner of Coming

As to the manner of His coming at the end of the age, Christ said:—

> And they shall see the Son of man coming in the clouds of heaven with power and great glory. And he shall send his angels with a great sound of a trumpet . . . then shall he sit upon the thrown of his glory: And before him shall be gathered all nations: and he shall separate them one from another, as a shepherd divideth his sheep from the goats.—Matt. xxiv, 30-31; xxv, 31-32.

Regarding these and similar passages Bahá'u'lláh writes in the *Book of Íqán:*—

> The term "heaven" denoteth loftiness and exaltation, inasmuch as it is the seat of the revelation of those Mani-festations of holiness, the Daysprings of ancient glory. These ancient Beings, though delivered from the womb of Their mother, have in reality descended from the heaven of the will of God. Though They be dwelling on this earth, yet Their true habitations are the retreats of glory in the realms above. Whilst walking amongst mortals, They soar in the heaven of the Divine presence. Without feet They tread the path of the spirit, and with-out wings They rise unto the exalted heights of divine unity. With every fleeting breath They cover the im-

mensity of space, and at every moment traverse the kingdoms of the visible and the invisible. . . .

By the term "clouds" is meant those things that are
contrary to the ways and desires of men. Even as He hath
revealed in the verse already quoted: "As oft as an
Apostle cometh unto you with that which your souls desire not, ye swell with pride, accusing some of being
impostors and slaying others." [Qur'án 55:56.] These
"clouds" signify, in one sense, the annulment of laws, the
abrogation of former Dispensations, the repeal of rituals
and customs current amongst men, the exalting of the
illiterate faithful above the learned opposers of the Faith.
In another sense, they mean the appearance of that immortal Beauty in the image of mortal man, with such
human limitations as eating and drinking, poverty and
riches, glory and abasement, sleeping and waking, and
such other things as cast doubt in the minds of men, and
cause them to turn away. All such veils are symbolically
referred to as "clouds."

These are the "clouds" that cause the heavens of the
knowledge and understanding of all that dwell on earth
to be cloven asunder. Even as He hath revealed: "On that
day shall the heaven be cloven by the clouds." [Qur'án
25:25.] Even as the clouds prevent the eyes of men from
beholding the sun, so do these things hinder the souls
of men from recognizing the light of the divine Luminary.
To this beareth witness that which hath proceeded out of
the mouth of the unbelievers as revealed in the sacred
Book: "And they have said: 'What manner of apostle is
this? He eateth food, and walketh the streets. Unless an
angel be sent down and take part in his warnings, we will
not believe.' " [Qur'án, 25:7.] Other Prophets, similarly,
have been subject to poverty and afflictions, to hunger,
and to the ills and chances of this world. As these holy
Persons were subject to such needs and wants, the people
were, consequently, lost in the wilds of misgivings and
doubts, and were afflicted with bewilderment and perplex-

ity. How, they wondered, could such a person be sent down from God, assert His ascendancy over all the peoples and kindreds of the earth, and claim Himself to be the goal of all creation—even as He hath said: "But for Thee, I would have not created all that are in heaven and on earth"—and yet be subject to such trivial things? You must undoubtedly have been informed of the tribulations, the poverty, the ills, and the degradation that have befallen every Prophet of God and His companions. You must have heard how the heads of Their followers were sent as presents unto different cities, how grievously they were hindered from that whereunto they were commanded. Each and every one of them fell a prey to the hands of the enemies of His Cause, and had to suffer whatsoever they decreed. . . .

The All-Glorious hath decreed these very things, that are contrary to the desires of wicked men, to be the touchstone and standard whereby He proveth His servants, that the just may be known from the wicked, and the faithful distinguished from the infidel. . . .

And now, concerning His words: "And He shall send His angels. . . ." By "angels" is meant those who, reinforced by the power of the spirit, have consumed, with the fire of the love of God, all human traits and limitations, and have clothed themselves with the attributes of the most exalted Beings and of the Cherubim. . . .

As the adherents of Jesus have never understood the hidden meaning of these words, and as the signs which they and the leaders of their Faith have expected have failed to appear, they therefore refused to acknowledge, even until now, the truth of those Manifestations of holiness that have since the days of Jesus been made manifest. They have thus deprived themselves of the outpourings of God's holy grace, and of the wonders of His divine utterance. Such is their low estate in this, the Day of Resurrection! They have even failed to perceive that were the signs of the Manifestation of God in every age to appear in the visible realm in accordance with the text of established traditions, none could possibly deny or turn away, nor would the blessed be distinguished from the miserable, and the transgressor from the God-fearing. Judge fairly: Were the prophecies recorded in the Gospel to be literally fulfilled; were Jesus, Son of Mary, accompanied by angels, to descend from the visible heaven upon the clouds; who would dare to disbelieve, who would dare to reject the truth, and wax disdainful? Nay, such consternation would immediately seize all the dwellers of the earth that no soul would feel able to utter a word, much less to reject or accept the truth.—*Kitáb-i-Íqán*, pp. 67, 71, 72, 73, 76, 78, 80-81.

According to the above explanation the coming of the Son of Man, in lowly human form, born of woman, poor, uneducated, oppressed, and set at naught by the great ones of the earth—this manner of coming is the very touchstone by which He judges the people of earth and separates them one from another, as a shepherd divides his sheep from the goats. Those whose spiritual eyes are opened can see through these clouds and rejoice in the "power and great glory"—the very glory of God—which He comes to reveal; the others, whose eyes are still holden by prejudice and error, can see but the dark clouds and continue to grope in gloom, deprived of the blessed sunshine.

Behold, I will send my messenger, and he shall prepare the way before me: and the Lord, whom ye seek, shall suddenly come to his temple, even the messenger of the covenant, whom ye delight in. . . . But who may abide the day of his coming? And who shall stand when he appeareth? For he is like a refiner's fire, and like fullers' soap. . . . For, behold, the day cometh, that shall burn as an oven; and all the proud, yea, and all that do wickedly, shall be stubble: . . . But unto you that fear my name shall the Sun of righteousness arise with healing in his wings.—Mal. iii, 1-2; iv, 1-2.

Note—The subject of fulfillment of prophecy is such an extensive one that many volumes would be required for its adequate exposition. All that can be done within the limits of a single chapter is to indicate the main outlines of the Bahá'í interpretations. The detailed Apocalypses revealed by Daniel and St. John have been left untouched. Readers will find certain chapters of these dealt with in *Some Answered Questions.* In the *Book of Íqán,* by Bahá'u'lláh, *Bahá'í Proofs,* by Mírzá Abu'l-Faḍl, and in many of the Tablets of Bahá'u'lláh and 'Abdu'l-Bahá further explanation of prophecies may be found.

Prophecies of Bahá'u'lláh and 'Abdu'l-Bahá/14

And if thou say in thine heart, "How shall we know the word which the Lord hath not spoken?" When a prophet speaketh in the name of the Lord, if the thing follow not, nor come to pass, that is the thing which the Lord hath not spoken, but the prophet hath spoken it presumptuously: thou shalt not be afraid of him.—Deut. xviii, 21-22.

Creative Power of God's Word

God, and God alone, has the power to do whatever He wills, and the greatest proof of a Manifestation of God is the creative power of His Word—its effectiveness to change and transform all human affairs and to triumph over all human opposition. Through the Word of the Prophets God announces His will, and the immediate or subsequent fulfillment of that Word is the clearest proof of the Prophet's claim and of the genuineness of His inspiration.

For as the rain cometh down, and the snow from heaven, and returneth not thither, but watereth the earth, and maketh it bring forth and bud, that it may give seed to the sower, and bread to the eater: so shall my word be that goeth forth out of my mouth: it shall not return unto me void, but it shall accomplish that which I please, and it shall prosper in the thing whereto I sent it.—Isa. lv, 10-11.

When the disciples of John the Baptist came to Jesus with the question: "Art thou he that should come, or do we look for another?" the answer of Jesus was simply to point to the effects wrought by His words:—

234

Go and show John again those things which ye do hear and see: The blind receive their sight, and the lame walk, the lepers are cleansed, and the deaf hear, the dead are raised up, and the poor have the gospel preached to them. And blessed is he, whosoever shall not be offended in me.—Matt. xi, 4-6.

Let us now see what evidence there is to show whether the words of Bahá'u'lláh have this creative power which is distinctive of the Word of God.

Bahá'u'lláh commanded the rulers to establish universal peace, and their prolongation of the policy of war since 1869-1870 has overthrown many ancient dynasties, while each successive war has produced less and less of the fruits of victory, until the European War of 1914-1918 revealed the historically startling fact that war has become disastrous to victor and vanquished alike.[1]

Bahá'u'lláh bade the rulers likewise to act as trustees of those under their control, making political authority a means to true general welfare. The progress toward social legislation has been unprecedented.

He commanded limitation of the extremes of wealth and poverty, and ever since, legislation for the establishment of minimum subsistence levels and for graduated taxation of wealth by income and inheritance taxes has been a constant concern. He commanded the abolition of both chattel and economic slavery, and ever since, the progress toward emancipation has been a ferment in all parts of the world.

Bahá'u'lláh declared the equality of men and women, expressed through equal responsibilities and equal rights and privileges, and since that declaration, the bonds by which women have been bound for ages have been breaking, and woman has rapidly been securing her rightful place as the equal and partner of man.

He declared the fundamental oneness of religions, and the succeeding interval has witnessed the most determined efforts of sincere souls in all parts of the world to achieve a new de-

---

[1] This has been further evidenced by the Second World War.

gree of tolerance, of mutual understanding, and of cooperation for universal ends. The sectarian attitude has everywhere been undermined, and its historical position has become more and more untenable. The basis of exclusiveness in religion has been destroyed by the same forces making nationalism of the self-contained type incapable of survival.

He commanded universal education, and made the independent investigation of truth a proof of spiritual vitality. Modern civilization has been stirred to its depths by this new leaven. Compulsory education for children, and the extension of educational facilities for adults, have become a primary policy of government. Nations which deliberately seek to restrict the independence of mind and spirit among their citizens by that very policy have aroused revolution within and suspicion and fear outside their boundaries.

Bahá'u'lláh commanded the adoption of a universal auxiliary language, and Dr. Zamenhof and others obeyed His call by devoting their lives and genius to this great task and opportunity.

Above all, Bahá'u'lláh imbued humanity with a new spirit, arousing new longings in minds and hearts and new ideals for society. Nothing in all history is so dramatic and impressive as the course of events since the dawn of the Bahá'í Era in 1844. Year by year, the power of a dead past prolonged through outworn ideas, habits, attitudes, and institutions has weakened, until at present every intelligent man and woman on earth realizes that humanity is passing through its most terrible crisis. On the one hand we see the new creation arising as the light of Bahá'u'lláh's teaching has revealed the true path of evolution. On the other hand we see naught but disaster and frustration in all realms where that light is resisted or ignored.

Yet, to the faithful Bahá'í, these and countless other evidences, impressive as they are, fail to give the real measure of the spiritual majesty of Bahá'u'lláh. His life on earth, and the irresistible force of His inspired words, stand as the only true criterion of the will of God.

A study of the more detailed prophecies of Bahá'u'lláh and

their fulfillment will give powerful corroborative evidence. Of these prophecies we shall now proceed to give a few examples, about the authenticity of which there can be no dispute. They were widely published and known before their fulfillment came about. The letters which He sent to the crowned heads of the world, in which many of these prophecies occur, were compiled in a book which was first published in Bombay in the late nineteenth century. Several editions have since been published. We shall also give some examples of noteworthy prophecies by 'Abdu'l-Bahá.

Napoleon III

In the year 1869 Bahá'u'lláh wrote to Napoleon III, rebuking him for his lust of war and for the contempt with which he had treated a former letter from Bahá'u'lláh. The epistle contains the following stern warning:—

> For what thou hast done, thy kingdom shall be thrown into confusion, and thine empire shall pass from thine hands, as a punishment for that which thou hast wrought. Then wilt thou know how thou hast plainly erred. Commotions shall seize all the people in that land, unless thou arisest to help this Cause, and followest Him Who is the Spirit of God (Jesus Christ) in this, the straight path. Hath thy pomp made thee proud? By My life! It shall not endure; nay, it shall soon pass away, unless thou holdest fast by this firm Cord. We see abasement hastening after thee, whilst thou art of the heedless.

Needless to say, Napoleon, who was then at the zenith of his power, paid no heed to this warning. In the following year he went to war with Prussia, firmly convinced that his troops could easily gain Berlin; but the tragedy foretold by Bahá'u'lláh overwhelmed him. He was defeated at Saarbruck, at Weissenburg, at Metz, and finally in the crushing catastrophe at Sedan. He was then carried prisoner to Prussia, and came to a miserable end in England two years later.

Germany

Bahá'u'lláh later gave an equally solemn warning to the conquerors of Napoleon, which also fell on deaf ears and received a terrible fulfillment. In the *Book of Aqdas*, which was begun in Adrianople, and finished in the early years of Bahá'u'lláh's imprisonment in 'Akká, He addressed the Emperor of Germany as follows:—

O King of Berlin! . . . Do thou remember the one whose power transcended thy power (Napoleon III), and whose station excelled thy station. Where is he? Whither are gone the things he possessed? Take warning, and be not of them that are fast asleep. He it was who cast the Tablet of God behind him, when We made known unto him what the hosts of tyranny had caused Us to suffer. Wherefore, disgrace assailed him from all sides, and he went down to dust in great loss. Think deeply, O King, concerning him, and concerning them who, like unto thee, have conquered cities and ruled over men. The All-Merciful brought them down from their palaces to their graves. Be warned, be of them who reflect. . . .

O banks of the Rhine! We have seen you covered with gore, inasmuch as the swords of retribution were drawn against you; and you shall have another turn. And We hear the lamentations of Berlin, though she be today in conspicuous glory.—*Kitáb-i-Aqdas*.

During the period of German successes in the Great War of 1914-1918, and especially during the last great German offensive in the spring of 1918, this well-known prophecy was extensively quoted by the opponents of the Bahá'í Faith in Persia, in order to discredit Bahá'u'lláh; but when the forward sweep of the victorious Germans was suddenly transformed into crushing, overwhelming disaster, the efforts of these enemies of the Bahá'í Cause recoiled on themselves, and the notoriety which they had given to the prophecy became a powerful means of enhancing the reputation of Bahá'u'lláh.

Persia

In the *Book of Aqdas* written when the tyrannical Náṣiri'd-Dín Sháh was at the height of his power, Bahá'u'lláh blesses the city of Ṭihrán, which is the capital of Persia, and His own birthplace, and says of it:—

Let nothing grieve thee, O Land of Ṭá (Ṭihrán), for God hath chosen thee to be the source of the joy of all mankind. He shall, if it be His will, bless thy throne with one who will rule with justice, who will gather together the flock of God which the wolves have scattered. Such a ruler will, with joy and gladness, turn his face towards, and extend his favors unto, the people of Bahá. He indeed is accounted in the sight of God as a jewel among men. Upon him rest forever the glory of God, and the glory of all that dwell in the kingdom of His Revelation.

Rejoice with great joy, for God hath made thee "the Dayspring of His light," inasmuch as within thee was born the Manifestation of His glory. Be thou glad for this name that hath been conferred upon thee—a name through which the Daystar of grace hath shed its splendor, through which both earth and heaven have been illumined.

Erelong will the state of affairs within thee be changed, and the reins of power fall into the hands of the people. Verily, thy Lord is the All-Knowing. His authority embraceth all things. Rest thou assured in the gracious favor of thy Lord. The eye of His loving-kindness shall everlastingly be directed towards thee. The day is approaching when thy agitation will have been transmuted into peace and quiet calm. Thus hath it been decreed in the wondrous Book.—*Gleanings from the Writings of Bahá'u'lláh,* pp. 110-111.

So far, Persia has only begun to emerge from the period of confusion foretold by Bahá'u'lláh, but already constitutional government has been started, and signs are not lacking that a brighter era is at hand.

Turkey

To the Sulṭán of Turkey and his Prime Minister 'Álí Páshá, Bahá'u'lláh, then (in 1868) confined in a Turkish prison, addressed some of His most solemn, grave warnings. To the Sulṭán He wrote from the Barracks at 'Akká:—

O thou who considerest thyself the greatest of all men . . . erelong thy name shall be forgotten and thou shalt find thyself in great loss. According to thy opinion, this Quickener of the world and its Peacemaker is culpable and seditious. What crime have the women, children and suffering babes committed to merit thy wrath, oppression and hate? You have persecuted a number of souls who have shown no opposition in your country, and who have instigated no revolution against the government; nay, rather, by day and by night they have been peacefully engaged in the mentioning of God. You have pillaged their properties, and through your tyrannical acts, all that they had was taken from them. . . . Before God, a handful of dust is greater than your kingdom, glory, sovereignty and dominion, and should He desire, He would scatter you as the sand of the desert. Erelong His wrath shall overtake you, revolutions shall appear in your midst and your countries will be divided! Then you will weep and lament and nowhere will you find help and protection. . . . Be ye watchful, for the wrath of God is prepared, and erelong you shall behold that which is written by the Pen of Command—*Star of the West,* vol. ii, p. 3.

And to 'Álí Páshá He wrote:—

Thou hast, O Chief, committed that which hath made Muḥammad, the Apostle of God, groan in the Most Exalted Paradise. The world hath made thee proud, so much so that thou hast turned away from the Face through Whose brightness the Concourse on high hath been illumined. Soon thou shalt find thyself in evident loss. Thou didst unite with the ruler of Persia for doing Me harm, although I had come to you from the Dawning-Place of the Almighty, the Great, with a Cause which refreshed the eyes of the favored ones of God. . . .

Didst thou think that thou couldst put out the fire which God hath enkindled in the universe? No! I declare by His true soul, wert thou of those who understand. More than that, by what thou hast done its blaze and flame have been increased. Soon it will encompass the world and its inhabitants. . . . The day is approaching when the Land of Mystery (Adrianople) and what is beside it shall be changed, and shall pass out of the hands of the king, and commotions shall appear, and the voice of lamentation shall be raised, and the evidences of mischief shall be revealed on all sides, and confusion shall spread by reason of that which hath befallen these captives [Bahá'u'lláh and His companions] at the hands of the hosts of oppression. The course of things shall be altered, and conditions shall wax so grievous, that the very sands on the desolate hills will moan, and the trees on the mountain will weep, and blood will flow out of all things. Then wilt thou behold the people in sore distress. . . .

Thus hath the matter been decreed on the part of the Designer, the Wise, Whose command the hosts of heaven and earth could not withstand, nor could all the kings and rulers withhold Him from that which He willeth. Calamities are the oil for this Lamp, and through them its light increaseth, were ye of those who know! All oppositions displayed by the oppressors are indeed as heralds to this Faith, and by them the appearance of God and His Cause have become widely spread among the people of the world.

Again in the *Book of Aqdas* He wrote:—

O Spot that art situate on the shores of the two seas (Constantinople)! The throne of tyranny hath, verily, been established upon thee, and the flame of hatred hath been kindled within thy bosom, in such wise that the Concourse on high and they who circle around the Exalted Throne have wailed and lamented. We behold in thee the foolish ruling over the wise, and darkness vaunting itself against the light. Thou art indeed filled with manifest pride. Hath thine outward splendor made thee vainglorious? By Him Who is the Lord of mankind! It shall soon perish, and thy daughters and thy widows and all the kindreds that dwell within thee shall lament. Thus informeth thee the All-Knowing, the All-Wise.

The successive calamities which have befallen this once great empire since the publication of these warnings have furnished an eloquent commentary on their prophetic significance.

America

In the *Book of Aqdas,* revealed in 'Akká in 1873, Bahá'u'lláh appealed to America as follows:—

. . . O rulers of America and the presidents of the Republics therein . . . Give ear unto that which hath been raised from the Dayspring of grandeur: Verily, there is none other God but Me, the Lord of Utterance, the All-Knowing. Bind ye the broken with the hands of justice, and crush the oppressor who flourisheth with the rod of the commandments of your Lord, the Ordainer, the All-Wise.

'Abdu'l-Bahá in His addresses in America and elsewhere frequently expressed the hope, the prayer, and the assurance that the banner of international peace would be first raised in America. At Cincinnati, Ohio, on November 5, 1912, He said:—

America is a noble nation, a standard-bearer of peace throughout the world, shedding her light to all regions. Other nations are not untrammeled and free of intrigues like the United States, and are unable to bring about universal peace. But America, thank God, is at peace with all the world, and is worthy of raising the flag of brotherhood and international peace. When the summons to international peace is raised by America, all the rest of the world will cry: "Yes, we accept." The nations of every clime will join in adopting the teachings of Bahá'u'lláh, revealed over fifty years ago. In His epistles He asked the parliaments of the world to send their best and wisest men to an international world parliament that should decide all questions between the peoples and establish peace . . . then we shall have the Parliament of Man of which the prophets have dreamed.—*Star of the West,* vol. vi, p. 81.

The appeals of Bahá'u'lláh and 'Abdu'l-Bahá have already been responded to, in a large measure, by the United States of America, and in no country of the world have the Bahá'í teachings met with readier acceptance. The role assigned to America, of summoning the nations to international peace, has as yet, however, been only partially played, and Bahá'ís are awaiting with interest the developments which the future has in store.[1]

The Great War

Both Bahá'u'lláh and 'Abdu'l-Bahá on many occasions foretold with surprising accuracy the coming of the Great War of 1914-1918. At Sacramento, California, on October 26, 1912, 'Abdu'l-Bahá said:—"Today the European continent is like an arsenal. It is a storehouse of explosives, ready for just a spark, and one spark could set aflame the whole of Europe, particularly at this time, when the Balkan question is before the world."

In many of His addresses in America and Europe He gave similar warnings. In another address in California in October 1912 He said:—

We are on the eve of the Battle of Armageddon referred to in the sixteenth chapter of Revelation. The time

---

[1] It is of interest that the charter meeting of the United Nations Organization was held in San Francisco.

is two years hence, when only a spark will set aflame the whole of Europe. The social unrest in all countries, the growing religious scepticism antecedent to the millennium, and already here, will set aflame the whole of Europe as is prophesied in the Book of Daniel and in the Book (Revelation) of John. By 1917 kingdoms will fall and cataclysms will rock the earth. (Reported by Mrs. Corinne True in *The North Shore Review,* September 26, 1914, Chicago, U.S.A.) On the eve of the great conflict He said:—

A general melee of the civilized nations is in sight. A tremendous conflict is at hand. The world is at the threshold of a most tragic struggle. . . . Vast armies—millions of men—are being mobilized and stationed at their frontiers. They are being prepared for the fearful contest. The slightest friction will bring them into a terrific crash, and there will be a conflagration, the like of which is not recorded in the past history of mankind (at Haifa, August 3, 1914).—*Star of the West,* vol. v. p. 163.

Social Troubles After the War

Both Bahá'u'lláh and 'Abdu'l-Bahá also foretold a period of great social upheaval, conflict, and calamity as an inevitable result of the irreligion and prejudices, the ignorance and superstition, prevalent throughout the world. The great international military conflict was but one phase of this upheaval. In a Tablet dated January 1920, He wrote:—

O ye lovers of truth! O ye servants of mankind! As the sweet fragrance of your thoughts and high intentions has breathed upon me, I feel that my soul is irresistibly prompted to communicate with you.

Ponder in your hearts how grievous is the turmoil in which the world is plunged; how the nations on earth are besmeared with human blood, nay their very soil is turned into clotted gore. The flame of war has caused so wild a conflagration that the world in its early days, in its middle ages, or in modern times has never witnessed its like. The millstones of war have ground and crushed many a human head, nay, even more severe has been the lot of these victims. Flourishing countries have been made desolate, cities have been laid level with the ground, and smiling villages have been turned into ruin. Fathers have lost their sons, and sons turned fatherless. Mothers have shed tears of blood in mourning for their youths, little children have been made orphans, and women left wanderers and homeless. In a word, humanity, in all its phases, has been debased. Loud is the cry and wailing of orphans, and bitter the lamentations of mothers which are echoed by the skies.

The prime cause for all these happenings is racial, national, religious, and political prejudice, and the root of all this prejudice lies in outworn and deepseated traditions, be they religious, racial, national, or political. So long as these traditions remain, the foundation of the human edifice is insecure, and mankind itself is exposed to continuous peril.

Now in this radiant age, when the essence of all beings has been made manifest, and the hidden secret of all created things been revealed, when the morning light of truth has broken and turned the darkness of the world into light, is it meet and seemly that such a frightful carnage which brings irretrievable ruin upon the world should be made possible? By God! that cannot be.

Christ summoned all the peoples of the world to reconciliation and peace. He commanded Peter to return his sword unto its scabbard. Such was His wish and counsel, and yet they that bear His name have unsheathed the sword! How great the difference between their deeds and the explicit text of the Gospel!

Sixty years ago Bahá'u'lláh, even as the shining sun, shone in the firmament of Persia, and proclaimed that the world is wrapt in darkness and this darkness is fraught with disastrous results, and will lead to fearful strife. In

His prison city of 'Akká, He apostrophized in unmistakable terms the Emperor of Germany, declaring that a terrible war shall take place, and Berlin will break forth in lamentation and wailing. In like manner, whilst the wronged prisoner of the Sulṭán of Turkey in the citadel of 'Akká, He clearly and emphatically wrote him that Constantinople will fall a prey to grave disorder, in such wise that the women and children will raise their moaning cry. In brief, He addressed epistles to all the chief rulers and sovereigns of the world, and all that He foretold has been fulfilled. From His pen of glory flowed teachings for the prevention of war, and these have been scattered far and wide.

His first teaching is the search after truth. Blind imitation, He declared, killeth the spirit of man, whereas the investigation of truth frees the world from the darkness of prejudice.

His second teaching is the oneness of mankind. All men are but one fold, and God the loving Shepherd. He bestoweth upon them His most great mercy, and considers them all as one. "Thou shalt find no difference amongst the creatures of God." They are all His servants, and all seek His bounty.

His third teaching is that religion is the most mighty stronghold. It should be conducive to unity, rather than be the cause of enmity and hate. Should it lead to enmity and hate better not have it at all. For religion is even as medicine, which if it should aggravate the disease, its abandonment would be preferred.

Likewise, religious, racial, national, and political prejudice, all are subversive of the foundation of human society, all lead to bloodshed, all heap ruin upon mankind. So long as these remain, the dread of war will continue. The sole remedy is universal peace. And this is achieved only by the establishment of a supreme tribunal, representative of all governments and peoples. All national and international problems should be referred to this tribunal, and whatsoever be its decision that should be enforced. Were a government or people to dissent, the world as a whole should rise against it.

And among His teachings is the equality in right of men and women, and so on with many other similar teachings that have been revealed by His pen.

At present it has been made evident and manifest that these principles are the very life of the world, and the embodiment of its true spirit. And now, ye, who are the servants of mankind, should exert yourselves, heart and soul, to free the world from the darkness of materialism and human prejudice, that it may be illumined with the light of the City of God.

Praise be to Him, ye are acquainted with the various schools, institutions and principles of the world; today nothing short of these divine teachings can assure peace and tranquillity to mankind. But for these teachings, this darkness shall never vanish, these chronic diseases shall never be healed; nay, they shall grow fiercer from day to day. The Balkans will remain restless, and its condition will aggravate. The vanquished will not keep still, but will seize every means to kindle anew the flame of war. Modern universal movements will do their utmost to carry out their purpose and intentions. The movement of the Left will acquire great importance, and its influence will spread.

Wherefore, endeavor that with an illumined heart, a heavenly spirit, and a divine strength, and aided by His grace, ye may bestow God's bountiful gift upon the world . . . the gift of comfort and tranquillity for all mankind.

In a talk given in November 1919, He said:—

Bahá'u'lláh frequently predicted that there would be a period when irreligion and consequent anarchy would prevail. The chaos will be due to too great liberty among people who are not ready for it, and in consequence there will have to be a temporary reversion to coercive government, in the interests of the people themselves and in order to prevent disorder and chaos. It is clear that each nation now wishes complete self-determination and freedom of action, but some of them are not ready for it. The prevailing state of the world is one of irreligion, which is bound to result in anarchy and confusion. I have always said that the peace proposals following the Great War were only a glimmer of the dawn, and not the sunrise.

Coming of the Kingdom of God

Amid these troublous times, however, the Cause of God will prosper. The calamities caused by the selfish struggle for individual existence, or for party or sectarian or national gain, will induce the people to turn in despair to the remedy offered by the Word of God. The more calamities abound, the more will the people turn to the only true remedy. Bahá'u'lláh says in His Epistle to the Sháh:—

> God hath made afflictions as a morning shower to this green pasture, and as a wick for His Lamp, whereby earth and heaven are illumined. . . . Through affliction hath His light shone and His praise been bright unceasingly; this hath been His method through past ages and bygone times.

Both Bahá'u'lláh and 'Abdu'l-Bahá predict in the most confident terms the speedy triumph of spirituality over materiality and the consequent establishment of the Most Great Peace. 'Abdu'l-Bahá wrote in 1904:—

> Know this, that hardships and misfortunes shall increase day by day, and the people shall be distressed. The doors of joy and happiness shall be closed on all sides. Terrible wars shall happen. Disappointment and the frustration of hopes shall surround the people from every direction until they are obliged to turn to God. Then the lights of great happiness shall enlighten the horizons, so that the cry of "Yá Bahá'u'l-Abhá!" may arise on all sides.—Tablet to L.D.B. quoted in *Compilation on War and Peace*, p. 187.

When asked, in February 1914, whether any of the Great Powers would become believers, He replied:—

All the people of the world will become believers. Should you compare the beginning of the Cause with its position today, you would see what a quick influence the Word of God has, and now the Cause of God has encompassed the world. . . . Unquestionably, all will come under the shadow of the Cause of God.—*Star of the West,* vol. ix, p. 31.

He declared that the establishment of world unity will come about during the present century. In one of His Tablets He wrote:—

All the members of the human family, whether peoples or governments, cities or villages, have become increasingly interdependent. For none is self-sufficiency any longer possible, inasmuch as political ties unite all peoples and nations, and the bonds of trade and industry, of agriculture and education, are being strengthened every day. Hence the unity of all mankind can in this day be achieved. Verily this is none other but one of the wonders of this wondrous age, this glorious century. Of this, past ages have been deprived, for this century—the century of light—has been endowed with the unique and unprecedented glory, power and illumination. Hence the miraculous unfolding of a fresh marvel every day. Eventually it will be seen how bright its candles will burn in the assemblage of man.

In the last two verses of the Book of Daniel occur the cryptic words:—"Blessed is he that waiteth and cometh to the thousand, three hundred and thirty-five days. But go thy way till the end be: for thou shalt rest, and stand in thy lot at the end of the days."

Many have been the attempts of learned students to solve the problem of the significance of these words. In a tabletalk at which the writer was present, 'Abdu'l-Bahá reckoned the fulfillment of Daniel's prophecy from the date of the beginning of the Muḥammadan Era.

'Abdu'l-Bahá's Tablets make it clear that this prophecy refers to the one hundredth anniversary of the Declaration of Bahá'u'lláh in Baghdád, or the year 1963:—

> Now concerning the verse in Daniel, the interpretation whereof thou didst ask, namely, "Blessed is he who cometh unto the thousand, three hundred and thirty-five days." These days must be reckoned as solar and not lunar years. For according to this calculation a century will have elapsed from the dawn of the Sun of Truth, then will the teachings of God be firmly established upon the earth, and the divine light shall flood the world from the East even unto the West. Then, on this day, will the faithful rejoice!

'Akká and Haifa

Mírzá Aḥmad Sohrab recorded in his diary the following prophecy about 'Akká and Haifa uttered by 'Abdu'l-Bahá while seated by the window of one of the Bahá'í pilgrim homes at Haifa on February 14, 1914:—

> The view from the pilgrim home is very attractive, especially as it faces the blessed Tomb of Bahá'u'lláh. In the future the distance between 'Akká and Haifa will be built up, and the two cities will join and clasp hands, becoming the two terminal sections of one mighty metropolis. As I look now over this scene, I see so clearly that it will become one of the first emporiums of the world. This great semicircular bay will be transformed into the finest harbor, wherein the ships of all nations will seek shelter and refuge. The great vessels of all peoples will come to this port, bringing on their decks thousands and thousands of men and women from every part of the globe. The mountain and the plain will be dotted with the most modern buildings and palaces. Industries will be established and various institutions of philanthropic nature will be

founded. The flowers of civilization and culture from all nations will be brought here to blend their fragrances together and blaze the way for the brotherhood of man. Wonderful gardens, orchards, groves and parks will be laid out on all sides. At night the great city will be lighted by electricity. The entire harbor from 'Akká to Haifa will be one path of illumination. Powerful searchlights will be placed on both sides of Mount Carmel to guide the steamers. Mount Carmel itself, from top to bottom, will be submerged in a sea of lights. A person standing on the summit of Mount Carmel, and the passengers of the steamers coming to it, will look upon the most sublime and majestic spectacle of the whole world.

From every part of the mountain the symphony of "Yá Bahá'u'l-Abhá!" will be raised, and before the daybreak soul-entrancing music accompanied by melodious voices will be uplifted towards the throne of the Almighty.

Indeed, God's ways are mysterious and unsearchable. What outward relation exists between Shiráz and Ṭihrán, Baghdád and Constantinople, Adrianople and 'Akká and Haifa? God worked patiently, step by step, through these various cities, according to His own definite and eternal plan, so that the prophecies and predictions as foretold by the Prophets might be fulfilled. This golden thread of promise concerning the Messianic millennium runs through the Bible, and it was so destined that God in His own good time would cause its appearance. Not even a single word will be left meaningless and unfulfilled.

Retrospect and Prospect/15

I bear witness, O friends! that the favor is complete, the argument fulfilled, the proof manifest, and the evidence established. Let it now be seen what your endeavors in the path of detachment will reveal. In this wise hath the divine favor been fully vouchsafed unto you and unto them that are in heaven and on earth. All praise to God, the Lord of all worlds.—
BAHÁ'U'LLÁH, *The Hidden Words.*

Progress of the Cause

Unfortunately it is impossible, within the space at our disposal, to describe in detail the progress of the Bahá'í Faith throughout the world. Many chapters might be devoted to this fascinating subject, and many thrilling stories related about the pioneers and martyrs of the Cause, but a very brief summary must suffice.

In Persia the early believers in this Revelation met with the utmost opposition, persecution, and cruelty at the hands of their fellow countrymen, but they faced all calamities and ordeals with sublime heroism, firmness, and patience. Their baptism was in their own blood, for many thousands of them perished as martyrs; while thousands more were beaten, imprisoned, stripped of their possessions, driven from their homes, or otherwise ill-treated. For sixty years or more anyone in Persia who dared to own allegiance to the Báb or Bahá'u'lláh did so at the risk of his property, his freedom, and even of his life. Yet this determined and ferocious opposition could no more check the progress of the Movement than a cloud of dust could keep the sun from rising.

From one end of Persia [1] to the other Bahá'ís are now to be

---

[1] Lord Curzon, in his book, *Persia and the Persian Question*, published in 1892, the year of Bahá'u'lláh's death, writes:—

252

found in almost every city and town, and even amongst the nomad tribes. In some villages the whole population is Bahá'í and in other places a large proportion of the inhabitants are believers. Recruited from many and diverse sects, which were bitterly hostile to each other, they now form a great fellowship of friends who acknowledge brotherhood, not only with each other, but with all men everywhere, who are working for the unification and upliftment of humanity, for the removal of all prejudices and conflict, and for the establishment of the Kingdom of God in the world.

What miracle could be greater than this? Only one, and that the accomplishment throughout the entire world of the task to which these men have set themselves. And signs are not lacking that this greater miracle, too, is in progress. The Faith is showing an astonishing vitality, and is spreading, like leaven, through the lump of humanity, transforming people and society as it spreads.[1]

The relatively small number of Bahá'ís may still seem insignificant in comparison with the followers of the ancient religions, but they are confident that a divine power has blessed them with the high privilege of serving a new order into which will throng the multitudes of East and West at no distant day.

While, therefore, it remains true that the Holy Spirit has reflected from pure hearts in all countries still unconscious of the Source, and the growth of the Faith can be witnessed in the many efforts outside the Bahá'í community to promote one or

---

"The lowest estimate places the present number of Bábís in Persia at half a million. I am disposed to think, from conversations with persons well qualified to judge, that the total is nearer one million. They are to be found in every walk of life, from the ministers and nobles of the Court to the scavenger or the groom, not the least arena of their activity being the Mussulman priesthood itself. . . .

"If Bábism continues to grow at its present rate of progression, a time may conceivably come when it will oust Mohammedanism from the field in Persia. This, I think, it would be unlikely to do, did it appear upon the ground under the flag of a hostile faith. But since its recruits are won from the best soldiers of the garrison whom it is attacking, there is greater reason to believe that it may ultimately prevail." (Vol. i, pp. 499-502.)

[1] The number of Bahá'ís is increasing every year and by 1969 the number of localities throughout the world where Bahá'ís reside has risen to over thirty-three thousand. (See Epilogue)

another of Bahá'u'lláh's teachings, nevertheless the lack of any enduring foundation in the old order is convincing proof that the ideals of the Kingdom can only become fruitful within the framework of the Bahá'í community.

Prophethood of Báb and Bahá'u'lláh

The more we study the lives and teachings of the Báb and Bahá'u'lláh, the more impossible does it seem to find any explanation of Their greatness, except that of divine inspiration. They were reared in an atmosphere of fanaticism and bigotry. They had only the most elementary education. They had no contact with Western culture. They had no political or financial power to back Them. They asked nothing from men, and received little but injustice and oppression. The great ones of earth ignored or opposed Them. They were scourged and tortured, imprisoned, and subjected to direst calamities in the fulfillment of Their mission. They were alone against the world, having no help but that of God, yet already Their triumph is manifest and magnificent.

The grandeur and sublimity of Their ideals, the nobility and self-sacrifice of Their lives; Their dauntless courage and conviction, Their amazing wisdom and knowledge, Their grasp of the needs of both Eastern and Western peoples, the comprehensiveness and adequacy of Their teachings, Their power to inspire wholehearted devotion and enthusiasm in Their followers, the penetration and potency of Their influence, the progress of the Movement They founded—surely these constitute proofs of Prophethood as convincing as any which the history of religion can show.

A Glorious Prospect

The Bahá'í glad tidings disclose a vision of the bounty of God and of the future progress of humanity, which is surely the greatest and most glorious Revelation ever given to mankind, the development and fulfillment of all previous Revelations. Its purpose is nothing less than the regeneration of mankind and the creation of "new heavens and a new earth." It is the same task to which Christ and all the Prophets have devoted Their lives, and between these great Teachers there is no rivalry. It is not by this Manifestation or by that, but by *all together,* that the task will be accomplished.

As 'Abdu'l-Bahá says:—

> It is not necessary to lower Abraham to raise Jesus. It is not necessary to lower Jesus to proclaim Bahá'u'lláh. We must welcome the truth of God wherever we behold it. The essence of the question is that all these great Messengers came to raise the divine standard of perfections. All of Them shine as orbs in the same heaven of the divine will. All of them give light to the world.—*Star of the West,* vol. iii, No. 8, p. 8.

The task is God's, and God calls not only the Prophets but all mankind to be His coworkers in this creative process. If we refuse His invitation, we shall not hinder the work from going on, for what God wills shall surely come to pass. If we fail to play our part He can raise up other instruments to perform His purpose; but we shall miss the real aim and object of our own lives. At-one-ment with God—becoming His lovers, His servants, the willing channels and mediums of His creative power, so that we are conscious of no life within us but His divine and abundant life—that, according to the Bahá'í teaching, is the ineffable and glorious consummation of human existence.

Humanity, however, is sound at heart, for it is made "in the image and likeness of God," and when at last it sees the truth, it will not persist in the paths of folly. Bahá'u'lláh assures us that erelong the call of God will be generally accepted, and mankind as a whole will turn to righteousness and obedience. "All sorrow will then be turned into joy, and all disease into health," and the kingdoms of this world shall become "the kingdoms of our Lord and of his Christ; and he shall reign for ever and ever" (Rev. xi, 15). Not only those on earth, but all in the heavens and on the earth, shall become one in God and rejoice eternally in Him.

Renewal of Religion

The state of the world today surely affords ample evidence that, with rare exceptions, people of all religions need to be reawakened to the real meaning of their religion; and that reawakening is an important part of the work of Bahá'u'lláh. He comes to make Christians better Christians, to make Muslims real Muslims, to make all men true to the spirit that inspired their Prophets. He also fulfills the promise made by all these Prophets, of a more glorious Manifestation which was to appear in the "fullness of time" to crown and consummate Their labors. He gives a fuller unfolding of spiritual truths than His predecessors, and reveals the will of God with regard to all the problems of individual and social life that confront us in the world today. He gives a universal teaching which affords a firm foundation on which a new and better civilization can be built up, a teaching adapted to the needs of the world in the new era which is now commencing.

Need for New Revelation

The unification of the world of humanity, the welding together of the world's different religions, the reconciliation of religion and science, the establishment of universal peace, of international arbitration, of an International House of Justice, of an international language, the emancipation of women, universal education, the abolition not only of chattel slavery, but of industrial slavery, the organization of humanity as a single whole, with due regard to the rights and liberties of each individual—these are problems of gigantic magnitude and stupendous difficulty in relation to which Christians, Muḥammadans, and adherents of other religions have held and still hold the most diverse and often violently opposed views, but Bahá'u'lláh has revealed clearly defined principles, the general adoption of which would obviously make the world a paradise.

Truth Is for All

Many are quite ready to admit that the Bahá'í teachings would be a splendid thing for Persia and for the East, but imagine that for the nations of the West they are unnecessary or unsuitable. To one who mentioned such a view, 'Abdu'l-Bahá replied:—

As to the meaning of the Cause of Bahá'u'lláh, whatever has to do with the universal good is divine, and whatever is divine is for the universal good. If it be true, it is for all; if not, it is for no one; therefore a divine cause of universal good cannot be limited to either the East or the West, for the radiance of the Sun of Truth illumines both the East and the West, and it makes its heat felt in the South and in the North—there is no difference between one pole and another. At the time of the manifestation of Christ, the Romans and Greeks thought His Cause was especially for the Jews. They thought they had a perfect civilization and nothing to learn from Christ's teachings, and by this false supposition many were deprived of His grace. Likewise know that the principles of Christianity and the commandments of Bahá'u'lláh are identical and that their paths are the same. Every day there is progress; there was a time when this divine institution (of progressive revelation) was in embryo, then newborn, then a child, then an intellectual youth; but today it is resplendent with beauty and shining with the greatest brilliancy.

Happy is he who penetrates the mystery and takes his place in the world of the illumined ones.

The Last Will and Testament of 'Abdu'l-Bahá

With the passing of its beloved Leader, 'Abdu'l-Bahá, the Bahá'í Faith entered on a new phase of its history. This new phase represents a higher state in the existence of the same spiritual organism, a more mature and consequently a more responsible expression of the faith felt by its members. 'Abdu'l-Bahá had devoted His superhuman energy and unique capacity to the task of spreading His love for Bahá'u'lláh throughout the East and West. He had lighted the candle of faith in countless souls. He had trained and guided them in the attributes of the personal spiritual life. In view of the momentous importance of the last *Will and Testament of 'Abdu'l-Bahá*, the gravity of the issues it raises, and the profound wisdom underlying its provisions, we give a few extracts which vividly portray the spirit and leading principles which animated and guided 'Abdu'l-Bahá and are transmitted as a rich heritage to His faithful followers:—

O ye beloved of the Lord! In this sacred Dispensation, conflict and contention are in no wise permitted. Every aggressor deprives himself of God's grace. It is incumbent upon everyone to show the utmost love, rectitude of conduct, straightforwardness and sincere kindliness unto all the peoples and kindreds of the world, be they friends or strangers. So intense must be the spirit of love and loving kindness, that the stranger may find himself a friend, the enemy a true brother, no difference whatsoever existing between them. For universality is of God and all limitations earthly. . . .

Wherefore, O my loving friends! Consort with all the peoples, kindreds and religions of the world with the utmost truthfulness, uprightness, faithfulness, kindliness, goodwill and friendliness, that all the world of being may be filled with the holy ecstasy of the grace of Bahá, that ignorance, enmity, hate and rancor may vanish from the world and the darkness of estrangement amidst the peoples and kindreds of the world may give way to the Light of unity. Should other peoples and nations be unfaithful to you, show your fidelity unto them, should they be unjust toward you, show justice towards them, should they keep aloof from you, attract them to yourself, should they show their enmity, be friendly towards them, should they poison your lives, sweeten their souls, should they inflict a wound upon you, be a salve to their sores. Such are the attributes of the sincere! Such are the attributes of the truthful.

O ye beloved of the Lord! It is incumbent upon you to be submissive to all monarchs that are just and to show your fidelity to every righteous king. Serve ye the sovereigns of the world with utmost truthfulness and loyalty. Show obedience unto them and be their well-wishers. Without their leave and permission do not meddle with political affairs, for disloyalty to the just sovereign is disloyalty to God Himself.

This is my counsel and the commandment of God unto you. Well is it with them that act accordingly.

Lord! Thou seest all things weeping me and my kindred rejoicing in my woes. By Thy Glory, O my God! Even amongst mine enemies, some have lamented my troubles and my distress, and of the envious ones a number have shed tears because of my cares, my exile, and my afflictions. They did this because they found naught in me but affection and care and witnessed naught but kindliness and mercy. As they saw me swept into the flood of tribulation and adversity and exposed even as a target to the arrows of fate, their hearts were moved with compassion, tears came to their eyes and they testified declaring: —"The Lord is our witness; naught have we seen from Him but faithfulness, generosity, and extreme compassion." The Covenant-breakers, foreboders of evil, however, waxed fiercer in their rancor, rejoiced as I fell a victim to the most grievous ordeal, bestirred themselves against me, and made merry over the heartrending happenings around me.

I call upon Thee, O Lord my God! with my tongue and with all my heart, not to requite them for their cruelty and their wrong-doings, their craft and their mischief, for they are foolish and ignoble and know not what they do. They discern not good from evil, neither do they distinguish right from wrong, nor justice from injustice. They follow their own desires and walk in the footsteps of the most imperfect and foolish amongst them. O my Lord! Have mercy upon them, shield them from all afflictions in these troubled times and grant that all trials and hardships may be the lot of this, Thy servant, that hath fallen into this darksome pit. Single me out for every woe and make me a sacrifice for all Thy loved ones, O Lord, Most High! May my soul, my life, my being, my spirit, my all, be offered up for them. O God, my God! Lowly, suppliant, and fallen upon my face, I beseech Thee with all the ardor of my invocation to pardon whosoever hath hurt me, forgive him that hath conspired against me and offended me, and wash away the misdeeds of them that have wrought injustice upon me. Vouchsafe unto them Thy goodly gifts, give them joy, relieve them from sorrow, grant them peace and prosperity, give them Thy bliss and pour upon them Thy bounty.

Thou art the Powerful, the Gracious, the Help in Peril, the Self-Subsisting!

The disciples of Christ forgot themselves and all earthly things, forsook all their cares and belongings, purged themselves of self and passion, and with absolute detachment scattered far and wide and engaged in calling the peoples of the world to the Divine Guidance, till at last they made the world another world, illumined the surface of the earth and, even to their last hour, proved self-sacrificing in the pathway of that beloved One of God. Finally in various lands they suffered glorious martyrdom. Let them that are men of action follow in their footsteps!

O God, my God! I call Thee, Thy Prophets and Thy Messengers, Thy saints and Thy holy ones, to witness that I have declared conclusively Thy proofs unto Thy loved ones and set forth clearly all things unto them, that they may watch over Thy Faith, guard Thy straight path, and protect Thy resplendent law. Thou art, verily, the All-Knowing, the All-Wise!

With 'Abdu'l-Bahá's passing, the time had come to establish the Administrative Order which has been termed the pattern and nucleus of the World Order which it is the special mission of the religion of Bahá'u'lláh to establish. The *Will and Testament of 'Abdu'l-Bahá* consequently marks a turning point in Bahá'í history, dividing the era of immaturity and irresponsibility from that era in which the Bahá'ís themselves are destined to fulfill their spirituality by enlarging its scope from the realm of personal experience to that of social unity and cooperation. The three principal elements in the administrative plan left by 'Abdu'l-Bahá are:—

1. The Guardian of the Cause of God,
2. The Hands of the Cause of God, and
3. The Houses of Justice, Local, National, and International.[1]

The Guardian of the Cause of God

'Abdu'l-Bahá appointed His eldest grandson, Shoghi Effendi, to the responsible position of Guardian of the Cause (Valíyy-i-Amru'lláh). Shoghi Effendi is the eldest son of Díyá'íyyih Khánum, the eldest daughter of 'Abdu'l-Bahá. His father, Mírzá Hádí, is a relative of the Báb (although not a direct descendant, as the Báb's only child died in infancy). Shoghi Effendi was twenty-five years of age, and was studying at Balliol College, Oxford, at the time of his Grandfather's passing. The announcement of his appointment is made in 'Abdu'l-Bahá's *Will* as follows:—

O my loving friends! After the passing away of this wronged one, it is incumbent upon the Aghsán

---

[1] The Local and National Houses of Justice are at the present time designated Local and National Spiritual Assemblies, as previously indicated.

(branches), the Afnán (twigs) of the sacred Lote-Tree, the Hands (pillars) of the Cause of God and the loved ones of the Abhá Beauty to turn unto Shoghi Effendi—the youthful branch branched from the two hallowed and sacred Lote-Trees and the fruit grown from the union of the two offshoots of the Tree of Holiness,—as he is the Sign of God, the Chosen Branch, the Guardian of the Cause of God, he unto whom all the Aghṣán, the Afnán, the Hands of the Cause of God and His loved ones must turn. He is the expounder of the words of God and after him will succeed the firstborn of his lineal descendants.

The sacred and youthful branch, the Guardian of the Cause of God, as well as the Universal House of Justice, to be universally elected and established, are both under the care and protection of the Abhá Beauty, under the shelter and unerring guidance of His Holiness, the Exalted One (may my life be offered up for them both). Whatsoever they decide is of God. . . .

O ye beloved of the Lord! It is incumbent upon the Guardian of the Cause of God to appoint in his own lifetime him that shall become his successor, that differences may not arise after his passing. He that is appointed must manifest in himself detachment from all worldly things, must be the essence of purity, must show in himself the fear of God, knowledge, wisdom and learning. Thus, should the firstborn of the Guardian of the Cause of God not manifest in himself the truth of the words:—"The child is the secret essence of its sire," that is, should he not inherit of the spiritual within him (the Guardian of the Cause of God) and his glorious lineage not be matched with a goodly character, then must he (the Guardian of the Cause of God) choose another branch to succeed him.

The Hands of the Cause of God must elect from their own number nine persons that shall at all times be occupied in the important services in the work of the Guardian of the Cause of God. The election of these nine must be carried either unanimously or by majority from the company of the Hands of the Cause of God and these, whether unanimously or by a majority vote, must give their assent to the choice of the one whom the Guardian of the Cause of God hath chosen as his successor. This assent must be given in such wise that the assenting and dissenting voices may not be distinguished (i.e., secret ballot).

Hands of the Cause of God

During His own lifetime Bahá'u'lláh appointed a few tried and trusted friends to assist in directing and promoting the work of the Movement, and gave them the title of *Ayádíyi-Amru'lláh* (lit. "Hands of the Cause of God"). 'Abdu'l-Bahá makes provision in His *Will* for the establishment of a permanent body of workers to serve the Cause and help the Guardian of the Cause. He writes:—

> O friends! The Hands of the Cause of God must be nominated and appointed by the Guardian of the Cause of God. . . .
> The obligations of the Hands of the Cause of God are to diffuse the divine fragrances, to edify the souls of men, to promote learning, to improve the character of all men and to be, at all times and under all conditions, sanctified and detached from earthly things. They must manifest the fear of God by their conduct, their manners, their deeds and their words.
> This body of the Hands of the Cause of God is under the direction of the Guardian of the Cause of God. He must continually urge them to strive and endeavor to the utmost of their ability to diffuse the sweet savors of God, and to guide all the peoples of the world, for it is the light of divine guidance that causeth all the universe to be illumined.[1]

---

[1] Of the Hands of the Cause appointed by Shoghi Effendi during his thirty-six year ministry, twenty-seven were living at the time of his passing. He also instituted, in 1954, Auxiliary Boards to be appointed by the Hands and to be their deputies, assistants, and advisors.

The Administrative Order [1]

It has been the general characteristic of religion that organization marks the interruption of the true spiritual influence and serves to prevent the original impulse from being carried into the world. The organization has invariably become a substitute for religion rather than a method or an instrument used to give the religion effect. The separation of peoples into different traditions unbridged by any peaceful or constructive intercourse has made this inevitable. Up to the present time, in fact, no Founder of a revealed religion has explicitly laid down the principles that should guide the administrative machinery of the Faith He has established.

In the Bahá'í Cause, the principles of world administration were expressed by Bahá'u'lláh, and these principles were developed in the Writings of 'Abdu'l-Bahá, more especially in His *Will and Testament.*

The purpose of this organization is to make possible a true and lasting unity among peoples of different races, classes, interests, characters, and inherited creeds. A close and sympathetic study of this aspect of the Bahá'í Cause will show that the purpose and method of Bahá'í administration is so perfectly adapted to the fundamental spirit of the Revelation that it bears to it the same relationship as body to soul. In character, the principles of Bahá'í administration represent the science of cooperation; in application, they provide for a new and higher type of morality worldwide in scope. . . .

A Bahá'í community differs from other voluntary gatherings in that its foundation is so deeply laid and broadly extended that it can include any sincere soul. Whereas other associations are exclusive, in effect if not in intention, and from method if not from ideal, Bahá'í association is inclusive, shutting the

---

[1] This section on the Administrative Order is taken from the article on *The Present-Day Administration of the Bahá'í Faith* by Horace Holley, published in 1933 in The *Bahá'í World,* Volume V, p. 191 et seq. Passages in this article quoting from Bahá'í writings have been replaced by newer translations where these are available.

gates of fellowship to no sincere soul. In every gathering there is latent or developed some basis of selection. In religion this basis is a creed limited by the historical nature of its origin; in politics this is party or platform; in economics this is a mutual misfortune or mutual power; in the arts and sciences this basis consists of special training or activity or interest. In all these matters, the more exclusive the basis of selection, the stronger the movement—a condition diametrically opposed to that existing in the Bahá'í Cause. Hence the Cause, for all its spirit of growth and progress, develops slowly as regards the numbers of its active adherents. For people are accustomed to exclusiveness and division in all affairs. The important sanctions have ever been warrants and justifications of division. To enter the Bahá'í Movement is to leave these sanctions behind— an experience which at first invariably exposes one to new trials and sufferings, as the human ego revolts against the supreme sanction of universal love. The scientific must associate with the simple and unlearned, the rich with the poor, the white with the colored, the mystic with the literalist, the Christian with the Jew, the Muslim with the Parsee: and on terms removing the advantage of long-established presumptions and privileges.

But for this difficult experience there are glorious compensations. Let us remember that art grows sterile as it turns away from the common humanity, that philosophy likewise loses its vision when developed in solitude, and that politics and religion never succeed apart from the general needs of mankind. Human nature is not yet known, for we have all lived in a state of mental, moral, emotional, or social defense, and the psychology of defense is the psychology of inhibition. But the love of God removes fear; the removal of fear establishes the latent powers, and association with others in spiritual love brings these powers into vital, positive expression. A Bahá'í community is a gathering where this process can take place in this age, slowly at first, as the new impetus gathers force, more rapidly as the members become conscious of the powers unfolding the flower of unity among men. . . .

The responsibility for and supervision of local Bahá'í affairs is vested in a body known as the spiritual assembly. This body (limited to nine members) is elected annually on April 21, the first day of Riḍván (the festival commemorating the Declaration of Bahá'u'lláh) by the adult declared believers of the community, the voting list being drawn up by the outgoing spiritual assembly. Concerning the character and functions of this body, 'Abdu'l-Bahá has written as follows:—

It is incumbent upon every one [every believer] not to take any step [of Bahá'í activity] without consulting the spiritual assembly, and they must assuredly obey with heart and soul its bidding and be submissive unto it, that things may be properly ordered and well arranged. Otherwise every person will act independently and after his own judgment, will follow his own desire, and do harm to the Cause.

The prime requisites for them that take counsel together are purity of motive, radiance of spirit, detachment from all else save God, attraction to His divine fragrances, humility and lowliness amongst His loved ones, patience and long-suffering in difficulties, and servitude to His exalted threshold. Should they be graciously aided to acquire these attributes, victory from the unseen Kingdom of Bahá shall be vouchsafed to them. In this day, assemblies of consultation are of the greatest importance and a vital necessity. Obedience unto them is essential and obligatory. The members thereof must take counsel together in such wise that no occasion for ill-feeling or discord may arise. This can be attained when every member expresseth with absolute freedom his own opinion and setteth forth his argument. Should any one oppose, he must on no account feel hurt for not until matters are fully discussed can the right way be revealed. The shining spark of truth cometh forth only after the clash of differing opinions. If after discussion, a decision be carried unanimously, well and good; but if, the Lord forbid, differences of opinion should arise, a majority of voices must prevail. . . .

The first condition is absolute love and harmony amongst the members of the assembly. They must be wholly free from estrangement and must manifest in themselves the unity of God, for they are the waves of one sea, the drops of one river, the stars of one heaven, the rays of one sun, the trees of one orchard, the flowers of one garden. Should harmony of thought and absolute unity be nonexistent, that gathering shall be dispersed and that assembly be brought to naught.

The second condition:—They must when coming together turn their faces to the Kingdom on high and ask aid from the Realm of Glory. . . . Discussions must all be confined to spiritual matters that pertain to the training of souls, the instruction of children, the relief of the poor, the help of the feeble throughout all classes in the world, kindness to all peoples, the diffusion of the fragrances of God and the exaltation of His holy Word. Should they endeavor to fulfill these conditions the grace of the Holy Spirit shall be vouchsafed unto them, and that assembly shall become the center of the divine blessings, the hosts of divine confirmation shall come to their aid, and they shall day by day receive a new effusion of Spirit.

Expounding on this subject, Shoghi Effendi writes:—

Nothing whatever should be given to the public by any individual among the friends, unless fully considered and approved by the spiritual assembly in his locality; and, if this (as is undoubtedly the case) is a matter that pertains to the general interest of the Cause in that land, then it is incumbent upon the spiritual assembly to submit it to the consideration and approval of the national body representing all the various local assemblies. Not only with regard to publication, but all matters without any exception whatsoever, regarding the interests of the Cause in that locality, individually or collectively, should be referred exclusively to the spiritual assembly in that locality, which shall decide upon it, unless it be a matter of national interest, in which case it shall be referred to the national [Bahá'í] body. With this national body also will rest the decision whether a given question is of local or national interest. (By national affairs is not meant matters that are political in their character, for the friends of God the world over are strictly forbidden to meddle with political affairs in any way whatever, but rather things that affect the spiritual activities of the body of the friends in that land.)

Full harmony, however, as well as cooperation among the various local assemblies and the members themselves, and particularly between each assembly and the national body, is of the utmost importance, for upon it depends the unity of the Cause of God, the solidarity of the friends, the full, speedy and efficient working of the spiritual activities of His loved ones.

The various assemblies, local and national, constitute today the bedrock upon the strength of which the Universal House [of Justice] is in future to be firmly established and raised. Not until these function vigorously and harmoniously can the hope for the termination of this period of transition be realized. . . . Bear in mind that the keynote of the Cause of God is not dictatorial authority but humble fellowship, not arbitrary power, but the spirit of frank and loving consultation. Nothing short of the spirit of a true Bahá'í can hope to reconcile the principles of mercy and justice, of freedom and submission, of the sanctity of the right of the individual and of self-surrender, of vigilance, discretion and prudence on the one hand, and fellowship, candor, and courage on the other.

The local spiritual assemblies of a country are linked together and coordinated through another elected body of nine members, the national spiritual assembly. This body comes into being by means of an annual election held by elected delegates representing the local Bahá'í communities. . . . The national convention in which the delegates are gathered together is composed of an elective body based upon the principle of proportional representation. . . . These national conventions

are preferably held during the period of Riḍván, the twelve
days beginning April 21 which commemorate the Declaration
made by Bahá'u'lláh in the Garden of Riḍván near Baghdád.
The recognition of delegates is vested in the outgoing national
spiritual assembly.

A national convention is an occasion for deepening one's
understanding of Bahá'í activities and of sharing reports of
national and local activities for the period of the elapsed
year. . . . The function of a Bahá'í delegate is limited to the
duration of the national convention and participation in the
election of the new national spiritual assembly. While gathered
together, the delegates are a consultative and advisory body
whose recommendations are to be carefully considered by the
members of the elected national spiritual assembly. . . .

The relation of the national spiritual assembly to the local
spiritual assemblies and to the body of the believers in the
country is thus defined in the letters of the Guardian of the
Cause:

> Regarding the establishment of "national assemblies,"
> it is of vital importance that in every country, where the
> conditions are favorable and the number of the friends
> has grown and reached a considerable size . . . that a
> "National Spiritual Assembly" be immediately estab-
> lished, representative of the friends throughout that
> country.
>
> Its immediate purpose is to stimulate, unify and co-
> ordinate by frequent personal consultations, the manifold
> activities of the friends as well as the local assemblies;
> and by keeping in close and constant touch with the Holy
> Land, initiate measures, and direct in general the affairs
> of the Cause in that country.
>
> It serves also another purpose, no less essential than
> the first, as in the course of time it shall evolve into the
> National House of Justice (referred to in 'Abdu'l-Bahá's
> *Will* as the "secondary House of Justice"), which accord-
> ing to the explicit text of the *Testament* will have, in con-
> junction with the other national assemblies throughout

the Bahá'í world, to elect directly the members of the International House of Justice, that supreme council that will guide, organize and unify the affairs of the Movement throughout the world. . . .

This national spiritual assembly, which, pending the establishment of the Universal House of Justice, will have to be reelected once a year, obviously assumes grave responsibilities, for it has to exercise full authority over all the local assemblies in its province, and will have to direct the activities of the friends, guard vigilantly the Cause of God, and control and supervise the affairs of the Movement in general.

Vital issues, affecting the interests of the Cause in that country such as the matter of translation and publication, the Mashriqu'l-Adhkár, the teaching work, and other similar matters that stand distinct from strictly local affairs, must be under the full jurisdiction of the national assembly.

It will have to refer each of these questions, even as the local assemblies, to a special committee, to be elected by the members of the national spiritual assembly, from among all the friends in that country, which will bear to it the same relation as the local committees bear to their respective local assemblies.

With it, too, rests the decision whether a certain point at issue is strictly local in its nature, and should be reserved for the consideration and decision of the local assembly, or whether it should fall under its own province and be regarded as a matter which ought to receive its special attention.

. . . It is the bounden duty, in the interest of the Cause we all love and serve, of the members of the incoming national assembly, once elected by the delegates at convention time, to seek and have the utmost regard, individually as well as collectively, for the advice, the considered opinion and the true sentiments of the assembled delegates. Banishing every vestige of secrecy, of undue reticence, of dictatorial aloofness, from their midst, they should radiantly and abundantly unfold to the eyes of the delegates, by whom they are elected, their plans, their hopes, and their cares. They should familiarize the delegates with the various matters that will have to be considered in the current year, and calmly and conscientiously study and weigh the opinions and judgments of the delegates. The newly elected national assembly, during the few days when the convention is in session and after the dispersal of the delegates, should seek ways and means to cultivate understanding, facilitate and maintain the exchange of views, deepen confidence, and vindicate by every tangible evidence their one desire to serve and advance the commonweal. . . .

The national spiritual assembly, however, in view of the unavoidable limitations imposed upon the convening of frequent and long-standing sessions of the convention, will have to retain in its hands the final decision on all matters that affect the interests of the Cause . . . such as the right to decide whether any local assembly is functioning in accordance with the principles laid down for the conduct and the advancement of the Cause.

Concerning the matter of drawing up the voting list to be used at the annual local Bahá'í elections, the responsibility for this is placed upon each local spiritual assembly, and as a guidance in the matter the Guardian has written the following:

To state very briefly and as adequately as present circumstances permit the principal factors that must be taken into consideration before deciding whether a person may be regarded a true believer or not: Full recognition of the station of the Forerunner, the Author, and the True Exemplar of the Bahá'í Cause, as set forth in 'Abdu'l-Bahá's *Testament;* unreserved acceptance of, and submission to, whatsoever has been revealed by Their pen; loyal and steadfast adherence to every clause of our Beloved's sacred *Will;* and close association with the spirit as well as the form of the present-day Bahá'í administration throughout the world—these I conceive to be the fundamental and primary considerations that must be fairly, discreetly and thoughtfully ascertained before reaching such a vital decision.

'Abdu'l-Bahá's instructions provide for the further development of Bahá'í organization:—

And now, concerning the House of Justice which God hath ordained as the source of all good and freed from all error, it must be elected by universal suffrage, that is, by the believers. Its members must be manifestations of the fear of God and daysprings of knowledge and understanding, must be steadfast in God's Faith and the well-wishers of all mankind. By this House is meant the Universal House of Justice, that is, in all countries a secondary House of Justice must be instituted, and these secondary Houses of Justice must elect the members of the Universal one.[1] Unto this body all things must be referred. It enacteth all ordinances and regulations that are not to be found in the explicit Holy Text. By this body all the difficult problems are to be resolved and the Guardian of the Cause of God is its sacred head and the distinguished member for life of that body. Should he not attend in person its deliberations, he must appoint one to represent him. . . . This House of Justice enacteth the laws and the government enforceth them. The legislative body must reinforce the executive, the executive must aid and assist the legislative body so that through the close union and harmony of these two forces, the foundation of fairness and justice may become firm and strong, that all the regions of the world may become even as Paradise itself. . . .

Unto the Most Holy Book every one must turn and all that is not expressly recorded therein must be referred to the Universal House of Justice. That which this body, whether unanimously or by a majority doth carry, that is

---

[1] The Universal House of Justice was elected for the first time in April 1963 by the members of fifty-six National Spiritual Assemblies.

verily the truth and the purpose of God Himself. Whoso doth deviate therefrom is verily of them that love discord, hath shown forth malice and turned away from the Lord of the Covenant.

Even at the present time, the Bahá'ís in all parts of the world maintain an intimate and cordial association by means of regular correspondence and individual visits. This contact of members of different races, nationalities, and religious traditions is concrete proof that the burden of prejudice and the historical factors of division can be entirely overcome through the spirit of oneness established by Bahá'u'lláh.

The World Order of Bahá'u'lláh

The larger implications of this order are explained by Shoghi Effendi in successive communications addressed to the Bahá'í community since February 1929:—

I cannot refrain from appealing to them who stand identified with the Faith to disregard the prevailing notions and the fleeting fashions of the day, and to realize as never before that the exploded theories and the tottering institutions of present-day civilization must needs appear in sharp contrast with those God-given institutions which are destined to arise upon their ruin. . . .

For Bahá'u'lláh . . . has not only imbued mankind with a new and regenerating Spirit. He has not merely enunciated certain universal principles, or propounded a particular philosophy, however potent, sound and universal these may be. In addition to these He, as well as 'Abdu'l-Bahá after Him, has, unlike the Dispensations of the past, clearly and specifically laid down a set of laws, established definite institutions, and provided for the essentials of a divine economy. These are destined to be a pattern for future society, a supreme instrument for the establishment of the Most Great Peace, and the one agency for the unification of the world, and the proclamation of the reign of righteousness and justice upon the earth. . . .

Unlike the Dispensation of Christ, unlike the Dispensation of Muḥammad, unlike all the Dispensations of the past, the apostles of Bahá'u'lláh in every land, wherever they labor and toil, have before them in clear, in unequivocal and emphatic language, all the laws, the regulations, the principles, the institutions, the guidance, they require for the prosecution and consummation of their task. . . . Therein lies the distinguishing feature of the Bahá'í Revelation. Therein lies the strength of the unity of the Faith, of the validity of a Revelation that claims not to destroy or belittle previous Revelations, but to connect, unify, and fulfill them. . . .

Feeble though our Faith may now appear in the eyes of men, who either denounce it as an offshoot of Islám, or contemptuously ignore it as one more of those obscure sects that abound in the West, this priceless gem of divine Revelation, now still in its embryonic state, shall evolve within the shell of His law, and shall forge ahead, undivided and unimpaired, till it embraces the whole of mankind. Only those who have already recognized the supreme station of Bahá'u'lláh, only those whose hearts have been touched by His love, and have become familiar with the potency of His spirit, can adequately appreciate the value of this divine economy—His inestimable gift to mankind.—*March 21, 1930.*

It is towards this goal—the goal of a new World Order, divine in origin, all-embracing in scope, equitable in principle, challenging in its features—that a harassed humanity must strive. . . .

How pathetic indeed are the efforts of those leaders of human institutions who, in utter disregard of the spirit of the age, are striving to adjust national processes, suited to the ancient days of self-contained nations, to an age which must either achieve the unity of the world, as adumbrated by Bahá'u'lláh, or perish. At so critical an hour in the history of civilization it behooves the leaders of all the nations of the world, great and small, whether in the East or in the West, whether victors or vanquished, to give heed to the clarion call of Bahá'u'lláh and, thoroughly imbued with a sense of world solidarity, the *sine qua non* of loyalty to His Cause, arise manfully to carry out in its entirety the one remedial scheme He, the Divine Physician, has prescribed for an ailing humanity. Let them discard, once for all, every preconceived idea, every national prejudice, and give heed to the sublime counsel of 'Abdu'l-Bahá, the authorized Expounder of His teachings. *"You can best serve your country,"* was 'Abdu'l-Bahá's rejoinder [1] to a high official in the service of the federal government of the United States of America, who had questioned Him as to the best manner in which he could promote the interests of his government and people, *"if you strive, in your capacity as a citizen of the world, to assist in the eventual application of the principle of federalism underlying the government of your own country to the relationships now existing between the peoples and nations of the world."*. . .

Some form of a world superstate must needs be evolved, in whose favor all the nations of the world will have willingly ceded every claim to make war, certain rights to impose taxation and all rights to maintain armaments, except for purposes of maintaining internal order within their respective dominions. Such a state will have to include within its orbit an international executive adequate to enforce supreme and unchallengeable authority on every recalcitrant member of the commonwealth; a world parliament whose members shall be elected by the people in their respective countries and whose election shall be confirmed by their respective governments; and a Supreme Tribunal whose judgment will have a binding effect even in such cases where the parties

---

[1] In the year 1912.

concerned did not voluntarily agree to submit their case to its consideration. A world community in which all economic barriers will have been permanently demolished and the interdependence of capital and labor definitely recognized; in which the clamor of religious fanaticism and strife will have been forever stilled; in which the flame of racial animosity will have been finally extinguished; in which a single code of international law—the product of the considered judgment of the world's federated representatives—shall have as its sanction the instant and coercive intervention of the combined forces of the federated units; and finally a world community in which the fury of a capricious and militant nationalism will have been transmuted into an abiding consciousness of world citizenship—such indeed, appears, in its broadest outline, the Order anticipated by Bahá'u'lláh, an Order that shall come to be regarded as the fairest fruit of a slowly maturing age. . . .

Let there be no misgivings as to the animating purpose of the worldwide law of Bahá'u'lláh. Far from aiming at the subversion of the existing foundations of society, it seeks to broaden its basis, to remold its institutions in a manner consonant with the needs of an ever-changing world. It can conflict with no legitimate allegiances, nor can it undermine essential loyalties. Its purpose is neither to stifle the flame of a sane and intelligent patriotism in men's hearts, nor to abolish the system of national autonomy so essential if the evils of excessive centralization are to be avoided. It does not ignore, nor does it attempt to suppress, the diversity of ethnical origins, of climate, of history, of language and tradition, of thought and habit, that differentiate the peoples and nations of the world. It calls for a wider loyalty, for a larger aspiration than any that has animated the human race. . . .

The call of Bahá'u'lláh is primarily directed against all forms of provincialism, all insularities and prejudices. . . . For legal standards, political and economic theories are solely designed to safeguard the interests of humanity as a whole, and not humanity to be crucified for the preservation of the integrity of any particular law or doctrine. . . .

The principle of the oneness of mankind—the pivot round which all the teachings of Bahá'u'lláh revolve—is no mere outburst of ignorant emotionalism or an expression of vague and pious hope. . . . Its implications are deeper, its claims greater than any which the Prophets of old were allowed to advance. Its message is applicable not only to the individual, but concerns itself primarily with the nature of those essential relationships that must bind all the states and nations as members of one human family. . . .

It represents the consummation of human evolution. . . .

That the forces of a world catastrophe can alone precipitate such a new phase of human thought is, alas, becoming increasingly apparent. . . .

Nothing but a fiery ordeal, out of which humanity will emerge, chastened and prepared, can succeed in implanting that sense of responsibility which the leaders of a newborn age must arise to shoulder. . . .

Has not 'Abdu'l-Bahá Himself asserted in unequivocal language that *"another war, fiercer than the last, will assuredly break out"? —November 28, 1931.*

This Administrative Order . . . will, as its component parts, its organic institutions, begin to function with efficiency and vigor, assert its claim and demonstrate its capacity to be regarded not only as the nucleus but the very pattern of the new World Order destined to embrace in the fullness of time the whole of mankind. . . .

Alone of all the Revelations gone before it this Faith has . . . succeeded in raising a structure which the bewildered followers of bankrupt and broken creeds might well approach and critically examine, and seek, ere it is too late, the invulnerable security of its world-embracing shelter. . . .

To what else if not to the power and majesty which this Administrative Order—the rudiments of the future all-enfolding Bahá'í Commonwealth—is destined to manifest, can these utterances of Bahá'u'lláh allude: *"The world's equilibrium hath been upset through the vibrating influence of this most great, this new World Order. Mankind's ordered life hath been revolutionized through the agency of this unique, this wondrous System—the like of which mortal eyes have never witnessed."* . . .

The Bahá'í Commonwealth of the future, of which this vast Administrative Order is the sole framework, is, both in theory and practice, not only unique in the entire history of political institutions, but can find no parallel in the annals of any of the world's recognized religious systems. No form of democratic government; no system of autocracy or of dictatorship, whether monarchical or republican; no intermediary scheme of a purely aristocratic order; nor even any of the recognized types of theocracy, whether it be the Hebrew Commonwealth, or the various Christian ecclesiastical organizations, or the Imamate or the Caliphate in Islám—none of these can be identified or be said to conform with the Administrative Order which the master-hand of its perfect Architect has fashioned. . . .

Let no one, while this system is still in its infancy, misconceive its character, belittle its significance or misrepresent its purpose. The bedrock on which this Administrative Order is founded is God's immutable purpose for mankind in this day. The Source from which it derives its inspiration is no one less than Bahá'u'lláh Himself. . . . The central, the underlying aim which animates it is the establishment of the new World Order as adumbrated by Bahá'u'lláh. The methods it employs, the standard it inculcates, incline it to neither East nor West, neither Jew nor Gentile, neither rich nor poor, neither white nor colored. Its watchword is the unification of

the human race; its standard the "Most Great Peace."
. . . *February 8, 1934.*

The contrast between the accumulating evidences of steady consolidation that accompany the rise of the Administrative Order of the Faith of God, and the forces of disintegration which batter at the fabric of a travailing society, is as clear as it is arresting. Both within and outside the Bahá'í world the signs and tokens which, in a mysterious manner, are heralding the birth of that World Order, the establishment of which must signalize the Golden Age of the Cause of God, are growing and multiplying day by day. . . .

"*Soon,*" Bahá'u'lláh's own words proclaim it, "*will the present-day Order be rolled up, and a new one spread out in its stead.*". . .

The Revelation of Bahá'u'lláh . . . should . . . be regarded as signalizing through its advent the *coming of age of the entire human race.* It should be viewed not merely as yet another spiritual revival in the ever-changing fortunes of mankind, not only as a further stage in a chain of progressive Revelations, nor even as the culmination of one of a series of recurrent prophetic cycles, but rather as marking the last and highest stage in the stupendous evolution of man's collective life on this planet. The emergence of a world community, the consciousness of world citizenship, the founding of a world civilization and culture . . . should . . . be regarded, as far as this planetary life is concerned, as the furthermost limits in the organization of human society, though man, as an individual, will, nay must indeed as a result of such a consummation, continue indefinitely to progress and develop. . . .

The unity of the human race, as envisaged by Bahá'u'lláh, implies the establishment of a world commonwealth in which all nations, races, creeds and classes are closely and permanently united, and in which the autonomy of its state members and the personal freedom and initiative of the individuals that compose them are definitely and completely safeguarded. This commonwealth must, as far as we can visualize it, consist of a world legislature, whose members will, as the trustees of the whole of mankind, ultimately control the entire resources of all the component nations, and will enact such laws as shall be required to regulate the life, satisfy the needs and adjust the relationships of all races and peoples. A world executive, backed by an international force, will carry out the decisions arrived at, and apply the laws enacted by, this world legislature, and will safeguard the organic unity of the whole commonwealth. A world tribunal will adjudicate and deliver its compulsory and final verdict in all and any disputes that may arise between the various elements constituting this universal system. A mechanism of world intercommunication will be devised, embracing the whole planet, freed from national hindrances and restrictions, and functioning with marvelous swiftness and perfect regularity. A world metropolis will act as the nerve center of a world civilization, the focus towards which the unifying forces of life will converge and from which its energizing influences will radiate. A world language will either be invented or chosen from among the existing languages and will be taught in the schools of all the federated nations as an auxiliary to their mother tongue. A world script, a world literature, a uniform and universal system of currency, of weights and measures, will simplify and facilitate intercourse and understanding among the nations and races of mankind. In such a world society, science and religion, the two most potent forces in human life, will be reconciled, will cooperate, and will harmoniously develop. The press will, under such a system, while giving full scope to the expression of the diversified views and convictions of mankind, cease to be mischievously manipulated by vested interests, whether private or public, and will be liberated from the influence of contending governments and peoples. The economic resources of the world will be organized, its sources of raw materials will be tapped and fully utilized, its markets will be coordinated and developed, and the distribution of its products will be equitably regulated.

National rivalries, hatreds, and intrigues will cease, and racial animosity and prejudice will be replaced by racial amity, understanding, and cooperation. The causes of religious strife will be permanently removed, economic barriers and restrictions will be completely abolished, and the inordinate distinction between classes will be obliterated. Destitution on the one hand, and gross accumulation of ownership on the other, will disappear. The enormous energy dissipated and wasted on war, whether economic or political, will be consecrated to such ends as will extend the range of human inventions and technical development, to the increase of the productivity of mankind, to the extermination of disease, to the extension of scientific research, to the raising of the standard of physical health, to the sharpening and refinement of the human brain, to the exploitation of the unused and unsuspected resources of the planet, to the prolongation of human life, and to the furtherance of any other agency that can stimulate the intellectual, the moral, and spiritual life of the entire human race.

A world federal system, ruling the whole earth and exercising unchallengeable authority over its unimaginably vast resources, blending and embodying the ideals of both the East and the West, liberated from the curse of war and its miseries, and bent on the exploitation of all the available sources of energy on the surface of the planet, a system in which force is made the servant of justice, whose life is sustained by its universal recognition of one God and by its allegiance to one common Revelation—such is the goal towards which humanity, impelled by the unifying forces of life, is moving.

The whole of mankind is groaning, is dying to be led to unity, and to terminate its agelong martyrdom. And yet it stubbornly refuses to embrace the light and acknowledge the sovereign authority of the one Power that can extricate it from its entanglements, and avert the woeful calamity that threatens to engulf it. . . .

Unification of the whole of mankind is the hallmark of the stage which human society is now approaching. Unity of family, of tribe, of city-state, and nation have been successively attempted and fully established. World unity is the goal towards which a harassed humanity is striving. Nation-building has come to an end. The anarchy inherent in state sovereignty is moving towards a climax. A world, growing to maturity, must abandon this fetish, recognize the oneness and wholeness of human relationships, and establish once for all the machinery that can best incarnate this fundamental principle of its life.— *March 11, 1936.*

[The above letters have been published in one volume entitled *The World Order of Bahá'u'lláh.*]

Epilogue

Under the inspired guidance of Shoghi Effendi, the Bahá'í
Cause grew steadily in size and in the establishment of its Administrative Order, so that by 1951 there were eleven functioning national spiritual assemblies. At that point the Guardian
turned to the development of the institutions of the Faith at its
international level, appointing the International Bahá'í Council, the forerunner of the Universal House of Justice, and,
shortly thereafter, the first contingent of Hands of the Cause
of God. Hitherto Shoghi Effendi had raised certain eminent
Bahá'ís to the rank of Hands of the Cause posthumously, one
of them being Dr. John E. Esslemont, but it was only in 1951
that he adjudged the time ripe to begin the full development
of this important institution. In rapid succession between 1951
and 1957 he appointed thirty-two Hands and extended the
range of their activities, instituting in each continent Auxiliary
Boards consisting of believers appointed by the Hands to be
their deputies, assistants, and advisors. Twenty-seven of these
Hands were living at the time of his passing.

Through a series of letters, some addressed to Bahá'ís
throughout the world, and others to those in specific countries,
the Guardian deepened their understanding of the teachings,
built up the administrative institutions of the Faith, trained
the believers in their correct and effective use, and in 1937
launched the American Bahá'í Community on the implemen-
tation of the Divine Plan for the diffusion of Bahá'u'lláh's
Message. This Divine Plan had been revealed by 'Abdu'l-Bahá
in a number of Tablets written during the years of the First
World War and constitutes the charter for the propagation of
the Faith.

Within the framework of this charter a number of teaching
plans were carried out, first in the Western Hemisphere, then
also in Europe, Asia, Australasia, and Africa until in 1953

283

the Guardian called for a "decade-long, world-embracing, spiritual crusade" to carry the Faith to all the remaining independent states and principal dependencies of the world. In 1957, as the midway point of the crusade approached, the Guardian, exhausted by thirty-six years of unremitting labor, died while on a visit to London.

As Shoghi Effendi had no heir, the work of the Faith after November 1957 was coordinated and directed by the twenty-seven Hands of the Cause until the victorious completion of the crusade in April 1963, at which time the first Universal House of Justice was elected by the members of fifty-six national spiritual assemblies convened at the Bahá'í World Center in Haifa by the Hands of the Cause.

Immediately following this historic election, Bahá'ís from all parts of the globe gathered in London at the first World Congress of the Faith to celebrate the Centenary of the Declaration of Bahá'u'lláh and to rejoice in the worldwide spread of His Faith.

The supreme institution of the Faith today is the Universal House of Justice, created by Bahá'u'lláh in His Most Holy Book, invested with authority to legislate on all matters not covered in the Bahá'í Writings, and assured divine guidance in the Sacred Text itself. 'Abdu'l-Bahá, in His Will and Testament, lays down the method of election of the Universal House of Justice, defines its station and duties more clearly, and asserts that it is under the direct guidance of the Báb and Bahá'u'lláh and is the body to which all must turn.

The unique and distinguishing feature of the Bahá'í Faith is the Covenant of Bahá'u'lláh, the bedrock upon which the Faith raises all its structures and bases its development. Its uniqueness is that for the first time in religious history the Manifestation of God, in clear and unambiguous language, provides for the authorized interpretation of His Word, and ensures the continuity of the divinely appointed authority which flows from the Source of the Faith.

Interpretation of Scripture has always in earlier religions been a most fertile source of schism. Bahá'u'lláh, in the Book of His Covenant, vested in His eldest son, 'Abdu'l-Bahá, full powers for the interpretation of His Writings and for the direction of His Cause. 'Abdu'l-Bahá, in His Will and Testament, appointed His eldest grandson, Shoghi Effendi, Guardian of the Faith and sole interpreter of the Writings. There is no priesthood within the Faith and no individual may claim special station or guidance; authority is vested in institutions created within the Bahá'í Scriptures.

By virtue of these unique provisions, the Faith of Bahá'u'lláh has been preserved from schism, from the depredations of unauthorized leadership, and above all from the infiltration of man-made doctrines and theories, which in the past have shattered the unity of religions. Pure and inviolate, the revealed Word of Bahá'u'lláh, with its authorized interpretation, remains throughout the Dispensation the uncorrupted and incorruptible source of spiritual life to men.

In 1968 the Universal House of Justice took action to provide for the future carrying out of the specific functions of protection and propagation vested in the Hands of the Cause, by the establishment of Continental Boards of Counsellors. Each Board consists of a number of Counsellors appointed by the Universal House of Justice, and they work in close collaboration with the Hands of the Cause of God. The appointment and direction of Auxiliary Boards is now the duty of the Boards of Counsellors, and the activities of the Hands, of whom nineteen are still living, have been extended to be worldwide.

The Guardian had written of future global teaching plans to be carried out under the direction of the Universal House of Justice, and the first of these, a Nine Year Plan, was launched in 1964. At the present time, 1969, the Bahá'í Faith has been established in 139 independent states. There are Bahá'ís living in over thirty-three thousand localities throughout the world; Bahá'í literature has been translated into 421 languages; the fifth Bahá'í temple is being built in the city of Panama; land for fifty other temples has been acquired; there are eighty-three national spiritual assemblies and over sixty-eight hundred local spiritual assemblies.

Most encouraging of all has been the response of the masses in such places as Africa, India, Southeast Asia, and Latin

America, where large numbers of the indigenous peoples have begun to enter the Cause, bringing about a new stage in the development of the administrative and social activities of the worldwide Bahá'í community.

Basic References on the Bahá'í Faith

Bahá'í Prayers.
Epistle to the Son of the Wolf, by Bahá'u'lláh. 1969
Gleanings from the Writings of Bahá'u'lláh. 1969
The Hidden Words of Bahá'u'lláh. 1969
The Kitáb-i-Iqán (The Book of Certitude), by Bahá'u'lláh. 1960
The Seven Valleys and the Four Valleys, by Bahá'u'lláh. 1968
Bahá'í World Faith (Writings of Bahá'u'lláh and 'Abdu'l-Bahá). 1969
Foundations of World Unity (talks by 'Abdu'l-Bahá). 1968
The Secret of Divine Civilization, by 'Abdu'l-Bahá. 1957
Some Answered Questions (talks by 'Abdu'l-Bahá). 1964
God Passes By, by Shoghi Effendi. 1965
The Promised Day Is Come, by Shoghi Effendi. 1967
The World Order of Bahá'u'lláh, by Shoghi Effendi. 1969
The Dawn-Breakers, Nabíl's Narrative (and translation of the French footnotes). 1962

The above titles are available from the Bahá'í Publishing Trust, Wilmette, Illinois, U. S. A.

Index

'Abbás Effendi (*see* 'Abdu'l-Bahá)
'Abdu'l-'Azíz, Sulṭán of Turkey, 36, 37, 217, 240
'Abdu'l-Bahá, xi, 51-70
  appointed Shoghi Effendi as Guardian, 130, 261-62, 285
  arranged for Bahá'u'lláh to go to Mazra'ih, 35-37
  birth, 14, 51, 182n, 183
  "Center of the Covenant," 55, 67, 128-31
  characteristics, 52, 53, 56-59, 64, 65, 68, 70, 259
  correspondence, 56, 62, 64, 66
  death, 65-66, 182, 183
  developed Administrative Order (*see* B. adm.) *
  early years, 51-53
  in Europe and America, 60, 67, 187, 242, 243
  Exemplar, 68, 69-70, 271
  Expounder, 40, 55, 67, 68, 129, 275
  healing power, 109
  imprisonment of, 55-56, 58
  investigation by Commissions, 58-59
  knighted, 63-64
  marriage, 53-54
  "Master," 53, 55, 56
  "Most Great Branch," 55, 129
  "Mystery of God," 52, 53
  named by Bahá'u'lláh as His representative, 40, 55
  never attended school or college, 53
  prayers revealed by, 98-100
  recognized station of Bahá'u'lláh, 52
  released from prison, 59

---

* Bahá'í administration

'Abdu'l-Bahá—*Cont.*
  services during wartime, 62-63
  station, 40, 55, 67-70, 129
  visitors to, 56, 57-58
  Will and Testament, 68-69, 130, 257-67, 271-73, 284, 285
  worked to free Bahá'u'lláh for writing, 38, 53
  writings and addresses, 10n, 53, 60, 66-67, 129, 242-44
'Abdu'l-Ḥamíd, 59
Abraham, 116, 255
Acquiescence (joy), radiant, 45, 50, 77, 96, 210
Adam and Eve, 207
Administration (*see* B. adm.)
Adrianople, 27, 30, 31, 32, 126, 241, 251
Agnosticism, true, 201-2
'Akká, 31, 32, 33, 38, 49, 56, 57, 58, 59, 63, 166, 250-51
Alcohol, 21, 102, 104
'Alí Muḥammad (*see* Báb)
'Alí, son-in-law of Muḥammad, 11n, 15n, 197
America, 31, 60, 187, 242-43, 275
Angels, 219, 229, 231
Arbitration, international, 136, 145, 166-67
Armageddon, 243
Armaments, 136, 166, 167, 169, 215, 243, 275. *See also* Self-defense.
Arts and crafts, 21, 79, 102, 106, 140, 143, 153
Asceticism, 77, 102
Assemblies (*see* B. adm.)
Authority
  administration, 69, 130, 144, 180, 265-66, 267-68, 270

289

Authority—*Cont.*
God, 72, 77, 78, 124, 133, 136, 239
government, 136, 139, 235, 275, 281
Prophets, 72, 121, 124, 125, 128, 133
Auxiliary Boards, 263n, 283, 285

Báb, the (*i.e.,* Gate), 11-22, 284
Bayán, The (the Báb's Revelation), 14, 20, 21, 48, 176
characteristics, 13, 15, 16, 18, 22, 254
Declaration, 14-16, 24, 30, 182, 183
early years, 13, 182, 183, 254
education, only reading and writing, 13 and n
Forerunner, 13, 18, 20, 50, 69, 271
founded Bábí Faith, 14-16, 20, 252 and n
inaugurated new calendar, 16, 178
"Letters of the Living," 14
marriage and son, 13
martyrdom, 15, 17-18, 22, 24, 182, 183
persecutions, 15
proofs of claims, 16, 19, 22, 254
prophecies about, 15, 16, 17, 214, 223
Prophethood, 15-16, 20, 22, 69, 125, 173, 254, 271
Shoghi Effendi related to, 261
teaching and writings, 19-22, 48, 128, 176
tomb, 18, 55, 66
Bábís, martyrdom of, 18, 25, 169, 198, 252
persecution of, 16-18, 24-25, 169, 198, 252
Backbiting, 82-83
Badí, 31
Baghdád, 26, 27, 28, 29, 30, 51, 250, 251, 269
Bahá'í administration
Assemblies, local Spiritual, 178, 179-81, 186, 261 and n, 265-68, 271

Bahá'í administration—*Cont.*
Assemblies, National Spiritual, 180-81, 261 and n, 267-71, 283, 284
Auxiliary Boards, 263n, 283, 285
International House of Justice (*see* House of Justice, below)
basis of world order, 264-82
committees, 270
consultation, 139, 145, 180-81, 184, 266-68, 269
conventions, 188, 268-69, 270
cooperation, 145, 157, 173, 181, 209, 236, 264, 268, 280, 281
Counsellors, Boards of, 285
delegates, 268-69, 270
developed by 'Abdu'l-Bahá, 68, 69, 179, 261, 264, 272-73
established by Shoghi Effendi, 267-72
Feasts, Nineteen Day, 186
funds,
common treasury, 21, 142, 146, 151, 180
Mashriqu'l-Adhkár, 187
for teachers, 131
Guardianship, 68, 130, 261-63, 272, 283, 284, 285
Hands of the Cause of God, 261, 263 and n, 283, 284, 285. *See also* Counsellors, Boards of, and Auxiliary Boards, above.
House of Justice, 129, 130, 144, 151, 163, 165, 180, 256, 261, 262, 268, 269, 270, 272-73, 283, 284, 285
International Bahá'í Council, 283
meetings, 180, 181, 182, 184-85, 188
membership, 264-65, 266, 271
no priesthood or clergy, 93, 131, 285
ordinances (*see* B. Faith)
publications, 180, 181, 267, 270
revealed by Bahá'u'lláh (*see* World Order)
teaching plans, 283, 285
World Crusade, 284
Bahá'í Covenant, 55, 67, 128-31, 284

Bahá'í Faith
administration (*see* B. adm.)
Covenant, 55, 67, 128-31, 284
enemies of, 61, 130, 198, 238
Founders (*see* Báb) (*see* Bahá'u'-
  lláh)
fulfillment of prophecies (*see*
  Prophecies)
Golden Age, 114, 254-56, 279
ordinances, 122, 175-88
  alcohol, 21, 102, 104
  calendar, 16, 178-79
  divorce, 177-78
  fast, 182, 183-84
  feasts and anniversaries, 30,
    181-83, 186, 188
  marriage, 175-77
  Ma<u>sh</u>riqu'l-A<u>dh</u>kár, 153, 186-
    88, 270
  monasticism forbidden, 175-76
  narcotics, 102, 104
  prayer (*see* Prayer)
peace (*see* Peace)
regenerating spirit of, 49
Scriptures, authentic, 121, 127,
  128, 237, 273, 274
Revelation, divine, two parts, 123
  continuous, progressive, 122-24
  object of, 124
teachings (*see* B. teachings)
tests, 8, 9, 231, 235-37
unity (*see* Unity)
worship, 21, 72, 79, 92, 100, 120,
  126, 143, 184, 186, 188, 204
Bahá'í Faith, progress of, 49-50, 62,
  66, 68 and n, 169-71, 252-54,
  257, 265, 274, 279, 283-86
Bahá'í membership, 264-65, 266, 271
Bahá'í prayers, 97-100, 112
Bahá'í teachings
administrative order (*see* B. adm.)
Bahá'u'lláh, the Promised One
  (*see* Bahá'u'lláh)
capital and labor, rights of, 144-46
consultation (*see* B. adm.)
deeds, 78, 79, 80, 85, 139
economics, 21, 102, 140-46, 235,
  273, 280-81
education, universal (*see* Education)

Bahá'í teachings—*Cont.*
equality of men and women, 146-
  49, 235
healing (*see* Healing)
independent investigation, 8, 10
  and n, 73-74, 76, 117, 131,
  134, 201, 236, 246
international tribunal, 166-69,
  243, 246-47, 256, 275-76,
  280
justice (*see* Justice)
language, universal (*see* Language)
life after death, 21, 77, 188-95,
  207-8
love for humanity (*see* Love)
mercy, 79, 96, 135, 144, 172
moderation, 102, 144, 145, 184
nonresistance, 50, 149-50, 169-71
Manifestations of God (Prophets)
  (*see* Prophets)
obedience
  to administration, 266
  to government, 136, 139, 178,
    259
  to Prophets, 77-78, 87, 95, 104-
    5, 124, 125, 133, 161, 185
oneness of humanity (*see* Unity)
oneness of religion (*see* Religion)
ordinances (*see* B. Faith)
peace (*see* Peace)
prayer indispensable and obligatory (*see* Prayer)
prejudice, abandonment of, 3, 10,
  73, 74, 76, 120, 160-61, 201,
  245, 246, 253, 275, 276, 281
profit-sharing, 145, 146
religion and science in accord,
  106-7, 113, 117, 158, 188,
  197, 199-202, 209-10, 256,
  280
slavery, forbidden, 144, 235
social and ethical, 5, 21-22, 74-87,
  102-5, 113, 134-35, 139-41,
  143, 144, 145, 146-49, 153-
  55, 156, 177-78, 188, 256
teaching enjoined, 79, 80, 131
tyranny, oppression forbidden,
  139
unity (*see* Unity)

Bahá'í teachings—*Cont.*
  work for all, 102, 142-43
  work is worship, 79, 100, 143
Bahá'ís, characteristics, 49-50, 71-87
  "as one soul," 61, 75, 255-56
  cleanliness, 103, 104, 185
  courtesy, 21, 81, 186
  devotion to God, 69, 72-73, 76,
    77, 78, 89, 92, 125
  faithfulness, 133, 139, 161, 170,
    258
  forgiveness, 82, 154, 171
  healers of sick, 109, 113, 114
  humility, 83-84, 185
  joyousness, 77, 81, 103
  love (*see* Love)
  "living the life," 10, 70, 71, 74, 79,
    102, 196
  mercy, 79, 135, 144, 172
  obedience (*see* B. teachings)
  prayer (*see* Prayer)
  radiant acquiescence, 45, 50, 77,
    96, 210
  reverence, 72, 81, 121, 125, 204
  seekers of truth (*see* Investi-
    gation)
  self-realization, 74, 77, 79, 82, 83,
    86-87, 160
  serving humanity, 71, 78, 79, 84,
    133, 135, 152, 170
  severance, 76-77, 79
  teachers, 79-80, 131-32
  truthfulness, 85-86, 139, 155
  without prejudice (*see* Prejudice)
Bahá'ís, martyrdom and persecution
  of, 9, 50, 77, 169, 170, 171,
    198, 240, 252
Bahá'u'lláh, 23-50, 283, 284, 285
  'Abdu'l-Bahá, His representative,
    40, 55
  ascension, 4, 40, 182, 183
  at Bahjí, 37, 38
  at Mazra'ih, 35-37
  Bábís accepted, 31
  banished to 'Akká, 31, 32, 33, 49,
    216-17
  birth and early life, 4, 23-24, 182,
    183, 254
  characteristics, 23-24, 29, 30, 37,
    39, 44, 45, 49, 254

Bahá'u'lláh—*Cont.*
  confirmed claims of Báb, 22, 223
  Declaration at Riḍván, 30, 181,
    250, 269, 284
  exiled to Adrianople, 30
  exiled to Baghdád, 26
  exiled to Constantinople, 29-30
  "Father," 47, 125, 212, 214, 215,
    219, 220
  founded Bahá'í Dispensation, 20
  founded basis for world unity, 5,
    47, 116
  "Glory of God," 23, 50, 72, 73-74,
    126, 203, 216-17, 232, 239
  Greatest Name, 81, 113, 135, 211
  healing power, 108-9
  "Him Whom God shall make
    manifest," 20, 22, 48
  His wife, Navváb, 54
  imprisoned in Ṭihrán, 25, 51
  in the wilderness, 27-28, 52
  interpretation of Scriptures, 7, 48,
    190-91, 211-33
  knowledge inherent, 23, 24, 44, 48
  letters to kings, 31
  Message, Voice of God, 126
  mission of, 5, 31, 46-48, 105, 117-
    18, 125-26, 156, 196, 216,
    255, 256, 274
  opposed by mullás, 28-29
  persecutions of, 24, 31-32, 254
  Physician, Great, 105
  Prayers, 98, 112
  Prof. E. G. Browne's visit to, 39-
    40, 48, 117-18
  Promised One of all Prophets, 1,
    2, 5, 30, 47, 125-26, 211, 212,
    214, 216, 256
  proofs of Prophethood, 8-9, 48,
    124, 128, 236, 254
  prophecies, 34, 38, 47, 156, 234-50
  prophecies about, 46-47, 125-26,
    212-13, 214-18, 223, 251, 256
  Prophethood, 4, 41-46, 68-69, 72,
    87, 91, 125-26, 173, 218, 219,
    220, 254
  renewed religion, 123
  Revealer of God's will, 72, 80, 256
  Spirit of Truth, 125

Bahá'u'lláh—*Cont.*
  Tablets to (excerpts)
    America, 31, 242
    Christians, 125-26
    Emperor of Germany, 238, 246
    Kings and rulers, 31, 135-36,
      235, 246
    Napoleon III, 175-76, 237
    Pope, 31, 126, 196
    Queen Victoria, 121-22, 166
    Ra'ís (Chief), 11, 156, 196,
      240-41
    Shah, 31-32, 44-45, 248
    Sultán of Turkey, 31, 240, 246
    Tihrán (Persia), 239
  Teacher, Educator of mankind, 1,
    5, 72
  tent on Mount Carmel, 34, 38
  tomb, 18, 250
  treachery of Subh-i-Azal (Mírzá
    Yahyá), 26-27, 31, 55
  Will and Testament, 40, 55, 119-
    20, 129
  Writings (*see* Tablets to), 5, 9, 29,
    38, 48 and n-49, 127, 128
    comprehensive, 5, 48, 254, 274
    in Persian and Arabic, xii, 9,
      10n, 49
    translations, 9-10 and n
    two classes, 41, 45-46, 135
Bahjí, 37, 38
Bayán, 14, 20, 21, 48, 176
Begging, 21, 102, 143
Bequests, 146
Branch, Most Great, 55, 129
Browne, Prof. E. G., 39-40, 48, 117-
  18
Buddha, 105, 118, 128, 201
Buddhists, 116

Calamity, 95, 136, 178, 241, 242,
  244, 248
Calendar, 16, 178-79
Capital and labor, 144-46, 276
Celestial Concourse, 185, 194
Center of the Covenant, 55, 67, 128-
  31
Ceremonies, 117, 126, 131, 177, 228
Change, essential to life, 118-19
Character, 4, 104, 124, 151-52, 210

Chastity, 102, 104
Children
  education of, 131-32, 147, 150,
    151, 153, 181, 210, 236
  suffering of, 96
Christ, 12, 84, 88, 91, 105, 109, 110,
    116, 118, 125, 128, 171, 173,
    175, 176, 260
  prophecies of, 47, 125, 219-20,
    222-33
  Revelation denied, 6-7, 9, 16, 213
  station of Prophethood, 2, 6, 7,
    41, 72, 91, 123, 201, 212-17,
    219, 228, 234-35, 257
  teachings, 8, 44, 47, 72, 73, 78, 79,
    82, 116, 123, 154, 196, 219,
    220, 222, 223, 245
Christians, 9, 11, 12, 28, 47, 116,
    120, 125, 159, 176, 226, 256,
    260, 265
  Tablet to, 125-26
  denied later Manifestations, 214,
    226, 231
Civilization, 133-55, 166-67
  criminals, treatment of, 153-55,
    171
  economics (*see* Economics)
  education (*see* Education)
  equality of men and women, 146-
    49, 235
  goal, 274
  government (*see* Government)
  justice (*see* Justice)
  peace (*see* Peace)
  press, the, 117, 155, 280
  religion, the basis (*see* Religion)
  spiritual unity of humanity (*see*
    Unity)
  true, 166-67, 173
Cleanliness, 103, 104, 185
Clouds, 3, 219, 223, 229, 230, 232
"Coming of the Lord" (*see* Day of
  God)
Committees, 270
Communication
  spiritual, 88, 89, 94-95, 192-95,
    208
  universal, 4, 117, 127, 163-66,
    256, 280

Concord, 116, 156, 163, 181, 218
Confession, 84-85
Confirmation, 79, 185, 267
Conflict, 46, 78, 105, 116, 117, 120,
    137, 139, 145, 156, 158, 197,
    244, 258
Constantinople, 30, 241, 246, 251
Consultation (*see* B. adm.)
Contentment, 102, 108
Contributions (*see* Funds)
Conventions, 188, 268-69, 270
Cooperation (*see* B. adm.)
Counsellors, Boards of, 285
Courtesy, 21, 81, 186
Covenant of God, 92, 130-31, 139,
    187
Covenant, Bahá'í, 55, 67, 128-31,
    284
Covenant-breaker, 62, 130, 259
Creation, 75, 86, 103, 133, 196,
    204-5
Criminals, 153-55, 171
Crusades, 159
Cycles, 119, 157, 182, 218, 220, 222,
    224, 279

Daniel, 211, 244, 249-50
Dawn-Breakers, The, 31n
Day of God (new era)
    Bahá'u'lláh's coming fulfills, 2, 4,
        5, 47, 48, 72, 137, 218-19,
        220, 236
    "coming of the Lord," 46, 47, 212,
        214,229-33
    Day of Judgment, 5, 20, 21, 47,
        219-20, 228, 232
    Day of Resurrection, 5, 20, 21, 47,
        220-22, 225, 226, 228, 231
    "Last Day," 212, 214, 218, 219,
        224
    signs of, 6-8, 218, 224-29
Dead, spiritually, 4, 16, 21, 191, 221,
    235
Death, life after, 21, 77, 188-95,
    207-8
Declaration of Báb, 14-16, 24, 30,
    182, 183
Deeds, 78, 79, 80, 85, 139
Defense (*see* Self-defense)
Delegates, 268-69, 270

Devotion, 69, 72-73, 76, 77, 78, 89,
    92, 125
Disasters, 95, 101, 135, 236, 247,
    248
Disease due to disobedience, 95, 101,
    104, 105
Divine economy, 273, 274
Divorce, 123, 177-78
Drugs, 104, 106

East and West, 60, 61, 158, 164,
    173-74, 215, 257, 258, 275,
    281
Economics, 21, 102, 140-46, 235,
    273, 280-81
Economy, 102
Education, 150-51
    aim of Prophets, 2, 4, 121, 150,
        157, 189
    compulsory, 5, 131, 147, 151, 153,
        181, 236
    essential elements, 150-51
    for character, 4, 104, 152-55
    for profession, 102, 153
    funds for, 151, 180, 181
    importance, 137, 139, 147, 150,
        153, 155
    press, influence of, 117, 155, 280
    principles of, 118, 131-32, 139,
        150-53, 160, 163, 210
    teachers, 91, 131, 146, 150, 152
    through suffering, 95, 96, 277
    universal, 131, 147, 150, 151, 163,
        236, 280
    women, 146-49
Elias, 193, 223
Emancipation, 144, 147, 149, 235,
    256
Enemies of the Cause, 61, 130, 198,
    238
Equality, absolute, impossible, 140
Equality of men and women, 146-49,
    235
Era, new (*see* Day of God)
Era, old, decline of, 2-5, 119, 136,
    149, 150, 181, 219, 236, 273,
    274, 279
Esperanto, 60, 163-64, 165, 199, 236
Evil, 195-96, 208

Evolution and progress, 118-19, 156-57, 204, 206, 207, 209, 279

Faith, Bahá'í (*see* B. Faith)
Faith in God, 78, 110, 191
Faith, one, 2, 116, 117, 122, 126, 137, 218, 219, 281
Faithfulness, 133, 139, 161, 170, 258
Fast, 182, 183-84
Fault-finding forbidden, 82-84
Fear, 21, 108, 265
Feasts and anniversaries, 30, 181-83, 186, 188
Fellowship, 61, 81, 119, 253, 258, 265, 268
Flowers, 57-58, 74, 81, 123, 124, 202
Food, 102, 106, 107, 183, 184
Forerunner (*see* Báb)
Forgiveness, 82, 154, 171
  divine, 84-85, 191, 192, 194
  prayer for, 99
Founders of religion, 2, 16, 20, 116, 121, 124-25, 203, 219
Funds (*see* B. adm.)
  of Bahá'u'lláh, 38

Gambling, 103
Glad Tidings, 1-10, 103, 254
Glory of God, 23, 50, 72, 73-74, 126, 203, 216-17, 232, 239
Glory, cause of man's, 40, 46, 85, 209
God
  attributes revealed through Prophets, 41, 42, 46, 74, 90, 91, 203, 212
  authority, 72, 77, 78, 124, 133, 136, 239
  Cause of, 248, 249
  comprehension of, not possible, 91, 201-2
  Covenant of, 92, 130-31, 139, 187
  Day of (*see* Day of God)
  disobedience to, 95, 101, 104, 105
  faith in, 78, 110, 191
  forgiveness of, 84-85, 191, 192, 194
  intermediary of, 90-91, 195, 212
  Kingdom of (*see* Kingdom of God)

God—*Cont.*
  knowledge of (*see* Knowledge of God)
  love of (*see* Love)
  oneness of, 12, 195, 281
  power of, 97, 114, 170, 234
  source of command, 28, 44, 78, 125, 255
  speaks through Prophets, 2, 41-46, 50, 69, 72, 88, 121, 124, 126, 133, 212, 220, 221, 234
  universe manifests, 89, 201-2, 245
  will of, 10, 72, 77, 78, 80, 110, 122, 138, 203, 210, 229, 234, 236, 251, 255, 256
  Word of, 69, 80, 114, 170, 234, 235, 248, 249
  worship of, 79, 100, 120-21, 143, 219
Golden Age, 114, 254-56, 279
Government, 135-46, 171, 236
  appointments, 139-40
  divine law, requisite, 137, 141, 278
  economics, 21, 102, 140-46, 235, 273, 280-81
  freedom, 137-39, 144-45, 173, 247, 248
  league of nations, 166-68, 172, 275-76
  representative, 137
  rulers, subjects, 135, 136, 137, 139, 166, 173, 235, 259
  world, 215, 275, 281
Gratitude, 103
Greatest Name, 81, 113, 135, 211
Great Britain, 60
Greed, 134-35, 161
Grief, 81, 96, 108
Guardian (*see* Shoghi Effendi)
Guidance, 2, 79, 260

Hague, The, 142, 169
Haifa, 38, 55, 59, 60, 62, 63, 64, 250, 251
Hands of the Cause of God, 261, 263 and n, 283, 284, 285
Healing (*see also* Humanity)
  attitude of patient, 107-11
  duty of Bahá'ís, 109, 113, 114
  material, 106-7

Healing—*Cont.*
 mental, 107-8
 physician, Tablet to, 106, 108, 112
 power of Prophets, 105, 109, 125, 247, 275
 prayer, importance of, 101, 107-14
 science of, most important, 112
 through unity, 114, 122, 137
Health, 101-15 (*see also* Healing)
 character affected, 104
 emotions affect, 108
 social, 101, 113, 143, 167
 use of, 96, 114-15
Heaven, 4, 20, 21, 88, 189, 190-91, 219, 220, 229, 230
Hell, 20-21, 190-91, 220
Holy Land, 18, 216, 218, 228
Holy Spirit
 Bahá'u'lláh, channel of, 4, 5, 70
 confirmation of, 79, 185, 267
 healing power, 108-14
 influences all lives, 4, 195, 203, 253
 Prophets, channels of, 4, 46, 70, 91, 222
Honesty, 85-86, 139, 145, 155
House of Justice (*see* B. adm.)
House of Worship (*see* Mashriqu'l-Adhkár)
Human nature, 118-19
Humanity (*see also* Man)
 "coming of age," 126, 273, 279, 282
 degrees essential, 141
 one organism, 95, 141, 147, 192, 256
 progress limitless (*see* Progress)
 rebirth, 119
 spiritual ills, remedy, 1, 76, 95, 105, 121-22, 125, 135, 137, 138, 196, 246, 248, 255, 275
 unity of (*see* Unity)
Ḥusayn 'Alí (*see* Bahá'u'lláh)

Imám Mihdí, 15n, 17
Immortality (*see* Life)
Income tax, 141, 235
Individual interpretation of teachings, 130

Infallibility, 124-25
Inheritance, 146, 235
Intercalary Days, 178, 183
Intercession, 191, 193-94
Interest, 144
Internationalism, 3, 137, 166-67, 172, 275-82
Interpretation of prophecies, 211-33
Inventions, 4, 117, 281
Investigation
 difficulties, 9
 independent, 8, 10 and n, 73-74, 76, 117, 131, 134, 201, 236, 246
 Turkish Commissions of, 58-59
Írán (*see* Persia)
Isaiah, 49, 214-15, 216, 234
Islám, 11n, 128, 274

Jesus Christ (*see* Christ)
Jews, 11, 12, 28, 46, 116, 120, 125, 126, 159, 218, 226, 257, 265
 misinterpreted prophecies, 6-7, 15-16, 213-14
John the Baptist, 20, 54n, 216, 223, 234
Judgment Day (*see* Day of God)
Justice
 administration of, 131, 141, 153-54, 166, 171, 172-73, 191, 273-74
 enjoined, 73, 79, 134-35, 141, 144, 258
 establishment of, 2
 in suffering of innocent, 96

Kingdom of God, 21, 47, 50, 71, 80, 96, 125, 185, 188, 190, 210, 220, 221, 224, 248-50, 255
Knowledge (*see also* Education)
 bounty of God, 91
 learning, source of all, 74
 man's treasury, 153
 of God, 21, 74, 78, 158, 202, 203, 217
 of self, 74, 86
Krishna, 2, 128

Labor, 144-46, 276
Land, belongs to humanity, 161-62

Language
  Esperanto, 60, 163-64, 165, 199, 236
  of the spirit, 88, 89, 94-95, 192-95, 208
  universal auxiliary, 5, 127, 163-66, 256, 280
League of nations (leagues), 166-68, 172, 275-76
"Letters of the Living," 14
Liberty, 138, 247
Life, physical, 101, 102, 204
Life, spiritual
  after death, 21, 77, 188-94, 207-8
  rebirth, 49, 73, 119, 207, 221-22
  "Living the life," 10, 70, 71, 74, 79, 102, 196
Lord of Hosts, 46, 214, 218, 220
Love
  cause of creation, 75
  divine, 22, 112, 123, 175, 203
  for God, 2, 21, 22, 74-76, 105
  for humanity, 21, 22, 71, 75, 76, 78, 81, 82, 116, 119, 158, 159, 161, 162-63, 209, 258
  of self, 69, 105

Man
  body of, 101, 207
  heart of, belongs to God, 135
  innate qualities, 141, 151-52, 160, 190, 276
  perfect, 74, 204
  progress limitless, 21, 84, 192, 254-55, 279
  progress through sorrow, 96
  purpose of, 75, 98
  self-realization, 74, 77, 79, 82, 83, 86-87, 160
  soul of, 90, 101, 135, 207, 208
  will, human, 77, 131
Manifestation of God (*see* Prophets)
Marriage, 175, 176-77
Martyrdom
  Báb, 15, 17-18, 22, 24, 182, 183
  Bábís, 18, 25, 169, 198, 252
  Bahá'ís, 50, 77, 169, 170, 171, 198, 252
  Christians, 260
  Prophets and scientists, 198

Mary Magdalene, 110, 148 (*see also* Qurratu'l-'Ayn)
Mashriqu'l-Adhkár, 153, 186-88, 270
Mazra'ih, 35-37
Mediator, 90-91, 194, 195, 212
Medicine, 106-7
Meetings, spiritual, 93, 94, 181, 184-85, 188
Meetings (*see* B. adm.)
Mercy, 79, 96, 135, 144, 172
Messiah, 6, 7, 213
Millennium, 244, 251
Miracles, 4, 28, 200, 253
Mírzá Husayn 'Alí (Bahá'u'lláh), 23
Mírzá Yahyá (Subh-i-Azal), 26-27, 31, 55
Moderation, 102, 144, 145, 184
Monasticism, 175-76
Monogamy, 176
Moses, 2, 8, 9, 16, 17, 46, 105, 116, 118, 123, 125, 128, 159, 173, 201, 219, 228, 278
Mount Carmel, 18, 34, 38, 55, 66, 251
Muhammad, 11n, 13, 15, 16, 118, 125, 128, 173, 226, 250, 274
  station of Prophethood, 2, 72, 219
  teachings of, 41, 42, 47, 88, 105, 116, 175, 176, 225-26, 228
Muhammadans, 11, 12, 15, 28, 116, 120, 125, 126, 128, 150, 159, 256, 265
Mullá Husayn Bushrú'í, 14
Munírih Khánum, wife of 'Abdu'l-Bahá, 54

Nabíl's Narrative (*The Dawn-Breakers*), 31n
Narcotics, 102, 104
Násiri'd-Dín Sháh, 239
Nationalism, 161, 236, 276
Navváb, wife of Bahá'u'lláh, 54
Nature, world of, 156-57
  unaware of God, 157
Naw-Rúz (New Year), 179, 181, 182, 183
Neutrality, 172
New Day (*see* Day of God)
New era (*see* Day of God)

Nineteen Day Feast, 186
Nonresistance, 50, 149-50, 169-71

Obedience (*see* B. teachings)
Oneness (*see* Unity)
Oppression, 139
Ordinances (*see* B. Faith)

Paradise, meaning of, 21
  earth as, 156, 174
Parsees, 265
Partner (with God), 22
Peace
  America, 242-43
  arbitration, international,   136,
    145, 166-67
  armaments, limitation of, 169, 275
  Christ's words on, 47, 216
  establishment of, 2, 5, 46, 71, 136,
    149, 158, 162-63, 166, 172,
    173, 218, 246
  law, international, code of, 276
  league of nations (leagues), 166-
    68, 172, 275-76
  Lesser, 135, 137
  Most Great Peace, 40, 47, 135,
    137, 157-58, 163, 173, 210,
    248, 273, 279
  tribunal, international,   166-69,
    243, 246-47, 256, 275-76,
    280
  United Nations Org., 167n
Persia, 11, 12, 13, 15, 18, 23, 49,
  142, 148, 169, 171, 173, 183,
  187, 198, 216, 238, 239, 257
Philanthropy, 183
Pilgrims to Holy Land, 33-34, 37,
  56, 57, 58, 62, 63, 64, 67
Politics, 137-38, 259, 268
Poor, 21, 136, 140, 141, 142, 181,
  183, 194
Prayer, 88-100
  and natural law, 96-97, 197
  congregational, 93-94
  conversation with God, 88, 89
  devotional attitude, 89-90, 93, 96
  for the dead, 93, 193, 194, 208
  for forgiveness, 84-85, 99
  for healing, 101, 107-14
  indispensable, 92, 93, 97

Prayer—*Cont.*
  intercessory, 191, 193-94
  is answered, 33, 89, 96, 97, 110
  obligatory, 92-93
  releases flow of divine bounty, 97
  service is, 79, 100, 143
  through Manifestation, 91-92
  wisdom of, 92-93
Prayers revealed by 'Abdu'l-Bahá,
  98-100
Prayers revealed by Bahá'u'lláh, 98,
  112
Prejudices, 22, 127, 158-61, 245,
  276, 281
  abandonment of, 3, 10, 73, 74, 76,
    120, 160-61, 201, 245, 246,
    253, 275, 276, 281
Press, the, 117, 155, 280
Priesthood and clergy, 93, 131, 285
Primal Point (Báb), 16
Professions, 102, 143
Profit-sharing, 145, 146
Progress
  after death, 21, 77, 188-94, 207-8
  basis of, 118, 138, 156, 164, 189,
    203, 209
  evidence of, 2, 3, 49, 84, 117, 119,
    126-27, 199-200, 236
  greatest foe to, 133, 156-57, 197,
    199
  leading factor in, 1
  of Bahá'í Faith (*see* B. Faith)
  through prayer, 93
  through suffering, 95, 96, 277
Prophecies fulfilled, 6-8, 119, 211-33
  about Báb, 15, 16, 17, 214, 223
  about Bahá'u'lláh, 46-47, 125-26,
    212-13, 214-18, 223, 251,
    256
  about Christ, 6-7, 213-14
  about Day of God (*see* Day of
    God)
  misinterpreted, 6-7, 15-16, 198,
    213-14, 226, 231
Prophecies of
  'Abdu'l-Bahá, 157-58, 234, 243-51
  Báb, 26n
  Bahá'u'lláh, 34, 38, 47, 156, 234-
    50

Prophets
all from the East, 173
appearance awaited, 1, 12, 14
Báb (*see* Báb)
Bahá'u'lláh (*see* Bahá'u'lláh)
bring spiritual light, 4
Buddha (*see* Buddha)
called for love, unity, 116
Christ (*see* Christ)
Dispensation of (*see* Day of God)
dual station, 41-44
future, 130
infallibility, 124-25
inspire through "language of the
spirit," 88
Krishna, 2, 128
Mediator, 90-91, 194, 195, 212
mission of, 2, 72-74, 87, 104, 121,
133, 150, 153, 157, 204, 222,
255
Moses (*see* Moses)
Muḥammad (*see* Muḥammad)
perfect man, the, 74, 204
Physician, Great, 105, 109, 111,
122, 125, 137, 275
proofs of, 8-9, 22, 78, 124, 225,
234
rejected, 6-7, 15-16, 198, 213, 214,
226, 231
reveal attributes of God, 41, 42,
46, 74, 90, 91, 203, 212
reveal Word of God, 2, 41-46, 50,
69, 72, 88, 122-24, 125, 126,
133, 212, 220, 234, 248
sovereignty, 7, 16, 37
station of distinction, 42, 122, 223-
24
station of oneness, 41, 70, 116,
120, 123, 223-24, 255
successive, 2, 123-24, 197-98, 255
suffered for man, 95
sun, spiritual, 2, 4, 72, 91, 173,
185, 201, 219, 228, 232, 257
Sun of Truth, 4, 21, 257
visions of, 193
Zoroaster, 2, 11, 46, 128
Psychic faculties, 193
Publications, 180, 181, 267, 270
Punishment, 21, 123, 154, 171, 191,
208

Qualifications for Bahá'í membership, 271-72
Qur'án, 41, 42, 49, 128, 176, 225,
227, 230
Qurratu'l-'Ayn, 148

Radiant acquiescence, 45, 50, 77,
96, 210
Rebirth, spiritual, 49, 73, 119, 207,
221-22
Recreation, 102-3
Religion
basis of civilization, 2, 117-18,
133, 137, 150, 153, 157, 158
dependent upon obedience, 72-73,
125, 134
Founders, 2, 16, 20, 116, 121, 124-
25, 203, 219
ordinances, 122, 123, 175-88, 228
progressive, 122-31, 157, 175,
198, 210, 228, 256, 257
purpose, 118, 120, 122, 124, 134,
157
renewal, 4, 123
rites and ceremonies, 117, 126,
131, 177, 228
unity of, 2, 75-76, 116-32, 137
Religion and science (*see* B. teachings)
Repentance, 84
Resurrection Day (*see* Day of God)
Revelation, divine (*see* B. Faith)
Revenue, public, 141-42, 146, 151,
235
Reverence, 72, 81, 121, 125, 204
Revolution, Turkish, 59
Rewards, 21, 191, 208
Riḍván, 30 (*see also* Bahá'u'lláh,
Declaration)
at Bahjí, 38
Feast of, 30, 181, 183, 266
Rulers, 135, 136, 137, 139, 166, 173,
235, 259
Russian Minister, 26

Ṣádiq, 24
Satan, 84, 159
Scepticism, 117, 244
Schism (*see* Sectarianism)

Science, medical, 102, 106, 107, 111-12
Sciences, 79, 106, 117, 153, 173, 197-202, 209, 280, 281
Scientists, 117, 156, 197-202, 204, 209
Script, common, 163, 280
Scriptures, explained, 7-8, 19, 20-21, 48, 190-91, 211-33, 256
Search after truth (*see* Investigation)
Sectarianism, 11-12, 66, 116-18, 121, 128, 214, 216, 226, 284, 285
   in Bahá'í Faith, impossible, 41, 69, 116, 129-30, 131, 236
Self-defense, 50, 154, 170, 171-72, 265
Self-realization, 74, 77, 79, 82, 83, 86-87, 160
Selfishness, 76, 84, 105, 134, 135, 137, 248
Service, 71, 78, 79, 84, 133, 135, 152, 170
Severance, 76-77, 79
Sháh of Persia, 24, 26, 31, 44, 217, 239
Sharing, 76, 142, 145, 146, 182-83
Shíráz, 13, 251
Shoghi Effendi (Guardian), v, vii, ix, 10n, 66, 68, 69, 130, 180-81, 261-62, 267-68, 269-72, 273-82, 283, 284, 285
Signs attesting divine Revelation, 5-7, 16, 46-47, 213, 217-18, 224-33
Signs of the times, 2, 3-4, 5, 47, 119, 136, 199-200, 209, 225-26, 236, 248, 253, 256, 279, 281-82
Slavery, 144, 235
Social and ethical teachings, 5, 21-22, 74-87, 102-5, 113, 134-35, 139-41, 143, 144, 145, 146-49, 153-55, 156, 177-78, 188, 256
Sorrow, 96, 108, 255
Sovereignty, 7, 16, 37
"Spring," 3, 4, 119
Strikes, 145

Ṣubḥ-i-Azal (Mírzá Yaḥyá), 26-27, 31, 55
Suffering, educative, remedial, 95, 96, 277
Sulṭán 'Abdu'l-'Azíz, 36, 37, 217, 240
Sulṭán 'Abdu'l-Ḥamíd, 59

Tabríz, 17, 18
Tax, income, 141, 235
Teachers, 91, 131, 146, 150, 152
Teachings (*see* B. teachings)
Territorial ambitions, 161-63
Ṭihrán, 23, 25, 51, 239, 251
Tolerance, 82, 119, 121, 127, 236
Tomb of Báb, 18, 55, 66
Tomb of Bahá'u'lláh, 18, 250
Tribunal, international, 166-69, 243, 246-47, 256, 275-76, 280
Truth, oneness of, 122, 197, 201, 255, 257
   discoverers, revealers of, 1
   discovery, requires humility, 9
Truthfulness, 85-86, 139, 155
Turkey, 59, 240
Turkish Commissions, 58-59
Tyranny, oppression, 139, 141

United Nations Organization, 167n
Unity
   basis for, brought, 5, 47, 116
   how retarded, 11-12, 116-17, 120, 122, 127, 156, 157, 161, 164
   of all life, 101, 126, 209
   of God, 12, 120, 195, 281
   of mankind, 46, 70, 75, 78, 81, 95, 116, 117-18, 121, 126-27, 135, 137, 147, 156, 160, 173-74, 184, 192, 209, 246, 249, 256, 273, 282
   of nations, 2, 5, 40, 117-18, 166-69, 172, 173-74
   of Prophets (*see* Prophets)
   of religion (*see* Religion)
   of religion and science (*see* B. teachings)
   of truth, 122, 197, 201, 255, 257
   of two worlds, 192, 255-56
   prayers for, 98-99

Unity—*Cont.*
 steps toward, 114, 119-21, 125, 127, 128, 133, 134, 135, 162-64, 166-69, 172-74, 215, 249, 261, 279-82
 through World Order, 137, 261-82

Victory, 137, 235
Visions of Prophets, 193
Voluntary giving, 76, 142, 145, 146, 182-83

War
 abolishment of, 40, 47-48, 157, 168-69, 172
 cause of, 135-36, 145-46, 158, 160, 161, 243-46
 future, prophecied, 277
 religious, 159, 170
 righteous, 136, 166-67, 171-73, 246-47
 victory, 137, 235
 world, 215, 235, 243-44
Wealth, 74, 96, 105, 140, 141, 143, 235, 281

Will of God (*see* God)
Will, human, 77, 131
Will and Testament (*see* 'Abdu'l-Bahá; Bahá'u'lláh)
Wills, 146
Women
 emancipation of, 147, 149, 235, 256
 equality of, with men, 146-49, 235
 in the new age, 21, 149
Word of God, 69, 80, 114, 170, 234, 235, 248, 249
Work, 79, 100, 102, 143
World citizenship, 276, 279
World commonwealth, 164, 274-82
World Congress, 284
World executive, 275, 280
World order, 137, 179-80, 215, 261-82
Worship (*see* B. Faith)

Zamenhof, 163, 165 and n, 199, 236
Zoroaster, 2, 11, 46, 128
Zoroastrians, 11, 12, 28, 49, 116, 126